A BEGINNER'S GUIDE TO COPY CATALOGING ON OCLC/PRISM

DA

| 12-9 |
| 11-1-04 |

A BEGINNER'S GUIDE
TO COPY CATALOGING
ON OCLC/PRISM

LOIS MASSENGALE SCHULTZ
Northern Kentucky University

1995
Libraries Unlimited, Inc.
Englewood, Colorado

To
Gerald, Matthew, and Sarah

LIBRARIES UNLIMITED, INC.
P.O. Box 6633
Englewood, CO 80155-6633
(800) 237-6124

Production Editor: Kevin W. Perizzolo
Copy Editor: D. Aviva Rothschild
Indexer: Nancy Fulton
Typesetting and Interior Design: Judy Gay Matthews

Library of Congress Cataloging-in-Publication Data

Schultz, Lois Massengale.
    A beginner's guide to copy cataloging on OCLC/PRISM / by
Lois Massengale Schultz.
    xvii,288 p. 17x25 cm.
    Includes index.
    ISBN 1-56308-308-6 (softbound)
    1. Copy cataloging. 2. OCLC PRISM (Information retrieval
system)
    I. Title.
Z693.3.C67S38   1995
025.3--dc20   95-32325
                                                        CIP

Contents

Part II
PERFORMING COPY CATALOGING

Part III
PRACTICE IN COPY CATALOGING

Preface

Having traincd many copy catalogers at the three libraries where I have worked, I have long seen a need for a manual for training copy catalogers. In 1993 I was granted a sabbatical by Northern Kentucky University to prepare such a manual. *Beginner's Guide* is a revised and expanded version of that manual.

This book has been written for the beginning copy cataloger in the catalog department of a library. It assumes that the individuals using it have very little knowledge of libraries, especially of activities relating to cataloging. It could also be used in schools that offer an associate degree program in library science or as a supplementary text in a cataloging class at the graduate level.

The book concentrates on copy cataloging of monographs. Other types of materials are covered in less detail. Terminology foreign to a new employee but used daily in a catalog department is explained in simple terms. Bibliographic utilities are discussed briefly, and the MARC record is explained in detail. Also provided is a suggested plan for teaching a new employee how to use the OCLC PRISM system.

I am especially grateful to OCLC for granting me permission to use OCLC bibliographic records in this manual. I have modified these records to illustrate the editing of various elements. The major part of the book consists of more than 50 examples of title pages, versos of title pages, and other relevant information, followed by an unedited OCLC bibliographic record that I modified. Next comes a discussion of the bibliographic area under review, along with an edited OCLC bibliographic record.

Some practice exercises are provided for the reader in chapter 10; the answers are in chapter 11. In chapters 7 and 8, the reader is given the option of working on the exercises for monographs found in chapter 10 as each area is discussed. A short bibliography of useful tools and a glossary of cataloging terminology come after the exercises.

The assistance of a number of people who spent many hours reading the manual in detail made the writing of this book possible: Barbara Pfeifle at the University of Kentucky, who made numerous helpful comments; Donna Smith and Jennifer Kluener, library technicians at Northern Kentucky University (Jennifer Kluener is now at Clermont County Public Library in Ohio), who made useful suggestions from a library technician's viewpoint; and Dwayne Smith, who read the manual and gave valuable comments from the point of view of an individual with no library experience. Michael Flannery, director of Lloyd Library and Museum in Cincinnati, Ohio, provided encouragement and moral support.

Many of my colleagues at Northern Kentucky University helped me in various ways. I am grateful for the support of Marian Winner, director of Steely Library at Northern Kentucky University. Cheryl Edelen helped me find many publishers' addresses. I was able to test the manual on Peggy King and Sally Bjork when they started their employment in the Catalog Department at Northern Kentucky University.

My husband, Gerald Schultz, deserves a special thanks for his support through the whole process.

I wish to thank the following authors, publishers and associations for permission to reprint from their works.

All OCLC Online Union Catalog bibliographic record examples are used with permission from OCLC Online Computer Library Center, Inc., Dublin, OH.

Figures 4.4a-4.4b. Reprinted with permission of McGraw-Hill from **Financial Accounting** by Walter B. Meigs and Robert F. Meigs. New York: McGraw-Hill. Copyright (c) 1979 by McGraw-Hill.

Figures 7.1a-7.1b. MacDonald, Scott B., **Dancing on a Volcano: The Latin American Drug Trade**, reprinted with permission of Greenwood Publishing Group, Inc., Westport, CT. Copyright © 1988 by Scott B. MacDonald.

Figures 7.2a-7.2b. Reprinted with permission of K. Thienemanns Verlag from **Die Unendliche Geschichte** by Michael Ende. Stuttgart: K. Thienemanns Verlag. Copyright © 1979 by K. Thienemanns Verlag, Stuttgart-Wien.

Figures 7.3a-7.3b. Reprinted from **Satanstoe, or The Littlepage Manuscripts: A Tale of the Colony** by James Fenimore Cooper in **The Writings of James Fenimore Cooper** by permission of The State University of New York Press.

Figures 7.4a-7.4b. Reprinted with permission of Mr. Anthony Tischhauser from **Dynamische Gleichgewichte, Neue Projekte, Dynamic Equilibrium, Recent Projects** by Santiago Calatrava. Zurich: Verlag fur Architektur. Copyright © 1992 Anthony Tischhauser.

Figures 7.5a-7.5b. Reprinted with permission of Random House from **A Natural History of the Senses** by Diane Ackerman. New York: Random House. Copyright © 1990 by Diane Ackerman.

Figures 7.6a-7.6b. Reprinted with permission of Libraries Unlimited/Teacher Ideas Press from **Introduction to Cataloging and Classification** by Bohdan S. Wynar. Englewood, CO: Libraries Unlimited. Copyright © 1992 by Bohdan S. Wynar. Additional material for the 8th ed. copyright © 1992 by Arlene G. Taylor.

Figures 7.7a-7.7b. Reprinted with permission of Routledge from **Changing Educational Assessment** edited by Patricia Broadfoot, Roger Murphy, and Harry Torrance. London, New York: Routledge. Copyright © 1990 British Comparative and International Educational Society.

Figures 7.8a-7.8b. Reprinted by permission of Oxford University Press from **The Gestapo and German Society** by Robert Gellately. New York: Clarendon Press/Oxford University. Copyright © 1990 by Robert Gellately.

Figures 7.9a-7.9b. Bancilhon, Francois and Peter Buneman, **Advances in Database Programming Languages.** Copyright © 1990 by the Association for Computing Machinery. Reprinted by permission of Addison-Wesley Publishing Co., Inc. Reading, MA.

Figure 7.10a. Reprinted with permission of Jack Daniels Distillery from **Back Home** by Joe Clark. Kingsport, Tenn.: privately printed for the Tennessee Squire Association by Kingsport Press. Copyright © 1965 Tennessee Squire Association, Lynchburg, TN 37352.

Figures 7.11a-7.11d. "Modified and reproduced by special permission of the Publisher, Consulting Psychologists Press, Inc., Palo Alto, CA 94303 from **Handbook of Industrial and Organizational Psychology** by M. D. Dunnette and L. M. Hough (eds.). Copyright © 1991 by Consulting Psychologists Press, Inc. All rights reserved. Further reproduction is prohibited without the Publisher's written consent."

Figures 7.12a-7.12b. Reprinted from Barry Lopez, **The Rediscovery of North America**, copyright © 1990 by The University Press of Kentucky, by permission of the publishers.

Figures 7.13a-7.13b. Reprinted with the permission of Cambridge University Press from **Fichte's Theory of Subjectivity** by Frederick Neuhouser. New York: Cambridge University Press. Copyright © 1990 Cambridge University Press.

Figures 7.14a-7.14b. Reprinted by permission of the publishers from **The Diversity of Life** by Edward O. Wilson, Cambridge, Mass.: The Belknap Press of Harvard University Press, Copyright © 1992 by Edward O. Wilson.

Figures 7.15a-7.15b. Reprinted with permission of University of Chicago Press from **Sisters and Workers in the Middle Ages** edited by Judith M. Bennett, Elizabeth A. Clark, Jean E. O'Barr, B. Anne Vilen, and Sarah Westphal-Wihl. Chicago: The University of Chicago Press. Copyright © 1976, 1980, 1982, 1987, 1989 by the University of Chicago.

Figures 7.16a-7.16b. Reprinted from "Operations Analysis in the U.S. Army Eighth Air Force in World War II," by Charles W. McArthur, **History of Mathematics,** Volume 4, by permission of the American Mathematical Society. Copyright © 1990 by the American Mathematical Society.

Figures 7.17a-7.17c. Reprinted with permission of St. Martin's Press from **Parliament Today** by Andrew Adonis. New York: Manchester University Press. Copyright © 1990 Andrew Adonis.

Figures 7.18a-7.18c. Reprinted with permission of Plenum Press from **Solid State Microbatteries** edited by James K. Akridge and Minko Balkanski. New York: Plenum Press. Copyright © 1990 Plenum Press, New York.

Figures 7.19a-7.19b. Jensen, Joli, **Redeeming Modernity: Contradictions in Media Criticism,** copyright © 1990 by Sage Publications, Inc. Reprinted by permission of Sage Publications, Inc.

Figures 7.20a-7.20c. Reprinted with permission of Spring Publications from **Color Symbolism: Six Excerpts from the Eranos Yearbook, 1972** by Adolf Portmann and others. Dallas, Tex.: Spring Publications. Copyright © 1977 by Spring Publications, Inc.

Figures 7.21a-7.21b. Reprinted with permission of The Globe Pequot Press from **Backyard Adventure: How to Create Outdoor Play Spaces** by Paula Brook. Chester, Conn.: Globe Pequot Press. Copyright © 1988 by Paula Brook.

Figures 7.22a-7.22b. Reprinted with permission of KTAV Publishing House from **The Holocaust: An Annotated Bibliography and Resource Guide** edited by David M. Szonyi. New York: KTAV Publishing House for The National Jewish Resource Center. Copyright © 1985 National Jewish Resource Center.

Figures 7.23a-7.23d. Reprinted with permission of Ashgate Publishing Group from **The First World War.** Charles à Court Repington. Hampshire, England: Gregg Revivals in association with Department of War Studies, King's College London. Reprinted in 1991 by Gregg Revivals. Copyright © 1991 preface, Brian Bond.

Figures 7.24a-7.24b. Reprinted with permission of H. W. Wilson from **Facts about the Cities** by Allan Carpenter. Bronx, N.Y.: H. W. Wilson. Copyright © 1992 by Allan Carpenter.

Figures 8.1a-8.1b. Reprinted with permission of Chapman & Hall from **Organic Polymer Chemistry** by K. J. Saunders. New York: Chapman and Hall. Copyright © 1973, 1988 K. J. Saunders.

Figures 8.2a-8.2b. Reprinted with permission of Oxford University Press from **Human Biology: An Introduction to Human Evolution, Variation and Growth** by Geoffrey Harrison and others. New York: Oxford University Press. Copyright © 1964 Oxford University Press.

Figures 8.3a-8.3b. Reprinted with permission of American Psychological Association from **Sleep and Cognition** by Richard R. Bootzin, John F. Kihlstrom and Daniel L. Schacter. Washington, D.C.: American Psychological Association, 1990. Copyright © 1990 by the American Psychological Association. Reprinted by permission.

Figures 8.4a-8.4b. Reprinted with permission of Greenwood Publishing Group from **The Corporation, Ethics, and the Environment** edited by W. Michael Hoffman, Robert Frederick, and Edwards S. Petry. New York: Quorum Books. Copyright © 1990 by the Center for Business Ethics at Bentley College.

Figures 8.5a-8.5b. Printed by permission of Jain Publishing Co. from **Toward a Superconsciousness: Meditational Theory & Practice** by Hiroshi Motoyama. Berkeley, Calif.: Asian Humanities Press. Copyright © 1990 by Hiroshi Motoyama.

Figures 8.6a-8.6b. Reprinted with permission of the Indiana Historical Society from **The Journals of William A. Lindsay: An Ordinary Nineteenth-century Physician's Surgical Cases** edited by Katherine Mandusic McDonell. Indianapolis: Indiana Historical Society. Copyright © 1989 Indiana Historical Society.

Figures 8.7a-8.7b. Reprinted with permission of Scholars Press from **Bonds of Unity: Women, Theology, and the Worldwide Church** by Melanie A. May. Atlanta, Ga.: Scholars Press. Copyright © 1989 The American Academy of Religion.

Figures 8.8a-8.8b. Reprinted with the permission of Cambridge University Press from **River Towns in the Great West: The Structure of Provincial Urbanization in the American Midwest, 1820-1870** by Timothy R. Mahoney. Cambridge, New York; Cambridge University Press. Copyright © 1990 Cambridge University Press.

Figures 8.9a-8.9b. Reprinted with permission of Spring Publications from **Women's Dionysian Initiation: The Villa of Mysteries in Pompeii** by Linda Fierz-David. Dallas, Tex.: Spring Publications. Copyright © 1988 by Spring Publications.

Figures 8.10a-8.10b. Reprinted with permission of Garland Publishing from **Contemporary Legend: A Folklore Bibliography** by Gillian Bennett and Paul Smith. New York: Garland Publishing. Copyright © 1993 Gillian Bennett and Paul Smith,

Figures 9.1a-9.1b. Reprinted with permission of Kentucky Department of Travel Development from **The Uncommon Wealth of Kentucky** by Kentucky Transportation Cabinet, 1992. Frankfort, Ky.: Kentucky Department of Travel Development, Frankfort.

Figures 9.2a-9.2c. Reprinted by permission of C. F. Peters Corporation, sole agents for Hinrichsen Edition, London from **Theme and Variations in A Minor** by Dimitri Kabalewski. New York: Edition Peters & Hinrichsen Edition. Copyright © 1960 by Hinrichsen Edition, Peters Edition, London.

Figures 9.3a-9.3b. Reprinted with courtesy of BMG International from Roger Whittaker CD "Greatest Hits" 09026-61986-2.

Figures 9.4a-9.4b. Reprinted with permission of PJS Publications from **Kids Are Crafters, Too, with Cindy Groom Harry**. Peoria, Ill.: PJS Publications. Copyright © 1987 PJS Publications.

Figures 9.5a-9.5b. Reprinted with permission from Microsoft Corporation from **Microsoft ® Works**. Version 3.0 for MS-DOS. Redmond, Wash.: Microsoft Corporation. Copyright © 1987-1992 Microsoft Corporation.

Figures 9.6a-9.6b. Reprinted with permission of Folkmanis from **Kangaroo Hand Puppet**. Emeryville, Calif.: Folkmanis. Copyright © Folkmanis.

Figures 9.7a-9.7b. Reprinted with permission of Aristoplay, Ltd. from **Our Town: Your Town** created by Jan Parker. Ann Arbor: Aristoplay. Copyright © 1989 Aristoplay.

Figures 9.8a-9.8c. Reprinted with permission of **American City & County** from January 1994 issue. Atlanta, Ga.: Argus Business. Copyright © 1994 by Argus Business.

Introduction

A library's purpose is to provide service to its users. This service includes collecting, preserving, and making accessible recorded information that comes in various formats (e.g., books, microforms, computer disks, videorecordings). In today's electronic age this information may not even be permanently stored in the user's local library. A library with more than two employees is often divided into units that provide different aspects of this service. It is important for every library employee to understand the purpose of the library and to realize how each unit interconnects with other units to accomplish the library's purpose. For instance, collection development and acquisitions are the two main units in collection building.

The catalog department is the key unit in making recorded information accessible through bibliographic control. For each item in the collection the catalog department prepares a bibliographic record that describes the item in detail. Elements included in the record are author, title, edition, publication information, physical description, series, subjects, and more. The bibliographic records for all the items comprise the catalog, which may be in card, book, microform, or electronic format. The catalog is necessary for the other departments of the library to perform various duties. The collection development department analyzes the collection through the catalog to determine what materials are needed. The acquisitions department uses the catalog before placing orders to determine if the library already owns the title. The reference department uses it to answer patrons' questions. In an automated environment, the circulation department is unable to check out an item until an item record exists in the catalog. (The bibliographic records are used to produce the item records.) The interlibrary loan department uses the catalog to retrieve a requested item.

Thus, it is essential the data in the catalog be correct; otherwise, other departments will not be able to function. For example, an incorrect date or edition can cause the acquisitions department to order a duplicate book or the interlibrary loan department to supply the wrong item.

With the emergence of computers and bibliographic utilities in the 1970s, much of the work of the cataloging unit has been transferred from catalogers to high-level technicians. The specific duties of library technicians vary from library to library. What level of work the library technician performs depends upon the library's philosophy. In some libraries technicians perform high-level functions, while in others, the technicians' functions are more restricted. In many libraries today library technicians do a large percentage of the copy cataloging for monographs (books).

This book doesn't cover the pros and cons of different levels of personnel performing copy cataloging; it is written for the beginning copy cataloger who may be a beginning professional cataloger or a library technician. If the latter, a supervisor will need to give guidance on when to use the various sections. For instance, the chapter on other types of materials would not be used until the trainee was ready to begin copy cataloging of materials other than monographs.

Few manuals have been written for training the beginning copy cataloger, who lacks the basic cataloging and library terminology. Often a trainer assumes the trainee knows terminology that is a part of the trainer's everyday vocabulary, when such is not the case. This manual was written to overcome this problem. Its purpose is to help make the training of a beginning copy cataloger more effective and less frustrating. More than 50 examples are used to illustrate various cataloging rules and OCLC-MARC guidelines.

Because beginning copy catalogers are not likely to catalog formats other than monographs, this manual concentrates on copy cataloging for monographs. Other types of materials are covered in less detail. Besides, copy cataloging of monographs is considered by many to be the basic groundwork for moving into the other formats.

The first section explains the basic concepts of copy cataloging. The second section, which is the major section of the book, consists of examples of title pages, versos of title pages, and the like; unedited OCLC bibliographic records that have been modified by the author; discussions on the editing of those records; and edited records. This manual uses a conservative approach and verifies and edits every field if needed. Because some libraries do not edit every field, the copy cataloger will need to be instructed on the specific verifying and editing policies of the library.

The third section consists of exercises for the reader to perform. An option to perform the monographic exercises is given in chapters 7 and 8; the reader may choose to edit each area as it is completed. A short selected bibliography of useful cataloging tools and a glossary of selective cataloging terms complete the book.

For the most effective use of this manual, it is suggested that from chapter 7 on *Anglo-American Cataloging Rules*, 2d edition, 1988 revision (*AACR2R*); *Anglo-American Cataloguing Rules, Second Edition, 1988 Revision. Amendments* (1993); and OCLC's *Bibliographic Formats and Standards*, 1993 with updates, be consulted as one moves through the examples. (Libraries should have the 1993 amendments integrated into *AACR2R*; therefore, in the rest of this book the use of *AACR2R* means *AACR2R* plus 1993 amendments.) *Bibliographic Formats and Standards* also periodically receive updated pages. The copy cataloger should also discuss the examples with the supervisor to resolve any questions or confusion and to learn the library's policies and procedures on the various issues.

Part

I

Basic Concepts
of Copy Cataloging

Cataloging Terminology

The cataloging world contains words and terms that are not a part of one's everyday vocabulary. In the last two decades, library terminology has changed significantly due to the emergence of automation in libraries. Thus, during the first week on the job, the copy cataloger is confronted with unfamiliar terminology pertaining to books, bibliographic records, the MARC format, and perhaps computers. If the copy cataloger consults the literature for definitions, even more confusion may result. A dictionary of library terminology may contain many terms that have been replaced with newer terms (i.e., collation has been replaced with physical description).

In this section, some common cataloging terminology pertaining to books and bibliographic records is discussed. Terminology relating to the MARC format will be discussed in chapter 4. Computer terminology is not discussed in this manual, because the copy cataloger probably has some computer expertise through the wide use of computers in everyday activities. (If the copy cataloger has no computer experience, a supervisor needs to provide a general explanation or some reading materials. Manuals that come with microcomputers or that are provided by bibliographic utilities or commercial vendors are good choices.)

Terminology relating to the book will be discussed first. Right away, the copy cataloger may encounter a problem with the term *book*, because in many libraries, *monograph* may be used synonymously with *book*. A monograph is an item complete in one part or complete—or intended to be completed—in a finite number of parts.

Monograph is used in contrast with *serial*, which is a publication issued in parts and intended to continue indefinitely. Magazines, journals, newspapers, annuals, and yearbooks are serials. Sometimes the terms *work* and *item* are also used to refer to a book. *Work* is used mainly when referring to the book's intellectual content, while *item* is employed when referring to the physical book. *Volume* is another word occasionally used for *book*.

A group of related books may be either a *set* or a *series*. A set refers to a group that is closely related by content. One might think of a set as having too much information to fit into a single book or volume. A multivolume encyclopedia is a good example of a set of books.

A series refers to a group that is more loosely related than a set. A series usually covers one subject and is issued by one publisher. Books in a series will each have an individual title as well as the *series title*. For instance, the book *SongCite: An Index to Popular Songs* by William D. Goodfellow has the series title Garland Reference Library of the Humanities. The series title may be on the title page, the verso of the title page, the cover, or on a separate page called a *series title page*.

As a publisher begins creating a book, huge sheets of paper are used. First, the text is printed on the sheets of paper. The sheets are then folded and cut into pages. The height of a book depends on how many times the sheets are folded (between one and four times). A folded sheet is called a *signature*. If the text is printed on both sides of the fold, each side is called a *page*. If the text is printed on only one side of the fold, it is called a *leaf*. Thus, a sheet folded once has two leaves or four pages, and a sheet folded twice has four leaves or eight pages. Most books have signatures of either 16 or 32 pages. Each signature may be sewn before it is bound into a casing or cover.

The back edge of the cover is called the *spine*. The papers glued to the inside front and back covers are called *lining papers* or *end papers*. Half of each lining paper is not glued and looks like two pages of the book.

The *pagination* (page numbering) of a book is often in two sections. The first section of pages in a book is often unnumbered or numbered in Roman numerals. These pages contain introductory material about the book: the preface, acknowledgments, introduction, and table of contents. This section may be referred to as *preliminary paging*.

The next section of pages is the *text*. In many books, the page numbering begins again in Arabic numerals. The text may be followed by units of related information (e.g., index, appendices). The pagination of these units often is a continuation of the Arabic numerals used for the text. There are exceptions to these pagination arrangements. Each chapter or section of a book may have its own set of numerals. Another possibility is that a two- or three-volume set may be continuously paged from one volume to the next. In some books, all the pages may be unnumbered, or part of the pages may be unnumbered. Often, all the pages in books for preschool children are unnumbered.

The pages are sometimes referred to as *recto* and *verso*. The *recto* is the right side of an open book, usually bearing an odd page number. The *verso* is the left side of an open book and usually has an even page number. *Verso* may be used for the back side of a leaf or the back of the recto page. *Verso* is often used to indicate the back of the title page.

Some books contain *plates*. These are leaves or pages bearing illustrations, with or without text, that are not part of the pagination of the text. Often these are on higher-quality paper. Plates may be grouped together or scattered throughout the text.

Some publishers place a statement at the end of a book containing information about the author, title, and publication particulars. This is called a *colophon*, which means "summit" or "final touch." Colophons are found in older books and in books published outside the United States. Today, the information once contained in the colophon is usually found on the title page.

Books printed before the mid-fifteenth century did not have title pages. Title pages came into use around 1480, but they usually only contained the title. Today, the title page and its verso supply much of the information used in a bibliographic record.

The individual description of an item in the library's catalog is known as a *bibliographic record*. A bibliographic record consists of eight major bibliographic description areas plus access points and call number. A *MARC bibliographic record*, one that can be understood and used by a computer—MARC stands for *MAchine-Readable Cataloging*—contains other fields of information. The eight areas in a bibliographic record are title and statement of responsibility, edition, material-specific (or type of publication) details, publication/distribution and other such information, physical description, series, notes, and standard number. Each area is further subdivided.

On the surface, *title* sounds simple, but it has some confusing components. It is further broken down into *title proper, other title information, alternative title, half title, parallel title, caption title, running title, spine title, binder's title,* and *collective title.* The *title proper* is the main title. *Other title information,* formerly called *subtitle,* is information that qualifies or further expands the title proper. An *alternative title* is another title by which the work may be known. The alternative title is always preceded by "or" or its equivalent in another language. A *half title* is a brief title on a page preceding the title page. A *parallel title* is the title in another language. A *caption title* is the title on the first page of the text. A *running title* is the title listed on each leaf or page. It may be either at the top or bottom. A *spine title* is the title written on the spine of the book. A *binder's title* is the title put on the cover or spine of a book when it is rebound. A *collective title* is a title assigned to a group of previously separately published works that have been published together in one or more volumes. Common examples of collective titles are books of plays and short stories.

The *statement of responsibility* is the list of the individuals and groups responsible for the intellectual content of the item. This includes authors, editors, illustrators, translators, compilers, and the like.

The *edition* of a book refers to all copies made from the same type setup or from the same plates and issued by the same entity. If the content of the item is changed, this constitutes a new edition. New editions may be called second, third, new, revised, abridged, enlarged, and so forth. Sometimes the same content may be published in different casings—hardcover, paperback, library binding, and so on.

Printings, impressions, issues, reprints, and *facsimiles* add complexity and confusion to determining the edition. *Printing* or *impression* is an exact copy made at a different time. An *issue* is a copy with minor but well-defined variations incorporated into the original type setup. A *reprint* refers to either a copy made from the original type setup, often by photographic processes, or a new edition with substantially unchanged text. Reprints are often issued by a different publisher. A *facsimile* is a reproduction of a book's exact content and a simulation of its original appearance.

The *material-specific (or type of publication) details* area is not used for books. It is used for cartographic materials, music, computer files, serial publications, and microforms to record details that are specific to those formats.

Publication/distribution contains the place, name, and date of all publication, distribution, and issuing activities. This was formerly called the *imprint* area.

The *extent of the item* (pagination for books), illustrative matter, and dimensions comprise the *physical description* area. This was formerly called the *collation* area.

Series lists the series of which the item is a part. It may contain the series number, International Standard Serial Number (ISSN), subseries, and statement of responsibility. An item can be in more than one series.

Notes contains general information. Anything that is deemed important to the user and is not already in the bibliographic record may be placed in a note. There may be as many notes as necessary.

Standard number refers to internationally agreed-upon numbers. This mainly refers to International Standard Book Number (ISBN) and International Standard Serial Number (ISSN).

A book will have several *access points*. An *access point* is a name, term, code, or similar element that may be used to search for the item. Most books will have author, title, and subject access points. *Entry* and *heading* are synonyms for *access point*. Entries are often identified as *main entries* and *added entries*. The *main entry* is the major access point—author or title—used to cite the item. There have been debates over the need for a main entry, because automation has reduced its role significantly. However, a main entry is needed for consistent citation of the bibliographic item.

Added entries comprise all other access points. On a catalog card, all the added entries are listed at the bottom of the card and are called *tracings*. The added entries for sub-jects are called *subject entries* or *subject headings*.

The *call number* is composed of a *classification number* and a *Cutter number*. It may also contain a *date, workmark, volume number*, and *copy number*. The *classification number* places the item with other items on the same subject. There are several classification systems, but the two used most frequently in the United States are *Dewey Decimal Classification* (*DDC*) and *Library of Congress Classification* (*LCC*). The *Cutter number*, also known as *author number* or *book number*, arranges items with the same classification number in alphabetical order by main entry. Libraries using DDC use one of the three following Cutter Tables to determine the Cutter number: Two-Figure

Author Table, Three-Figure Author Table, or Cutter-Sanborn Table. Most libraries using LCC use a table prepared by the Library of Congress for composing Cutter numbers.

The *date* represents the publication date of the item. In *DDC*, a *workmark* consists of one or two lowercase letters at the end of the Cutter number; these represent the title. This allows titles by the same author in the same classification number to be arranged alphabetically. In *LCC*, a *workmark* is one or two lowercase letters following the publication date that identify the item as a facsimile or a variant edition published in the same year. The *volume number* distinguishes the physical units of the item. *Copy numbers* are needed if the library has more than one copy of the item.

Cataloging is the process of preparing the bibliographic record. Often, part of this bibliographic record appears in the book, usually on the verso of the title page. This partial record is called CIP (Cataloging-in-Publication). It is prepared by the Library of Congress from the publisher's galley proof so it can be included in the book. A galley proof is a copy of a work, before it is made into pages, that is used for examination and correction.

If new terminology is encountered, do not hesitate to ask a supervisor for a definition. The words and terms listed above are not exhaustive, and each library may have coined terms that are used only in that library.

2

Copy Cataloging—What Is It?

Before discussing copy cataloging, it is necessary to explain the term *cataloging*. Cataloging may be defined as the process of describing an item in a collection. It includes assigning name, title, and subject access points and determining a call number. Cataloging enables a user to determine whether an item is in the collection if the author, title, or subject is known. It also allows a user to determine the item's suitability for a need and serves as a location device via the call number. The product of cataloging is a bibliographic record.

Cataloging may be divided into two parts: *descriptive* and *subject*. Descriptive cataloging involves physically describing the item and assigning author and title access points. Subject cataloging involves assigning subject headings and a classification number.

Cataloging is often discussed in terms of *original* and *copy cataloging*. Original cataloging means creating a bibliographic record without reference to other bibliographic records for the same item or for different editions of the item. Copy cataloging means preparing a bibliographic record by using or adapting a bibliographic record already prepared by someone in another library or organization.

Some individuals use *shared* and *cooperative* cataloging synonymously with copy cataloging. While these terms are closely related, there are some important differences. Shared and cooperative cataloging indicate that there is a give and take, a two-way street. Copy cataloging may not be a two-way street. The library may not contribute any originally cataloged records to be used by others. This is usually the case if the library uses copy from CIP (Cataloging in Publication), library reference sources, commercial processing and cataloging services, or catalog cards that accompany purchased titles.

Bibliographic utilities, nonprofit organizations that produce databases and provide other services, encourage libraries to input originally cataloged bibliographic records; this increases the size of their database for copy cataloging and resource sharing. Thus, those libraries using a bibliographic utility share cataloging copy. However, the bibliographic records being added to the utility are usually entered by a higher-level individual than the one doing the copy cataloging. Libraries may need to be reminded to contribute records to the utility as they move to local online catalogs that allow bibliographic records to be input directly and easily into the local catalog. Many libraries will face this temptation to enter records directly into the local online catalog without entering them into the utility's database. Almost every cataloger will spend more time checking and verifying a record going into a national or international database than on a record only going into a local database.

Shared and cooperative cataloging are not new ideas. Charles C. Jewett was a proponent of cooperative cataloging in the 1800s while he was librarian at the Smithsonian Institution. At that time, the lack of rules or standards for cataloging inhibited the development of shared cataloging. Progress was greatly enhanced in 1901, when the Library of Congress started distributing catalog cards. The publication of *A Catalog of Books Represented by Library of Congress Printed Cards* and its successors also furthered standardization and shared cataloging. The biggest boost to shared cataloging came in the 1970s with the development of the USMARC format and the establishment of bibliographic utilities.

Today, the most widely used method of copy cataloging is through a bibliographic utility. Other methods include using CIP, purchasing cataloging copy or cards from a commercial processing and cataloging service, using copy found in library sources such as *National Union Catalog*, or using card sets supplied with the purchased item. Even though a large percentage of this copy is based on Library of Congress (LC) copy, the quality of cataloging ranges from excellent to poor, a result of individuals with various backgrounds and levels of expertise preparing and working with the copy.

The Online Computer Library Center (OCLC) is the largest bibliographic utility in the world and is used by more 20,000 libraries; hence, this manual is based on the copy cataloging being performed on the OCLC PRISM system. A further discussion of bibliographic utilities can be found in chapter 3.

Cataloging copy can be divided into two groups: *exact match* and *close copy*. Other names for close copy are *near copy*, *kindred copy*, or *variant copy*. Exact copy means copy for that edition of the item. Close copy is copy for another edition of the item. With exact copy, libraries make decisions, based on the administrative philosophy of each library, as to the amount of verifying and editing necessary. Some libraries will accept copy without any verification or editing. Other libraries check every field in the record.

Some libraries approach the acceptance of cataloging copy on the basis of its originator. For instance, Library of Congress copy, often referred to as *DLC* (the OCLC symbol for the Library of Congress) *copy*, will be accepted with little or no verification, while copy prepared by other libraries, referred to as *member copy*, will be thoroughly scrutinized.

Cataloging copy for a different edition of an item is referred to as *close copy*. Close copy requires editing or creating a new record. If a library is using pre-prepared card sets, editing may be the most practical way to proceed. (The library has to be willing to tolerate cards containing corrections.) If a library belongs to a bibliographic utility, there will be guidelines from the utility as to when to edit and when to create a new record. Because the library's symbol is attached to the bibliographic record on the utility, the bibliographic record needs to accurately reflect what the library owns. If not, problems will be created for the interlibrary loan department, and resource sharing, a necessity in today's economic climate, will be hindered.

Editing a bibliographic record for a different edition so that it matches the edition at hand has also caused libraries problems when they implemented an online catalog. Many online systems will only permit a bibliographic record to be in the system once. If the library used the bibliographic record twice, once for the first edition and again for the second, only one edited version may appear in the local online catalog. Because both records retained the same bibliographic control number, one edited version was overlaid on the other.

It is easy to create a new record when close copy is available as a reference, because in many cases only the edition, publication data, and physical description change. In OCLC, the NEW command allows much of the old data to be automatically transferred to a new record. The disadvantage is that without very careful proofing, errors will slip through. For this reason, in some libraries the use of the NEW command may be reserved only for original catalogers.

It is not always easy to tell when one has a different edition. Publishers have not been consistent with the words *printing* and *impression* or with their use of dates. Also, the meanings and uses of these words have changed with different sets of cataloging rules. Foreign publishers often use *printing* and *impression* in different contexts than U.S. publishers. For some items, a significant amount of experience is needed to be able to decipher the publication information. The copy cataloger should always consult a supervisor until he or she is comfortable in making a decision regarding editions and imprints.

OCLC's *Bibliographic Formats and Standards* lists guidelines as to when to create a new bibliographic record. Each field is discussed in detail. The copy cataloger needs to consult with a supervisor on procedures to follow for inputting a new record. A new record is usually needed when there are:

> differences in wording of the title proper
>
> variations in editions
>
> different places of publication
>
> different publishers
>
> different dates of publication
>
> major differences in the extent of the item (paging for books)
>
> differences of more than two centimeters in size

A truly different edition will usually differ in more than one field.

If a library does have a different edition, a new bibliographic record should be created. However, a library does not want to add duplicate records to a bibliographic utility, or even to its own catalog, if the edition is not truly different. One needs to proceed cautiously when deciding between editing an old record and creating a new one. Libraries have varying policies on who can decide when a new record is needed. Copy catalogers will need to consult supervisors on this issue.

3

Bibliographic Utilities

The long-time desire of librarians to share cataloging copy to reduce costs and increase cataloging speed, coupled with the development of the MARC format in the 1960s, gave rise to bibliographic utilities in the 1970s. Bibliographic utilities are sometimes called *bibliographic networks*, and sometimes the term *bibliographic* is even dropped. These nonprofit organizations produce bibliographic databases and provide many other services. The constituent members provide the bibliographic records, and the utility supplies the computer hardware, software, and communications to produce a database from the bibliographic records.

Bibliographic utilities can be differentiated from other networks in that they produce databases, while the other networks may be defined as groups of libraries banded together to secure services from a third party. Such services may consist of compiling a database of the members' bibliographic records. These networks are usually regional or state in nature, such as AMIGOS Bibliographic Council, Inc. (AMIGOS), serving the southwestern United States; Indiana Cooperative Library Services Authority (INCOLSA), serving the state of Indiana; Kentucky Library Network (KLN), a state network; OHIONET, which serves the state of Ohio; and Southeastern Library Network (SOLINET), serving the southeastern United States. They may also be subject-oriented, such as those for medical or law libraries.

Four bibliographic utilities were developed during the 1970s in North America: OCLC, Research Libraries Information Network (RLIN), Western Library Network (WLN), and ISM Library Information Services, a Canadian utility. Each grew from a need for shared cataloging rather than "reinventing the wheel" every time a library cataloged the same title. Although each bibliographic utility was established originally for a specific group of libraries, each has grown and broadened its membership criteria and services.

Due to the rapidly changing automation environment, each utility has experienced growing pains as it has moved from infancy to adolescence and on to adulthood. Interestingly, OCLC, WLN, and ISM have changed their names one or more times. Both OCLC and WLN managed to find names that matched their old initials or acronym. OCLC started as the Ohio College Library Center and is now Online Computer Library Center. For a short period, its name was just OCLC, Inc., with OCLC standing for nothing. WLN started as the Washington Library Network and in 1986 changed its name to Western Library Network. ISM traces its origins back to the University of Toronto Library Automation Systems. In between it was Utlas International and Utlas International Canada. In the literal sense, RLIN has not changed its name, but it resulted from the adoption of Stanford University's BALLOTS system.

If one is interested in the history of or more information on any of these bibliographic utilities, information is readily available in the professional literature.

4

MARC Record

MARC stands for MAchine-Readable Cataloging. It is a series of protocols for coding bibliographic data into a form that can be understood and used by a computer. It was developed by the Library of Congress in the 1960s. The MARC format revolutionized cataloging and brought automation within the grasp of many libraries. Readers, who have not seen an OCLC-MARC or MARC bibliographic record, may at this time want to look at the OCLC-MARC record in figure 4.6 (page 21) and the MARC record in figure 4.7 (page 22).

MARC was first developed for books. As demand grew, the format was adapted for archival and manuscript materials, computer files, maps, music, serials, and visual materials. Because the different formats were developed over a period of time, there are inconsistencies between them. Even as they were being developed, catalogers talked about integrating all of them. This integration was to have occurred in 1993, but it was delayed. It will now be implemented in phases. Some of the changes have already been implemented. For instance, the second indicator for the 100 field for books, serials, and music was made obsolete. At one time, the second indicator determined whether a subject entry was generated for the main entry. Another change is the 740 field, which now has very restricted use. A title traced differently now goes in field 246.

Through the MARC format, standardization in the library field has made great strides. However, bibliographic utilities, vendors, and agencies in other countries have made slight modifications in the MARC format. Thus we have USMARC, OCLC-MARC, UKMARC, CANMARC, so forth. These modifications are often additions that facilitate the use of the record in the specific system.

The MARC bibliographic record has mystified many librarians. Upon analysis, the MARC record can be broken into three elements: *record structure, content designation,* and *content.* They may be defined as follows:

> *Record Structure*: the codes used to identify the elements of information in a MARC record (e.g., tags, indicators, subfield codes)

> *Content Designation*: the definition of the codes in the record structure (i.e., 100 is for personal author main entry)

> *Content*: the data (text) of the record

Each MARC bibliographic record is divided into three parts—*leader, record directory,* and *variable fields.* The leader is the first 24 positions in the record. It contains coded information that enables the computer to process the record (e.g., record length, type of record). The record directory lists the fields by tag, stating their lengths and starting positions. The variable fields are the subunits of the data (text). Each variable field begins with a tag of three digits.

Variable fields are divided into two types: *variable control fields* and *variable data fields.* Variable control fields contain single data elements or a series of fixed-length data elements identified by relative character position. Tags range from 001 to 009 and contain no indicators or subfield codes. Usually the information is in coded form. Variable data fields have tags from 010 to 999. Each field is further defined by indicators, and the data is further subdivided into subfields. The information is in textual form.

Fixed field is a term used in many libraries because of a slight modification to the MARC record applied by bibliographic utilities and vendors. The fixed field is the MARC 008 field plus some of the leader items. This field is usually displayed at the top of the screen as a single paragraph with mnemonic tags.

The leader and record directory are not displayed on the screen. All of the directory and most of the leader are system-generated. Thus, the cataloger is mainly concerned with the data or the variable fields. That in itself is a big task, as the variable fields with their tags, indicators, and subfield codes are complex. Figure 4.1 lists some widely used variable fields and their meanings.

Fig. 4.1. Widely used variable fields.

010	Library of Congress Control (card) number
020	ISBN
100	Main entry, personal name
110	Main entry, corporate name
111	Main entry, conference name
245	Title and statement of responsibility
250	Edition statement
260	Publication, distribution information
300	Physical description
440	Traced series
490	Series untraced or traced in a different form
500	General note
504	Bibliography note
600	Subject access, personal name
610	Subject access, corporate name
611	Subject access, conference name
650	Subject access, topical heading
651	Subject access, geographic heading
700	Additional access point, personal name
710	Additional access point, corporate name
711	Additional access point, conference name
830	Additional access point, series uniform title

For ease in communication, some fields can be grouped by function based on the first character of the tag. For instance, the 100s are main entries and the 600s are subjects. Usually the last two characters of the tag are represented by xx. Thus, the 1xxs are main entries and the 6xxs are subjects (see figure 4.2).

Fig. 4.2. First character of tag.

1xx	Main entry—Name
4xx	Series statement
5xx	Notes
6xx	Subjects
7xx	Added entries
8xx	Series added entries
9xx	Local implementation

The meaning of the last two characters of a tag is maintained in some groups. For instance, in the 1xx, 4xx, 6xx, 7xx, and 8xx fields, 00 as the last two characters means personal name, and 10 in the same position means corporate name (see figure 4.3).

Fig. 4.3. Last two characters of tag.

```
x00    Personal names
x10    Corporate names
x11    Conference names
x30    Uniform titles—Main entry
x40    Uniform titles
```

As stated earlier, the variable fields are further defined by indicators. Each MARC bibliographical record contains two indicators at the beginning of each variable data field. Indicators are either lowercase alphabetic or numeric characters. Because numeric characters are defined first, most of the indicators in use at the present time are numeric. In some cases, indicators may be undefined and represented by blank positions. An indicator may tell the computer how many positions to skip before it begins sorting and filing. This is the case with the second indicator in the 245 field, as initial articles in a title are disregarded in filing. Thus, if a title begins with "The," the second indicator would be 4. The computer would disregard the three positions for "The" plus the blank space following it when indexing the entry.

Subfield codes consists of two characters that further subdivide the data in a field. The first position of a subfield code is a *delimiter*. A delimiter is one of the characters standardized by the American Standard Code for Information Interchange (ASCII). These characters were standardized so computers could communicate with each other. An example of a delimiter is ASCII $1F_{16}$. On paper, a delimiter may be displayed as ‡, $, :, or "\." In this manual, $ will be used for the delimiter. The second position is a lowercase alphabetic or numeric character. If the first subfield code in a field is $a, it is often not displayed. Subfield codes are defined for each field. For instance, subfield b in the 245 field contains other title information, while subfield c contains the statement of responsibility.

For a basic understanding of the MARC format, see the analysis of a simple bibliographic record that follows. (The examples in the rest of this manual will be in the OCLC-MARC format.) Figures 4.4a and 4.4b show the title page and title page verso of a book. Figure 4.5 depicts a catalog card for the book. Figure 4.6 illustrates the OCLC bibliographic record display as modified by the author. Figure 4.7 represents the MARC bibliographic record.

As figure 4.7 illustrates, a MARC bibliographic record is composed of fields strung together, with no breaks between fields or subfields. Each letter, mark of punctuation, and space counts as a position. In this example, as in all MARC records, the first 24 positions comprise the leader. The next 157 positions comprise the record directory. The last 322 positions contain the variable fields. Positions in the MARC record are defined in the tables Analysis of Leader, Analysis of Directory, and Analysis of Variable Fields.

Fig. 4.4a. Title page. Figures 4.4a–4.4b. Reprinted with permission of McGraw-Hill. From *Financial Accounting* by Walter B. Meigs and Robert F. Meigs. New York: McGraw-Hill. Copyright (c) 1979 by McGraw-Hill.

Financial Accounting

THIRD EDITION

WALTER B. MEIGS, Ph.D., C.P.A.
Professor of Accounting
University of Southern California

ROBERT F. MEIGS, D.B.A.
Professor of Accounting
School of Accountancy
San Diego State University

McGRAW-HILL BOOK COMPANY
New York   St Louis   San Francisco   Auckland   Bogotá   Dusseldorf
Johannesburg   London   Madrid   Mexico   Montreal   New Delhi   Panama
Paris   São Paulo   Singapore   Sydney   Tokyo   Toronto

Fig. 4.4b. Verso of title page.

Financial Accounting

1 2 3 4 5 6 7 8 9 0   K P K P   7 8 3 2 1 0 9 8

Library of Congress Cataloging in Publication Data

Meigs, Walter B.
    Financial accounting.

      1. Accounting. I. Meigs, Robert F., joint author.
II. Title.
HF5635.M492   1979   657   78-17818
ISBN 0-07-041220-0

This book was set in Vega by York Graphic Services, Inc.
The editors were Donald E. Chatham, Jr., Marjorie Singer,
Annette Hall, and M. Susan Norton;
the designer was Anne Canevari Green;
the cover painting was done by Glen Heller;
the production supervisor was Dennis J. Conroy.
Kingsport Press, Inc., was printer and binder.

Fig. 4.5. Catalog card.

```
HD          Meigs, Walter B.
5635           Financial accounting / Walter B.
.M492       Meigs, Robert F. Meigs. — 3rd ed. —
1979        New York : McGraw-Hill, c1979.
               xviii, 750 p. : ill. ; 24 cm.
               Includes index.




            1.  Accounting.  I.  Meigs, Robert F.
            II.  Title.
```

Fig. 4.6. OCLC bibliographic record.

```
OCLC: 3965811          Rec stat:   n
Entered: 19780522      Replaced: 19801220    Used: 19930302
Type: a  Bib lvl:  m  Source:         Lang:    eng
Repr:    Enc lvl:     Conf pub:  0    Ctry:    nyu
Indx: 1  Mod rec:     Govt pub:       Cont:
Desc: a  Int lvl:     Festschr:  0    Illus:   a
         F/B        0 Dat tp:    s    Dates:   1979,
1    010        78-17818
2    040        DLC $c DLC [Modified by author]
3    020        0070412200
4    050  0     HD5635 $b .M492 1979
5    082 00     657
6    049        KHNN
7    100 1      Meigs, Walter B.
8    245 10     Financial accounting / $c Walter B. Meigs,
Robert F. Meigs.
9    250        3rd ed.
10   260        New York : $b McGraw-Hill, $c c1979.
11   300        xviii, 750 p. : $b ill. ; $c 24 cm.
12   500        Includes index.
13   650  0     Accounting.
14   700 1      Meigs, Robert F.
```

Fig. 4.7. MARC bibliographic record.

```
Leader                        Record Directory
00504namƀƀ2200181ƀaƀ450000100130000000080041000130200150
0                   24                          48


00540500002300069082000800092100002000100245006200120250 0
    60                          96


01200182260003700194300003600231500002000267650001600287
                132                         156

                LC control number
700001900303Fƀƀƀ78017818ƀF780522s1979ƀƀƀƀnyuaƀƀƀƀƀƀƀƀƀƀ0
                181
                0
                              LC call number
01ƀ0ƀengƀƀFƀƀ$a0070412200F0ƀ$aHD5635$b.M492ƀ1979F00$a657
        54              69                   92

                     Title
F1ƀ$aMeigsƀWalterƀB.F10$aFinancialƀaccountingƀ/$cWalterƀ
   100                120

                          Edition
B.ƀMeigs,ƀRobertƀF.ƀMeigs.Fƀƀ$a3rdƀed.Fƀƀ$aNewƀYorkƀ:$bM
                       182              194

                    Physical description
cGraw-Hill,$cc1979.Fƀƀ$axviii,ƀ750ƀp.ƀ:$bill.ƀ;$c24ƀcm.F
                   231

                     Subject
ƀƀ$aIncludesƀindex.Fƀ0$aAccounting.F1ƀ$aMeigsƀRobertƀF.R
                   287                                322
```

Analysis of Leader

Position	Definition	Data
0–4	length of record	504 characters
5	status of record	new
6	type of record	printed language
7	bibliographic level	monograph
8–9	blanks	undefined
10	indicator count	indicator is composed of two characters
11	subfield count	subfield code is composed of two characters
12–16	starting character of variable field	181
17	encoding level	full level
18	descriptive cataloging form	AACR2
19	linked record requirement	related record not required
20–21	map for record directory	4 positions allocated for length 5 positions allocated for starting position
22	length of the implementation defined position	no implementation defined position
23	undefined entry map character position	undefined position

Analysis of Directory

Position	Definition	Tag	Length	Starting Position
24–35	1st variable field	001	13	0
36–47	2nd variable field	008	41	13
48–59	3rd variable field	020	15	54
60–71	4th variable field	050	23	69
72–83	5th variable field	082	8	92
84–95	6th variable field	100	20	100
96–107	7th variable field	245	62	120
108–119	8th variable field	250	12	182
120–131	9th variable field	260	37	194
132-143	10th variable field	300	36	231
144–155	11th variable field	500	20	267
156–167	12th variable field	650	16	287
168–179	13th variable field	700	19	303

Interpreting the directory for the seventh variable field, position 96–107, reveals that field 245 is the seventh variable field. It has 62 characters and starts in position 120. Note that numbering starts over with 0 at the beginning of the variable fields. The R in position 322 represents a record terminator.

Analysis of Variable Fields

Position	Field	Data
0–12	001	LC control number
13–53	008	general information
54–68	020	ISBN
69–91	050	LC call number; "0" in first indicator position means item is in LC collection; a blank in the second indicator position means no information provided on source of number; subfield b contains item portion of call number
92–99	082	Dewey call number
100–119	100	main entry, personal name; "1" in first indicator position means name is a single surname; the second indicator position is blank because the position is undefined
120–181	245	title statement; "1" in first indicator position means there is an added entry for title; "0" in second indicator position means there are zero nonfiling characters in title; subfield c contains statement of responsibility
182–193	250	edition statement; indicators are blank because the positions are undefined
194–230	260	publication, distribution area; indicators are blank because the positions are undefined; subfield b contains publisher; subfield c contains date of publication
231–266	300	physical description; indicators are blank because the positions are undefined; subfield b contains other physical details (e.g., illustrations); subfield c contains dimensions
267–286	500	note; indicators are blank because the positions are undefined
287–302	650	subject heading; the first position is blank because the position is undefined; "0" in second indicator position indicates that subject is an LC subject heading
303–321	700	added entry, personal name; "1" in first indicator position means name is a single surname; "ƀ" in second indicator position means entry is not for an analytic
322		record terminator

For ease in readability, bibliographic utilities and vendors display the MARC bibliographic record with each variable field on a separate line, with the tag in front of the field. The OCLC bibliographic record display in figure 4.6 is much easier to decipher even though it is not considered user-friendly. Note that the LC control number has been moved to the 010 field in the OCLC display; bibliographic utilities and vendors place their own bibliographic control number in the 001 field and move the LC control number to the 010 field. As stated earlier, the remaining examples in this manual will be in the OCLC-MARC format as modified by the author.

5

OCLC

Using OCLC

To be effective and efficient at editing cataloging copy, one must have an understanding of cataloging rules and the use of the OCLC PRISM system. OCLC is a bibliographic utility located in Dublin, Ohio. It was organized in 1967 by 54 Ohio college and university libraries. The online database began operation in 1971. In November 1990, OCLC launched its new online system, PRISM. Most libraries did not start using PRISM until 1991. PRISM is a new computer architecture that provides several new features that enhance cataloging and other OCLC activities. The other subsystems, such as interlibrary loan and union listing, have migrated to PRISM since 1991.

Membership in OCLC is composed of libraries and organizations from more than 50 countries, and the bibliographic database contains more than 30 million records. It is a sophisticated system that requires extensive training for efficient use. To ensure finding the correct record as quickly as possible with minimum cost, one must be able to comprehend and apply the various search strategies. Editing the bibliographic record on OCLC for production of cards or exporting to a local system requires many steps.

OCLC has documentation that covers all aspects of using its system. A supervisor should prepare a strategy for teaching OCLC that is appropriate to the workflow in the library. For instance, editing the bibliographic record may be done on the local system in some libraries. In that case, the copy cataloger will only need to know how to search and export (download) on OCLC.

Teaching the OCLC system may be accomplished by a variety of methods: demonstrating, reading, hands-on practicing, using a computer-based training (CBT) package, or a combination of these. The author suggests the strategy listed below for a trainee who has had no experience with OCLC.

A. Supervisor does a general demonstration of OCLC that lasts approximately one hour.

B. Supervisor sits next to the trainee while the trainee performs some basic activities on the OCLC workstation. The supervisor tells the trainee which commands to use and which keys to press, giving the trainee a general feel for using OCLC.

C. As indicated below, the trainee, supervisor, or both perform the following sessions using OCLC's *PRISM Basics CBT* course.

1. Trainee completes section 1.

2. Supervisor and trainee discuss section 1.

3. Trainee completes the first half of section 2.
   (Because of its length, section 2 should be split into two sessions. A good place to divide the section is after the part about numeric search keys.)

4. Supervisor and trainee discuss the first part of section 2.

5. Trainee completes the second half of section 2.

6. Supervisor and trainee discuss the second half of section 2.

7. Trainee completes section 3.

8. Supervisor and trainee discuss section 3.

D. As indicated below, the trainee, supervisor, or both perform the following sessions using OCLC's *Cataloging User Guide*, 2d edition:

1. Trainee reads chapters 1 and 2.

2. Supervisor and trainee discuss chapters 1 and 2.

3. Trainee reads chapter 3.

4. Supervisor and trainee discuss chapter 3.

5. Trainee practices on OCLC workstation.

6. Trainee reads chapter 4.

7. Supervisor and trainee discuss chapter 4.

8. Trainee practices on OCLC workstation.

9. Trainee reads chapter 7.

10. Supervisor and trainee discuss chapter 7.

11. Trainee reads chapters 8 and 9.

12. Supervisor and trainee discuss chapters 8 and 9.

13. Trainee practices on OCLC workstation.

14. Trainee reads chapter 10.

15. Supervisor and trainee discuss chapter 10.

16. Supervisor demonstrates expected workflow on OCLC for two or three items.

17. Supervisor sits beside trainee while trainee does the expected workflow for five to six items.

18. Trainee begins performing library's copy cataloging and is encouraged to ask questions as they arise. Cataloging is checked for an extensive time.

Some of the information in *Cataloging User Guide* overlaps the information presented in *PRISM Basics CBT*. The author feels that this helps the trainee's retention rate.

It takes time to learn to use the OCLC system effectively, but it is time well spent. Supervisors need to make sure adequate time is allowed for accomplishing this task.

Analyzing an OCLC Bibliographic Record

The copy cataloger must possess a basic understanding of the current cataloging rules and the OCLC-MARC format to be able to verify and edit copy cataloging.

To help the beginning copy cataloger understand what is involved with verifying and editing, the OCLC-MARC bibliographic record for *Financial Accounting* will be analyzed using *Anglo-American Cataloguing Rules*, 2d edition, 1988 revision and the 1993 amendments (noted as *AACR2R* in the rest of this book) and OCLC's *Bibliographic Formats and Standards* (noted as *Bibliographic Formats* in the rest of this book). See figures 4.4a and 4.4b on pages 19-20 for the title page and title page verso.

Fig. 5.1. OCLC bibliographic record.

```
OCLC: 3965811          Rec stat:   n
Entered: 19780522    Replaced: 19801220     Used: 19930302
Type: a  Bib lvl:  m  Source:         Lang:    eng
Repr:    Enc lvl:     Conf pub:  0    Ctry:    nyu
Indx: 1  Mod rec:     Govt pub:       Cont:
Desc: a  Int lvl:     Festschr:  0    Illus:   a
         F/B        0 Dat tp:    s    Dates:   1979,
1     010          78-17818
2     040          DLC $c DLC [Modified by author]
3     020          0070412200
4     050  0       HD5635 $b .M492 1979
5     082 00       657
6     049          KHNN
7     100 1        Meigs, Walter B.
8     245 10       Financial accounting / $c Walter B. Meigs,
Robert F. Meigs.
9     250          3rd ed.
10    260          New York : $b McGraw-Hill, $c c1979.
11    300          xviii, 750 p. : $b ill. ; $c 24 cm.
12    500          Includes index.
13    650  0       Accounting.
14    700 1        Meigs, Robert F.
```

The variable fields will be discussed first, because the Fixed Field contains codes based on the variable fields. Unless otherwise noted, the first subfield is always subfield a, and the delimiter "a" is not displayed.

010 78-17818: This is the Library of Congress control number field. *AACR2R* has no rules for recording system control numbers because it was not written for a specific system. *Bibliographic Formats* states that both indicators are blank and that subfield a lists the LC control number. The LC control number listed on the verso of the title page is 78-17818.

040 DLC $c DLC: This field identifies the institution that prepared the bibliographic record (cataloging institution) and the institution that input the record into the OCLC database. As might be expected, *AACR2R* does not address this area because it is for the source of cataloging. *Bibliographic Formats* notes that both indicators are blank. Subfield a contains the OCLC symbol of the institution that created the bibliographic record. Subfield b contains the language of cataloging and is only used by libraries where English is not the language of the cataloging agency. Subfield c contains the OCLC symbol of the institution that input the record into OCLC. The symbol DLC stands for Library of Congress; thus, this record was cataloged and input through tapeload into the OCLC database by the Library of Congress. Codes for OCLC members may be found in *OCLC Participating Institutions.*

020 0070412200: This is the International Standard Book Number field. *AACR2R* Rules 1.8 and 2.8 describe how to record the ISBN. *Bibliographic Formats* states that both indicators are blank. The ISBN listed on the verso of the title page is 0-07-041220-0. Hyphens and the letters ISBN are omitted when entering the number into the 020 field. The print program supplies "ISBN" and hyphens upon printing. Subfield a contains the ISBN.

050 0 HD5635 $b .M492 1979: This is the Library of Congress call number assigned by the Library of Congress, the British Library, or other agency. (An LC call number assigned by an OCLC member goes in the 090 field.) This call number is the one listed in the CIP on the verso of the title page. Because *AACR2R* only covers descriptive cataloging, this field is not addressed in *AACR2R*. According to *Bibliographic Formats,* a "0" in the first indicator position indicates that the item is in LC's collection. A blank in the second indicator position means that no information is provided on the source of the number. Subfield a contains the classification number. Subfield b contains the item number. Verifying and editing the call number varies greatly among libraries. The copy cataloger will need to consult a supervisor for local practices. The number may be accepted as is; it may be verified (checked) in the local shelflist; or it may be verified in the LC classification schedules.

082 00 657: This is the Dewey Decimal Classification (DDC) number assigned by LC. (A DDC number assigned by an OCLC member goes in the 092 field.) Because *AACR2R* only addresses descriptive cataloging, this field is not discussed in *AACR2R*. According to *Bibliographic Formats*, a zero in the first indicator position means that the full edition of DDC was used to assign the call number. A zero in the second indicator position means that the number was assigned by the Library of Congress. Subfield a contains the DDC number.

100 1 Meigs, Walter B.: This field is for a personal name main entry. In *AACR2R*, Rule 21.6C1 states that when responsibility is shared between two or three persons and principal responsibility is not indicated, the main entry should be for the person named first. In this case, Walter and Robert Meigs are responsible for the intellectual content of this book. There is no indication that one had principal responsibility; therefore, the main entry is under Walter, as he is listed first.

Bibliographic Formats states that a "1" in the first indicator position means a single surname. The second indicator at the present time is a blank. Subfield a contains the surname and forenames.

The copy cataloger may need to verify that the form of name is correct in an authority file. Authority work varies from library to library; the copy cataloger will need to follow the library's specific procedures on authority work. In many libraries, this will be done on the local system after the record is exported.

245 10 Financial accounting / $c Walter B. Meigs, Robert F. Meigs: This field contains the title and statement of responsibility. In *AACR2R*, Rules 1.1 and 2.1 state that the title is to be recorded as it appears on the title page as to wording, order, and spelling, but not necessarily as to punctuation and capitalization. Appendix A on capitalization states that the first word of a title is capitalized. Other words are capitalized as instructed in the rules for the language involved. In English, rules for the language mean that, after the first word, only proper names are capitalized. This explains why *accounting* is not capitalized. Rule 1.1F7 states that qualifications of names are omitted except for some specific cases. Thus, Ph.D. and C.P.A. are omitted from Walter B. Meigs and D.B.A. from Robert F. Meigs.

From *Bibliographic Formats* a "1" in the first indicator position will cause a title-added entry to be generated. The "0" in the second indicator position means that the computer will not skip any positions before it starts filing. Subfield a contains the title, and subfield c the statement of responsibility. Because there is no other title information, subfield b is not used.

250 3rd ed.: This field contains the edition statement. From Rules 1.2 and 2.2 and appendices B and C in *AACR2R*, one determines that Arabic numbers should be substituted for numbers expressed as words in the edition area, and that *edition* can be abbreviated. From *Bibliographic Formats*, one determines that both indicators are blank. Subfield a contains the edition statement.

260 New York : $b McGraw-Hill, $c c1979: This field contains the publication information. In *AACR2R*, one ascertains from Rules 1.4 and 2.4 that only the first place of publication needs to be listed for this book. The shortest form that can be understood internationally should be used for the publisher, so "Book Company" can be omitted from the publisher's name. The only dates given are copyright dates; thus, the latest copyright date is all that is listed. *Bibliographic Formats* states that both indicators are blank. Subfield a contains the place of publication, subfield b the publisher, and subfield c the date.

300 xviii, 750 p. : $b ill. ; $c 24 cm.: This field contains the physical description. Using Rule 2.5 and Appendix B in *AACR2R*, one determines that the last numbered page in each sequence of pages should be listed and that pages are abbreviated. Illustrations are listed as "ill." The height is given in centimeters. Part of a centimeter is always rounded to the next highest centimeter. *Bibliographic Formats* states that both indicators are blank. Subfield a contains the pagination, subfield b the illustrative statement, and subfield c the dimensions.

500 Includes index.: A 500 field is a general note. Rules 1.7 and 2.7 in *AACR2R* describe the note area. Notes contain any useful information that is not covered in one of the other areas. *Bibliographic Formats* states that both indicators are blank. Subfield a contains the general note.

650 0 Accounting.: A 650 field contains a topical subject heading. *AACR2R* does not contain rules for subject headings. The two main subject heading lists in use in the United States are *Sears List of Subject Headings* and *Library of Congress Subject Headings.* The copy cataloger will need to follow the procedures of the library for listing subject headings. Because this involves authority work, a wide variation exists in the amount of verification among libraries. *Bibliographic Formats* notes that the first indicator is blank except for technical reports. A "0" in the second indicator position indicates that it is an LC subject heading. Subfield a contains the topical subject.

700 1 Meigs, Robert F.: A 700 field is an added entry for a personal name. Rule 21.6C1 in *AACR2R* indicates that an added entry should be made for the author who is not listed as main entry when responsibility is shared between two persons and principal responsibility is not indicated. *Bibliographic Formats* notes that the first indicator of "1" indicates a single surname. The second indicator is blank, indicating the entry is not for an analytic. Subfield a contains the surname and forename of the author.

The fixed field displayed at the top of the record in paragraph style is in code form. *AACR2R* does not cover the fixed field; therefore, one only has to consult *Bibliographic Formats* for it.

Type: a	it is printed-language material
Bib lvl: m	it is a monograph
Source:	it was cataloged by LC
Lang: eng	it is in English
Repr:	it is not microform, Braille, large print, or regular-print reproduction
Enc lvl:	denotes full-level LC cataloging
Conf pub: 0	it is not a conference publication
Ctry: nyu	it was published in New York State
Indx: 1	it has an index
Mod red:	the record has not been modified for machine-readable form
Gov pub:	it is not a government publication
Cont:	it does not fit into a special contents type
Desc: a	it was cataloged according to *AACR2* rules
Int lvl:	it is not a work for juveniles
Festschr: 0	it is not a festschrift
Illus: a	it has illustrations
F/B: 0	it is not fiction or biography
Dat tp: s	there is a single publication date
Dates: 1979,	the publication date is 1979

6

Final Transactions

After editing the cataloging copy on a bibliographic utility, a final step is needed to transfer the bibliographic records into the local collection. (Some libraries with local automated systems will transfer first and then do the editing on their local systems.) This step may be producing catalog cards, or it may be transferring the MARC records to a local automated catalog. On OCLC, both are simple processes.

If one is producing cards, one need only press a couple of keys to request them from OCLC. The catalog cards will arrive in approximately a week, already sorted in alphabetical and shelflist order according to the library's profile.

If one is transferring the MARC record to a local automated system, a few more transactions are needed. This process is called *exporting* or *downloading*. The procedures will vary depending on the local system; a few steps on OCLC and a few steps on the local system may be necessary. In many cases, the record will be available for users to access that same day or the next day. Some libraries may leave the bibliographic record in a buffer in the local system until the book has been physically processed. (Physical processing includes attaching a call number and security label, stamping the book with an ownership stamp, etc.)

If the library has an automated system, an item record will need to be generated. This record contains information specific to that item, such as bar code number, volume number, copy number, and circulation parameters. If the library is still using a card catalog and shelflist, much of the information contained on the item record will be entered on the shelflist card.

At this point, the book is ready for use as specified by the library, either to be kept within the library or to be made available for circulation.

Part

Performing
Copy Cataloging

7

Description for Monographs

In copy cataloging, as well as original cataloging, one must know how to read the book to determine the information for the bibliographic record. One cannot take the time to read the book from cover to cover, so the key parts are read or scanned. This is called *technical reading*. These key parts are:

> title page
>
> verso of title page
>
> cover
>
> jacket
>
> preface
>
> introduction
>
> table of contents
>
> series title page
>
> index

These parts usually provide all the information needed to catalog a book except the physical description.

With book in hand, the copy cataloger decides on a search strategy to use for retrieving the bibliographic record for that book. In some libraries, the book may be accompanied by an OCLC control number found in preorder searching. If not, the copy cataloger chooses one of the following search strategies:

ISBN

LC control number

author

title

author/title

title phrase

combined search

The copy cataloger will want to use qualifiers on author, title, author/title, and combined searches.

Upon retrieving the record, the copy cataloger quickly checks two or three key fields to verify that the bibliographic record is the correct one for that book. Recommended key fields are 020, 245, and 260. If no exact copy is found, the copy cataloger follows the library's procedures for handling close copy.

After determining that the bibliographic record matches the book in hand, the copy cataloger verifies and edits fields required by the library. This manual uses a conservative approach and verifies and edits every field, if needed. Copy cataloging is illustrated in the following examples. The author has tried to use examples that a copy cataloger is likely to encounter in most libraries.

Each example has the following four parts:

1. A copy of the title page and verso of the title page are shown with a description of other relevant information, if needed.

2. A simulated OCLC record is shown. These records have been modified to illustrate editing; if anyone searches OCLC, these precise records will not be found.

3. The field(s) for the area under consideration is discussed.

4. A simulated edited OCLC record is shown.

The rules referred to will be from *AACR2R*. The field requirements will be taken from *Bibliographic Formats*. In some cases, the Library of Congress's interpretations of the rules have been noted, as many libraries in the United States follow LC's interpretations. These interpretations can be found in either *Cataloging Service Bulletin*, published quarterly by LC, or *Library of Congress Rule Interpretations*. In this book the reader will be referred to *Cataloging Service Bulletin*.

The copy cataloger needs to become familiar with these tools, as they contain useful information. The appendices in *AACR2R* are useful tools, and there is much helpful information at the front of *Bibliographic Formats* and at each field or at each element section. For instance, at the F/B element in the fixed field, one finds that poetry and drama are not considered fiction. Library of Congress's interpretations provide the most current information on changes and interpretations at LC.

Title and Statement of Responsibility Area (Rules 1.1 and 2.1; Field 245)

Fig. 7.1a. Title page. Figures 7.1a-7.1b. MacDonald, Scott B., *Dancing on a Volcano: The Latin American Drug Trade*, reprinted with permission of Greenwood Publishing Group, Inc., Westport, CT. Copyright © 1988 by Scott B. MacDonald.

DANCING
on a
VOLCANO

The Latin American Drug Trade

Scott B. MacDonald

PRAEGER

New York
Westport, Connecticut
London

Fig. 7.1b. Verso of title page.

Library of Congress Cataloging-in-Publication Data

MacDonald, Scott.
    Dancing on a volcano : the Latin American drug trade / Scott B.
MacDonald.
        p.   cm.
    Bibliography: p.
    Includes index.
    ISBN 0-275-92752-0 (alk. paper)
    ISBN 0-275-93105-6 (pbk : alk. paper)
    1. Drug traffic—Latin America.   2. Drug traffic—United States.
I. Title.
HV5840.L3M34   1988
363.4'5'098—dc19   88-9950

Library of Congress Catalog Card Number: 88-9950
ISBN: 0-275-92752-0
ISBN: 0-275-93105-6 (paperback)

First published in 1988

Praeger Publishers, One Madison Avenue, New York, NY 10010
A division of Greenwood Press, Inc.

Printed in the United States of America

The paper used in this book complies with the Permanent
Paper Standard issued by the National Information Standards
Organization (Z39.48—1984).

10 9 8 7 6 5 4 3 2 1

Fig. 7.1c. Unedited OCLC bibliographic record.

```
OCLC: 17765724        Rec stat:  c
Entered: 19880324    Replaced: 19900421     Used: 19910419
Type: a  Bib lvl:  m  Source:         Lang:    eng
Repr:    Enc lvl:     Conf pub:  0    Ctry:    nyu
Indx: 1  Mod rec:     Govt pub:       Cont:
Desc: a  Int lvl:     Festschr:  0    Illus:
         F/B:      0  Dat tp:    s    Dates:   1988,
1    010          88-9950//r90
2    040          DLC $c DLC $d OCL [Modified by author]
3    020          0275927520 (alk. paper)
4    020          0275931056 (pbk. : alk. paper)
5    043          cl----- $a n-us---
6    050 00       HV5840.L3 $b M34 1988
7    082 00       363.4/5/098 $2 19
8    049          KHNN
9    100 1        MacDonald, Scott B.
10   245 10       Dancing on a Volcano : $b the Latin
American Drug Trade / Scott B. MacDonald.
11   260          New York : $b Praeger, $c 1988.
12   300          xi, 166 p. ; $c 24 cm.
13   500          Includes index.
14   504          Includes bibliographical references (p.
[155]-160).
15   650  0       Drug traffic $z Latin America.
16   650  0       Drug traffic $z United States.
```

Discussion: Rules 1.1B1 and 1.1E1 state that the title should be transcribed exactly as to wording, order, and spelling, but not necessarily as to punctuation and capitalization. Capitalization should be in accordance with Appendix A. The title proper and other information are transcribed exactly as to wording, order, and spelling, but capitalization is not in accordance with Appendix A. As stated in Rule A.4A1, the first word should be capitalized, and the capitalization of the rest of the words in the title is dependent on the rules of the language involved. Rules for English require that only proper names be capitalized; thus, capitalization is incorrect. Only *Dancing* and *Latin American* should be capitalized. The statement of responsibility has been transcribed correctly according to Rule 1.1F1. The colon and slash are the correct prescribed punctuation for other title information and statement of responsibility.

The first indicator of "1" means the title will have a title added entry made. The second indicator of "0" means that no positions will be disregarded for sorting or filing processes. A subfield code of "b" is correct for the other title information. The

subfield code for statement of responsibility has been omitted.
It should be "c."

Fig. 7.1d. Edited OCLC bibliographic record.

```
OCLC: 17765724        Rec stat:  c
Entered: 19880324   Replaced: 19900421    Used: 19910419
Type: a  Bib lvl:  m  Source:        Lang:    eng
Repr:     Enc lvl:     Conf pub:  0   Ctry:    nyu
Indx: 1  Mod rec:     Govt pub:      Cont:
Desc: a  Int lvl:     Festschr:  0   Illus:
          F/B:      0  Dat tp:    s   Dates:   1988,
1    010          88-9950//r90
2    040          DLC $c DLC $d OCL [Modified by author]
3    020          0275927520 (alk. paper)
4    020          0275931056 (pbk. : alk. paper)
5    043          cl----- $a n-us---
6    050 00       HV5840.L3 $b M34 1988
7    082 00       363.4/5/098 $2 19
8    049          KHNN
9    100 1        MacDonald, Scott B.
10   245 10       Dancing on a volcano : $b the Latin
American drug trade / $c Scott B. MacDonald.
11   260          New York : $b Praeger, $c 1988.
12   300          xi, 166 p. ; $c 24 cm.
13   500          Includes index.
14   504          Includes bibliographical references (p.
[155]-160).
15   650  0       Drug traffic $z Latin America.
16   650  0       Drug traffic $z United States.
```

Fig. 7.2a. Title page.

Michael Ende

Die unendliche Geschichte

Von

A bis Z

mit Buchstaben und Bildern

versehen von

Roswitha Quadflieg

K. Thienemanns Verlag

Stuttgart

Fig. 7.2b. Colophon.

Ausgezeichnet mit dem
»Buxtehuder Bullen«
Deutscher Jugendbuchpreis (Auswahlliste)
Europäischer Jugendbuchpreis
Großer Preis der Deutschen Akademie für
Kinder- und Jugendliteratur, Volkach
Preis der Leseratten
Wilhelm-Hauff-Preis
Preis der Akademie der schönen Künste Florenz
»Lorenzo il Magnifico 82«
»Bronzi di Riace 82«
(Kiwanis Literatur-Preis)
»Silberner Griffel von Rotterdam 83«
Michael Ende
erhielt für sein literarisches Gesamtwerk
den Janusz-Korczak-Preis

Zu dem Buch »Die unendliche Geschichte«
gibt es auch Schallplatten oder Kassetten
und Aufnahmen in Blindenhörbüchereien
Es erschienen Übersetzungen in folgenden Sprachen:
Bulgarisch, Dänisch, Englisch (Weltrechte), Finnisch,
Französisch, Griechisch, Hebräisch, Holländisch, Isländisch,
Italienisch, Japanisch, Norwegisch, Polnisch, Portugiesisch,
Russisch, Rumänisch, Schwedisch, Slowenisch,
Spanisch, Tschechisch, Türkisch, Ukrainisch, Ungarisch

CIP-Kurztitelaufnahme der Deutschen Bibliothek
Ende, Michael
Die unendliche Geschichte
ISBN 3-522-12800-1
Gesamtausstattung Roswitha Quadflieg in Hamburg
Schrift Garamond Antiqua
Satz G. Müller
Druck und Bindung Franz Spiegel Buch GmbH in Ulm
Offsetreproduktionen Gustav Reisacher in Stuttgart
© 1979 by K. Thienemanns Verlag in Stuttgart
Printed in Germany
25   24   23   22

Fig. 7.2c. Unedited OCLC bibliographic record.

```
OCLC: 7460007          Rec stat:   c
Entered: 19810403     Replaced: 19870203      Used: 19910521
Type: a  Bib lvl:   m  Source:         Lang:    ger
Repr:       Enc lvl:      Conf pub:  0    Ctry:    gw
Indx: 0  Mod rec:      Govt pub:       Cont:
Desc: i  Int lvl:      Festschr:  0    Illus:   a
            F/B:      1  Dat tp:    s    Dates:   1979,
1     010          89-145722
2     040          DLC $c DLC [Modified by author]
3     015          GFR80-A3
4     019          6969541
5     020          3522128001 : $c DM24.80
6     050   0      PT2665.N27 $b U5
7     092          END
8     049          KHNN
9     100 1        Ende, Michael.
10   245 10       Die unendliche geschichte : $b von a bis z
/ $c Michael Ende mit buchstaben u. bildern vers. von
Roswitha Quadflieg.
11   260          Stuttgart : $b Thienemanns, $c c1979.
12   300          428 p. : $b col. ill. ; $c 21 cm.
13   700 1        Quadflieg, Roswitha.
```

Discussion: The title and other title information have been transcribed exactly as to wording, order, and spelling (Rules 1.1B1 and 1.1E1). The capitalization is not in accordance with the German language (Rule A.4A1). In German, all nouns are capitalized. Looking at Rules 1.1F1 and 1.1F6, the statement of responsibility should be transcribed in the form and order specified. The author's surname has been misspelled. It has also been misspelled in the 100 field, so anyone searching by author will not retrieve this record. In looking at Appendix B, the only abbreviations permitted in the title and statement of responsibility area are those found on the prescribed source of information and "i.e.," "et al.," and their equivalents (Rule B.4). Thus, *und* and *versehen* cannot be abbreviated. Looking at the fixed field, one notices that this record is not cataloged according to *AACR2*. Before *AACR2*, other abbreviations were allowed.

A slash is the correct prescribed punctuation to precede the first statement of responsibility. Rule 2.1A1 states that each subsequent statement of responsibility is preceded by a semicolon. Thus, a semicolon space (;)should be inserted before *mit*.

The first indicator of "1" means a title added entry will be generated. The second indicator is incorrect, as "0" means no positions will be omitted in sorting and filing processes. *Die* means "the" in German; therefore, the second indicator should be "4." The subfield codes are correct.

Fig. 7.2d. Edited OCLC bibliographic record.

```
OCLC: 7460007        Rec stat:  c
Entered: 19810403    Replaced: 19870203    Used: 19910521
Type: a  Bib lvl:  m  Source:        Lang:    ger
Repr:    Enc lvl:     Conf pub:  0    Ctry:    gw
Indx: 0  Mod rec:     Govt pub:       Cont:
Desc: a  Int lvl:     Festschr:  0    Illus:   a
         F/B:      1  Dat tp:    s    Dates:   1979,
1    010        89-145722
2    040        DLC $c DLC [Modified by author]
3    015        GFR80-A3
4    019        6969541
5    020        3522128001 : $c DM24.80
6    050  0     PT2665.N27 $b U5
7    092        END
8    049        KHNN
9    100  1     Ende, Michael.
10   245  14    Die unendliche Geschichte : $b von A bis Z
/ $c Michael Ende ; mit Buchstaben und Bildern versehen
von Roswitha Quadflieg.
11   260        Stuttgart : $b Thienemanns, $c c1979.
12   300        428 p. : $b col. ill. ; $c 21 cm.
13   700  1     Quadflieg, Roswitha.
```

Fig. 7.3a. Title page. Figures 7.3a-7.3b. Reprinted from *Satanstoe, or The Littlepage Manuscripts: A Tale of the Colony* by James Fenimore Cooper in *The Writings of James Fenimore Cooper* by permission of the State University of New York.

Satanstoe,

or The Littlepage Manuscripts

A Tale of the Colony

James Fenimore Cooper

Historical Introduction by

Kay Seymour House

Text Established, with Explanatory Notes

by Kay Seymour House and

Constance Ayers Denne

"The only amaranthine flower on earth

Is virtue; the only treasure, truth."

William Cowper, "The Task," iii, 268

State University of New York Press

Fig. 7.3b. Verso of title page.

The preparation of this volume was made possible (in part) by a grant from the Program for Editions of the National Endowment for the Humanities, an independent Federal agency.

The Center emblem means that one of a panel of textual experts serving the Center has reviewed the text and textual apparatus of the printer's copy by thorough and scrupulous sampling, and has approved them for sound and consistent editorial principles employed and maximum accuracy attained. The accuracy of the text has been guarded by careful and repeated proofreading according to standards set by the Center.

Published by
State University of New York Press, Albany

©1990 State University of New York

Printed in the United States of America

For information, address State University of New York
Press, State University Plaza, Albany, N.Y., 12246

Library of Congress Cataloging-in-Publication Data
Cooper, James Fenimore, 1789–1851.
    Satanstoe, or, The Littlepage manuscripts : a tale of the Colony /
James Fenimore Cooper ; historical introduction by Kay Seymour House
; text established, with explanatory notes by Kay Seymour House and
Constance Ayers Denne.
       p. cm. — (The Writings of James Fenimore Cooper)
    Includes bibliographies.
    ISBN 0–88706–903–7. ISBN 0–88706–904–5 (pbk.)
    1. New York (State)—History—Colonial period, ca. 1600–1775-
-Fiction. I. House, Kay Seymour. II. Denne, Constance Ayers.
III. Title. IV. Title: Satanstoe. V. Title: Littlepage
manuscripts. VI. Series: Cooper, James Fenimore, 1789–1851. Works.
   1980.
PS1417.S3 1989   88–12196
813′.2—dc19   CIP
10 9 8 7 6 5 4 3 2 1

Fig. 7.3c. Unedited OCLC bibliographic record.

```
OCLC: 17806804      Rec stat:   c
Entered: 19880401   Replaced: 19901027    Used: 19930303
Type: a  Bib lvl:  m  Source:         Lang:    eng
Repr:    Enc lvl:     Conf pub:  0    Ctry:    nyu
Indx: 0  Mod rec:     Govt pub:  s    Cont:    b
Desc: a  Int lvl:     Festschr:  0    Illus:   a
         F/B:       1 Dat tp:    s    Dates:   1990,
1    010         88-12196//r90
2    040         DLC $c DLC [Modified by author]
3    020         0887069037
4    020         0887069045 (pbk.)
5    043         n-us-ny
6    050 00      PS1417 $b .S3 1990
7    082 00      813/.2 $2 19
8    049         KHNN
9    100 1       Cooper, James Fenimore, $d 1789-1851.
10   245 10      Satanstoe : $b or the Littlepage
manuscripts : a tale of the Colony / $c James Fenimore
Cooper, historical introduction by Kay Seymour House.
11   260         Albany : $b State University of New York
Press, $c c1990.
12   300         xxxviii, 500 p. : $b ill. ; $c 24 cm.
13   490 1       The writings of James Fenimore Cooper
14   504         Includes bibliographies.
15   651  0      New York (State) $x History $y Colonial
period, ca. 1600-1775 $x Fiction.
16   740 01      Satanstoe.
17   740 01      Littlepage manuscripts.
18   800 1       Cooper, James Fenimore, $d 1789-1851. $t
Works. $f 1980.
```

Discussion: The "or" is a clue that there is an alternative title here. Rule 1.1B1 states that an alternative title is part of the title proper. In this case the alternative title is being treated as if it were other title information. Rule 1.1B1 also states that a comma should precede and follow the word "or." *Satanstoe* has been misspelled. This bibliographic record should have three statements of responsibility, but only two have been recorded. Rule 1.1A1 states that after the first statement of responsibility, each subsequent statement of responsibility should be preceded by a semicolon, but the second statement of responsibility is not. Two access points are missing because the third statement of responsibility was omitted.

Even though this is not a CIP record, it is not unusual for something like this to happen in a CIP record. The copy cataloger needs to be aware that this may happen and to follow the policy of the library for getting the access points added. Often this may be performed by someone at a higher level.

With the 1995 format integration changes, the 740 field is no longer valid for a title traced differently. The 740 field now is only used for analytical and titles of related items. The copy cataloger needs to be aware that the OCLC database will contain many records with 740 fields for titles traced differently. The copy cataloger will need to know the library's policy on whether 740 fields will be changed to 246 fields. In this book the 740 fields with titles traced differently will change to 246 fields.

The indicators are correct. The subfield code for other title information needs to be inserted before a tale. The subfield code for the statement of responsibility is correct.

Fig. 7.3d. Edited OCLC bibliographic record.

```
OCLC: 17806804      Rec stat:   c
Entered: 19880401   Replaced: 19901027     Used: 19930303
Type: a  Bib lvl:  m  Source:         Lang:    eng
Repr:    Enc lvl:     Conf pub:  0    Ctry:    nyu
Indx: 0  Mod rec:     Govt pub:  s    Cont:    b
Desc: a  Int lvl:     Festschr:  0    Illus:   a
         F/B:      1  Dat tp:    s    Dates:   1990,
1    010         88-12196//r90
2    040         DLC $c DLC [Modified by author]
3    020         0887069037
4    020         0887069045 (pbk.)
5    043         n-us-ny
6    050 00      PS1417 $b .S3 1990
7    082 00      813/.2 $2 19
8    049         KHNN
9    100 1       Cooper, James Fenimore, $d 1789-1851.
10   245 10      Satanstoe, or, The Littlepage manuscripts
: $b a tale of the Colony / $c James Fenimore Cooper ;
historical introduction by Kay Seymour House ; text
established, with explanatory notes by Kay Seymour House
and Constance Ayers Denne.
11   246 30      Satanstoe
12   246 30      Littlepage manuscripts
13   260         Albany : $b State University of New York
Press, $c c1990.
14   300         xxxviii, 500 p. : $b ill. ; $c 24 cm.
15   490 1       The writings of James Fenimore Cooper
16   504         Includes bibliographies.
17   651  0      New York (State) $x History $y Colonial
period, ca. 1600-1775 $x Fiction.
18   700 1       House, Kay Seymour.
19   700 1       Denne, Constance Ayers.
20   800 1       Cooper, James Fenimore, $d 1789-1851. $t
Works. $f 1980.
```

Fig. 7.4a. Title page.

SANTIAGO CALATRAVA

DYNAMISCHE GLEICHGEWICHTE

NEUE PROJEKTE

DYNAMIC EQUILIBRIUM

RECENT PROJECTS

Fig. 7.4b. Colophon.

Dieses Buch wurde von der "Holderbank" Financière Glarus AG, Schweiz.

und der Firma Hans Schmidlin AG, Fassaden-/Fenstersysteme, Aesch/BL, Schweiz,

mit einem Beitrag unterstützt

This book was supported by "Holderbank"

Financière Glaris Ltd., Switzerland,

and Hans Schmidlin AG,

windows and curtain walling,

Aesch, Switzerland

Konzeption/Concept: Anthony Tischhauser, Tristan Kobler

Layout: Quim Nolla

Photographien der Architekturmodelle/Model Photographs: Heinrich Helfenstein

Architekturmodelle/Architectural Models: Atelier Zaborowsky

Skulpturen und Objekte/Sculptures and Objects: Josef Gerig (Atelier Zaborowsky)

Übersetzungen/Translations: Leslie Schnyder, Alejandra Alvaredo,

Peter Grimshaw

Dieses Buch erscheint anlässlich

der Ausstellung/This book is published on

the occasion of the exhibition:

Santiago Calatrava: Dynamische Gleichgewichte/Dynamic Equilibrium

Museum für Gestaltung Zürich

Ausstellungsstrasse 60

25. 9 –10 11. 1991

Nederlands Architectuurinstituut

Westersingel 10, 3014 GM Rotterdam

1. 3.–3 5. 1992

Copyright 1991

Verlag für Architektur/Architectural Publishers

Artemis Verlags AG, Zürich

Printed in Switzerland

ISBN 3-7608-8092-4

ISBN 1-874056-05-6

2. Auflage 1992

Fig. 7.4c. Unedited OCLC bibliographic record.

```
OCLC: 26589834        Rec stat:  a
Entered: 19920513    Replaced: 19920912    Used: 19930318
Type: a  Bib lvl:  m  Source:        Lang:    ger
Repr:       Enc lvl:  8  Conf pub:  0   Ctry:    sz
Indx: 0  Mod rec:      Govt pub:      Cont:    c
Desc: a  Int lvl:      Festschr:  0   Illus:   a
         F/B:      0  Dat tp:    s   Dates:   1992,
1    010         92-159544
2    040         DLC $c DLC [Modified by author]
3    020         3760880924
4    020         1874056056
5    041 0       gereng
6    043         e-sp---
7    050 00      NA1313.C35 $b A4 1992
8    049         KHNN
9    100 1       Calatrava, Santiago, $d 1951-
10   245 00      Dynamische Gleichgewichte, neue Projekte
$b Dynamic equilibrium, recent projects / $c Santiago
Calatrava ; [Konzeption, Anthony Tischhauser, Tristan
Kobler].
11   250         2. Aufl.
12   260         Zurich : $b Verlag fur Architektur, $c
1992.
13   300         1 v. (unpaged) : $b ill. ; $c 28 cm.
14   500         Catalog of the exhibit presented at the
Museum fur Gestaltung Zurich, 09/25-11/10/1991, and at
the Nederlands Architectuurinstituut. Rotterdam, 03/01-
05/03/1992.
15   500         German and English.
16   600 10      Calatrava, Santiago, $d 1951- $x
Exhibitions.
17   650  0      Architecture, Modern $y 20th century $z
Spain $x Exhibitions.
18   700 1       Tischhauser, Anthony.
19   700 1       Kobler, Tristan.
20   710 2       Museum fur Gestaltung Zurich.
21   710 1       Nederlands Architectuurinstituut.
22   740 01      Dynamic equilibrium, recent projects.
```

Discussion: One quickly sees that the title page contains titles in German and English. This is a parallel title (Rule 1.1D). The equals sign that should precede a parallel title is missing (Rule 1.1A1). The second statement of responsibility is taken from outside the prescribed source of information; thus, it is enclosed in brackets (Rule 2.0B2). The slash and semicolon are the prescribed punctuation needed for the statement of responsibility.

The encoding level in the fixed field contains an "8," signifying that it is CIP. Because CIP records are prepared from galley proofs before the book is published, it is not unusual for changes to occur in the title or statement of responsibility after the CIP is prepared. The copy cataloger needs to know the library's policy on handling CIP records, as access to the record can be affected. Sometimes there are misspellings, or access points are missing. Some libraries may want their copy catalogers to pay closer attention to a CIP record than to a record with a full encoding level.

The first indicator of "0" in the 245 field means that no title card will be generated. A title entry is needed in this case, or a vital access point is lost. The first indicator should be "1." The subfield codes are correct. The title in the 740 field needs to be moved to a 246 field to comply with 1995 MARC format integration.

If desired, the reader may now practice the exercises in chapter 10 for the 245 field for monographs. Figures 10.1–10.3, 10.5, and 10.7 need editing in the 245 fields. Consult chapter 11 for the answers. (Figure 7.4d is on page 60.)

Fig. 7.4d. Edited OCLC bibliographic record.

```
OCLC: 26589834       Rec stat:   a
Entered: 19920513    Replaced: 19920912    Used: 19930318
Type: a  Bib lvl:   m  Source:          Lang:    ger
Repr:       Enc lvl:   8  Conf pub:  0    Ctry:    sz
Indx: 0  Mod rec:      Govt pub:       Cont:    c
Desc: a  Int lvl:      Festschr:  0    Illus:   a
         F/B:       0  Dat tp:    s    Dates:   1992,
1    010          92-159544
2    040          DLC $c DLC [Modified by author]
3    020          3760880924
4    020          1874056056
5    041 0        gereng
6    043          e-sp---
7    050 00       NA1313.C35 $b A4 1992
8    049          KHNN
9    100 1        Calatrava, Santiago, $d 1951-
10   245 10       Dynamische Gleichgewichte, neue Projekte =
$b Dynamic equilibrium, recent projects / $c Santiago
Calatrava ; [Konzeption, Anthony Tischhauser, Tristan
Kobler].
     246 11       Dynamic equilibrium, recent projects
12   250          2. Aufl.
13   260          Zurich : $b Verlag fur Architektur, $c
1992.
14   300          1 v. (unpaged) : $b ill. ; $c 28 cm.
15   500          Catalog of the exhibit presented at the
Museum fur Gestaltung Zurich, 09/25-11/10/1991, and at
the Nederlands Architectuurinstituut. Rotterdam, 03/01-
05/03/1992.
16   546          German and English.
17   600 10       Calatrava, Santiago, $d 1951- $x
Exhibitions.
18   650  0       Architecture, Modern $y 20th century $z
Spain $x Exhibitions.
19   700 1        Tischhauser, Anthony.
20   700 1        Kobler, Tristan.
21   710 2        Museum fur Gestaltung Zurich.
22   710 1        Nederlands Architectuurinstituut.
```

Edition Area (Rules 1.2 and 2.2; Field 250)

Fig. 7.5a. Title page.

Fig. 7.5b. Verso of title page.

Copyright © 1990 by Diane Ackerman

All rights reserved under International and Pan-American Copyright Conventions. Published in the United States by Random House, Inc., New York, and simultaneously in Canada by Random House of Canada Limited, Toronto.

Portions of this work were originally published as first-serial contributions to *Parade* magazine. Portions of this work were originally published in different form in *The New York Times Book Review* and *Condé Nast Traveler.*

Owing to limitations of space all acknowledgments for permission to reprint previously published material may be found on page v.

Library of Congress Cataloging-in-Publication Data

Ackerman, Diane.
A natural history of the senses/by Diane Ackerman.
p. cm.
Includes bibliographical references.
ISBN 0-394-57335-8
1. Senses and sensation. I. Title.
QP431.A26 1990
612.8—dc20 89-43416

Manufactured in the United States of America
24689753
First Edition

Book design by Debbie Glasserman

Fig. 7.5c. Unedited OCLC bibliographic record.

```
OCLC: 20799461         Rec stat:  c
Entered: 19890919    Replaced: 19901205    Used: 19910426
Type: a  Bib lvl:  m  Source:         Lang:    eng
Repr:    Enc lvl:     Conf pub: 0     Ctry:    nyu
Indx: 1  Mod red:     Govt pub:       Cont:    b
Desc: a  Int lvl:     Festschr: 0     Illus:
         F/B:      0  Dat tp:   s     Dates:   1990,
1    010         89-43416
2    040         DLC $c DLC $d VET [Modified by author]
3    020         0394573358 : $c $19.95
4    050 00      BF233 $b .A24 1990
5    082 00      612.8 $2 20
6    096         WL 700 A182 1990
7    049         KHNN
8    100 1       Ackerman, Diane.
9    245 12      A natural history of the senses / $c Diane
Ackerman.
10   260         New York : $b Random House, $c c1990.
11   300         xix, 331 p. ; $c 25 cm.
12   504         Includes bibliographical references (p.
[311]-315) and index.
13   650 0       Senses and sensation.
14   650 0       Manners and customs.
15   650 0       Human behavior.
16   650 2       Sensation
17   650 2       Sense Organs
18   650 2       Social Behavior
```

Discussion: This record has no 250 field. Individuals new to cataloging often feel that there is no need to list "first edition." The assumption is that, unless noted otherwise, all books are first editions; therefore, there is no need to list such an edition statement. However, Rule 1.2B1 states that one must transcribe the edition statement as found on the item. "First edition" is stated on the verso of the title page; thus, it should be listed in the edition area. The latter part of 1.2B1 tells the cataloger to use abbreviations and numerals as instructed in Appendices B and C, respectively.

When the 250 field is entered, both indicators will be blank. There will only be a subfield a.

Fig. 7.5d. Edited OCLC bibliographic record.

```
OCLC: 20799461        Rec stat:   c
Entered: 19890919    Replaced: 19901205     Used: 19910426
Type: a  Bib lvl:  m  Source:          Lang:    eng
Repr:    Enc lvl:     Conf pub:  0    Ctry:    nyu
Indx: 1  Mod red:     Govt pub:        Cont:    b
Desc: a  Int lvl:     Festschr:  0    Illus:
         F/B:      0  Dat tp:    s    Dates:   1990
1    010          89-43416
2    040          DLC $c DLC $d VET [Modified by author]
3    020          0394573358 : $c $19.95
4    050 00       BF233 $b .A24 1990
5    082 00       612.8 $2 20
6    096          WL 700 A182 1990
7    049          KHNN
8    100 1        Ackerman, Diane.
9    245 12       A natural history of the senses / $c Diane
Ackerman.
10   250          1st ed.
11   260          New York : $b Random House, $c c1990.
12   300          xix, 331 p. ; $c 25 cm.
13   504          Includes bibliographical references (p.
[311]-315) and index.
14   650  0       Senses and sensation.
15   650  0       Manners and customs.
16   650  0       Human behavior.
17   650  2       Sensation
18   650  2       Sense Organs
19   650  2       Social Behavior
```

Fig. 7.6a. Title page.

BOHDAN S. WYNAR

INTRODUCTION TO CATALOGING AND CLASSIFICATION

eighth edition

ARLENE G. TAYLOR

1992

LIBRARIES UNLIMITED, INC.

Englewood, Colorado

Fig. 7.6b. Verso of title page.

LIBRARIES UNLIMITED, INC.
P.O. Box 6633
Englewood, CO 80155-6633

Library of Congress Cataloging-in-Publication Data

Taylor, Arlene G., 1941-
    Introduction to cataloging and classification / Bohdan S. Wynar. -
- 8th ed. / by Arlene G. Taylor.
    xvii, 633p. 17x25 cm. -- (Library science text series)
    Includes bibliographical references and index.
    ISBN 0-87287-811-2 (cloth) -- ISBN 0-87287-967-4 (paper)
    1. Cataloging. 2. Classification--Books. 3. Anglo-American
cataloguing rules. I. Wynar, Bohdan S. Introduction to cataloging
and classification. II. Title. III. Series.
Z693.W94 1991
025.3--dc20   91-24851
                                        CIP

Fig. 7.6c. Unedited OCLC bibliographic record.

```
OCLC: 24067132        Rec stat:   c
Entered: 19910620    Replaced: 19920825     Used: 19930308
Type: a   Bib lvl:   m  Source:          Lang:      eng
Repr:     Enc lvl:      Conf pub:  0     Ctry:      cou
Indx: 1   Mod rec:      Govt pub:        Cont:      b
Desc: a   Int lvl:      Festschr:  0     Illus:     a
          F/B:       0  Dat tp:    s     Dates:     1992
1    010          91-24851//r92
2    040          DLC $c DLC $d COU [Modified by author]
3    020          0872878112 (cloth)
4    020          0872879674 (pbk.)
5    050 00       Z693 $b .W94 1991
6    082 00       025.3 $2 20
7    049          KHNN
8    100 1        Wynar, Bohdan S.
9    245 10       Introduction to cataloging and
classification / $c Bohdan S. Wynar.
10   250          8th ed.
11   260          Englewood, Colo. : $b Libraries Unlimited,
$c 1992.
12   300          xvii, 633 p. : $b ill. ; $c 24 cm.
13   440  0       Library science text series
14   504          Includes bibliographical references (p.
591-599)and index.
15   650  0       Cataloging.
16   650  0       Subject cataloging.
17   650  0       Classification $x Books.
18   630 00       Anglo-American cataloguing rules.
19   650  2       Cataloging $x methods
20   650  2       Book Classification $x methods
21   650  2       Subject Headings
```

Discussion: The edition statement has been transcribed as instructed in Rule 1.2B1 and Appendices B and C. On the title page, the chief source of information for books, Arlene G. Taylor is listed immediately under the 8th edition. Is this a statement of responsibility relating only to some of the editions (Rule 1.2C1)? Taylor needs to be listed either in a 245 or 250 field and given an access point. Using OCLC, one determines that Taylor was not involved with all the editions. Thus, "Arlene G. Taylor" is a statement of responsibility relating to the edition.

The indicators are correct. A new subfield code will be needed when the statement of responsibility is added.

Fig. 7.6d. Edited OCLC bibliographic record.

```
OCLC: 24067132        Rec stat:   c
Entered: 19910620    Replaced: 19920825      Used: 19930308
Type: a   Bib lvl:   m  Source:           Lang:     eng
Repr:     Enc lvl:      Conf pub:  0    Ctry:     cou
Indx: 1   Mod rec:      Govt pub:        Cont:     b
Desc: a   Int lvl:      Festschr:  0    Illus:    a
          F/B:       0  Dat tp:    s    Dates:    1992
1     010          91-24851//r92
2     040          DLC $c DLC $d COU [Modified by author]
3     020          0872878112 (cloth)
4     020          0872879674 (pbk.)
5     050 00       Z693 $b .W94 1991
6     082 00       025.3 $2 20
7     049          KHNN
8     100 1        Wynar, Bohdan S.
9     245 10       Introduction to cataloging and
classification / $c Bohdan S. Wynar.
10    250          8th ed. / $b Arlene G. Taylor.
11    260          Englewood, Colo. : $b Libraries Unlimited,
$c 1992.
12    300          xvii, 633 p. : $b ill. ; $c 24 cm.
13    440  0       Library science text series
14    504          Includes bibliographical references (p.
591-599)and index.
15    650  0       Cataloging.
16    650  0       Subject cataloging.
17    650  0       Classification $x Books.
18    630 00       Anglo-American cataloguing rules.
19    650  2       Cataloging $x methods
20    650  2       Book Classification $x methods
21    650  2       Subject Headings
22    700 1        Taylor, Arlene G., $d 1941-
```

If desired, the reader may now practice the exercise in chapter 10 for the 250 field for monographs. Figure 10.5 needs editing in the 250 field. Consult chapter 11 for the answer.

**Publication, Distribution, etc., Area
(Rules 1.4 and 2.4; Field 260)**

Fig. 7.7a. Title page.

Changing educational assessment

International perspectives and trends

Edited by Patricia Broadfoot,
Roger Murphy and Harry Torrance
for the British Comparative and
International Education
Society (BCIES)

London and New York

Fig. 7.7b. Verso of title page.

First published 1990
by Routledge
11 New Fetter Lane, London EC4P 4EE

Simultaneously published in the USA and Canada
by Routledge
a division of Routledge, Chapman and Hall, Inc.
29 West 35th Street, New York, NY 10001

Printed and bound in Great Britain by
Biddles Ltd, Guildford and King's Lynn

British Library Cataloguing in Publication Data

Changing educational assessment : international perspectives and trends.
  1. Education. Assessment
  I. Broadfoot, Patricia II. Murphy, Roger III. Torrance,
  Harry IV. British Comparative and International Education
  Society
  379.154

  ISBN 0-415-05293-9

Library of Congress Cataloging in Publications Data
0-415-05293-9

Fig. 7.7c. Unedited OCLC bibliographic record.

```
OCLC: 21226212        Rec stat:  p
Entered: 19901024    Replaced: 19901124    Used: 19910509
Type: a  Bib lvl:  m  Source:    d    Lang:   eng
Repr:    Enc lvl:      Conf pub:  0    Ctry:   enk
Indx: 1  Mod red:      Govt pub:       Cont:   b
Desc: a  Int lvl:      Festschr:  0    Illus:  a
         F/B:      0  Dat tp:    s    Dates:  1990,
1    010        gb90-14800
2    040        UKM $c UKM [Modified by author]
3    015        GB90-14800
4    020        0415052939 ι $c No price
5    050 14     LB3051
6    082 04     371.264 $2 20
7    090        LB3050.5 $b .C43 1990x
8    049        KHNN
9    245 00     Changing educational assessment : $b
international perspectives and trends / $c edited by
Patricia Broadfoot, Roger Murphy and Harry Torrance for
the British Comparative and International Education
Society (BCIES).
10   260        London : $b Routledge, $c 1990.
11   300        x, 236 p. : $b ill. ; $c 23 cm.
12   504        Includes bibliographical references (p.
222-223)and index.
13   650  0     Grading and marking (Students)
14   653        Students $a Academic achievement $a
Assessment
15   700 1      Broadfoot, Patricia.
16   700 1      Murphy, Roger.
17   700 1      Torrance, Harry.
18   710 2      British Comparative and International
Education Society.
19   886 2      $2 UK MARC $a 690 $b 00 $s 11030 $a
students $z p1030 $a academic achievement $z 20030 $a
assessment
20   886 2      $2 UK MARC $a 691 $b 00 $a 0180009
21   886 2      $2 UK MARC $a 692 $b 00 $a 0000612
22   886 2      $2 UK MARC $a 692 $b 00 $a 0022373
```

Discussion: According to Rule 1.4C5, if two or more places are listed for the publisher, the first-named place should be recorded. If the first-named place is not in the country of the cataloging agency, and one of the subsequent places is in that country, the subsequent place should also be recorded. Thus, "New York" should be added. From the 040 field one ascertains that the source of cataloging is British; thus, the record is correct for a British library. The publisher and date are in accordance with Rules 1.4D and 1.4F respectively. The prescribed punctuation is correct for the information listed. A semicolon will need to precede "New York" when it is added.

The two indicators and subfield codes are correct for the information listed. A subfield code of "a" will need to precede "New York" as each place is input into a separate subfield.

Fig. 7.7d. Edited OCLC bibliographic record.

```
OCLC: 21226212      Rec stat:  p
Entered: 19901024    Replaced: 19901124    Used: 19910509
Type: a  Bib lvl:  m  Source:    d    Lang:   eng
Repr:    Enc lvl:     Conf pub:  0    Ctry:   enk
Indx: 1  Mod red:     Govt pub:       Cont:   b
Desc: a  Int lvl:     Festschr:  0    Illus:  a
         F/B:      0  Dat tp:    s    Dates:  1990,
1    010        gb90-14800
2    040        UKM $c UKM [Modified by author]
3    015        GB90-14800
4    020        0415052939 : $c No price
5    050 14     LB3051
6    082 04     371.264 $2 20
7    090        LB3050.5 $b .C43 1990x
8    049        KHNN
9    245 00     Changing educational assessment : $b
international perspectives and trends / $c edited by
Patricia Broadfoot, Roger Murphy and Harry Torrance for
the British Comparative and International Education
Society (BCIES).
10   260        London ; $a New York : $b Routledge, $c
1990.
11   300        x, 236 p. : $b ill. ; $c 23 cm.
12   504        Includes bibliographical references (p.
222-223)and index.
13   650  0     Grading and marking (Students)
14   653        Students $a Academic achievement $a
Assessment
15   700 1      Broadfoot, Patricia.
16   700 1      Murphy, Roger.
17   700 1      Torrance, Harry.
18   710 2      British Comparative and International
Education Society.
19   886 2      $2 UK MARC $a 690 $b 00 $s 11030 $a
students $z p1030 $a academic achievement $z 20030 $a
assessment
20   886 2      $2 UK MARC $a 691 $b 00 $a 0180009
21   886 2      $2 UK MARC $a 692 $b 00 $a 0000612
22   886 2      $2 UK MARC $a 692 $b 00 $a 0022373
```

Fig. 7.8a. Title page.

THE GESTAPO AND GERMAN SOCIETY

Enforcing Racial Policy
1933–1945

ROBERT GELLATELY

CLARENDON PRESS · OXFORD
1990

Fig. 7.8b. Verso of title page.

Oxford University Press, Walton Street, Oxford OX2 6DP

Oxford New York Toronto
Delhi Bombay Calcutta Madras Karachi
Petaling Jaya Singapore Hong Kong Tokyo
Nairobi Dar es Salaam Cape Town
Melbourne Auckland

and associated companies in
Berlin Ibadan

Oxford is a trade mark of Oxford University Press

Published in the United States
by Oxford University Press, New York

© Robert Gellately 1990

All rights reserved. No part of this publication may be reproduced,
stored in a retrieval system, or transmitted, in any form or by any means,
electronic, mechanical, photocopying, recording, or otherwise, without
the prior permission of Oxford University Press

British Library Cataloguing in Publication Data
Gellately, Robert
The Gestapo and German society: enforcing racial policy
1933–1945.
1. Germany. Geheime Staatspolizei
I. Title
363.2'83'0943
ISBN 0–19–822869–4

Library of Congress Cataloging in Publication Data
Gellately, Robert, 1943–
p. cm.
The Gestapo and German society: enforcing racial policy 1935–1945/
Robert Gellately.
Includes bibliographical references.
1. Jews—Germany—History—1933–1945. 2. Germany. Geheime
Staatspolizei. 3. Jews—Germany (West)—Unterfranken—Persecutions.
4. Germany—Ethnic relations. 5. Unterfranken (Germany)—Ethnic
relations. I. Title.
DS135.G3315G45 1990
943'.004924—dc20 89-26534
ISBN 0–19–822869–4

Typeset by Butler & Tanner Ltd, Frome and London
Printed and bound in
Great Britain by Biddles Ltd,
Guildford and King's Lynn

Fig. 7.8c. Unedited OCLC bibliographic record.

```
OCLC: 20670549        Rec stat:'  c
Entered: 19891103    Replaced: 19901222    Used: 19910508
Type: a  Bib lvl:  m  Source:          Lang:    eng
Repr:       Enc lvl:  8  Conf pub:  0   Ctry:    enk
Indx: 1  Mod rec:     Govt pub:       Cont:    b
Desc: a  Int lvl:     Festschr:  0    Illus:   b
          F/B:       0  Dat tp:    s   Dates:   1990,
1    010         89-26534
2    040         DLC $c DLC [Modified by author]
3    020         0198228694 : $c $48.00 (U.S.)
4    043         e-gx--- $a e-gw---
5    050 00      DS135.G3315 $b G45 1990
6    082 00      943/.004924 $2 20
7    049         KHNN
8    100 1       Gellately, Robert, $d 1943-
9    245 14      The Gestapo and German society : $b
enforcing racial policy 1933-1945 / $c Robert Gellately.
10   260         Oxford : $b Clarendon Press, $c 1990
11   300         xiv, 297 p. : $b maps ; $c 25 cm.
12   504         Includes bibliographical references.
13   650  0      Jews $z Germany $x History $y 1933-1945.
14   610 10      Germany. $b Geheime Staatspolizei.
15   650  0      Jews $Z Germany (West) $z Unterfranken $x
Persecutions.
16   651  0      Germany $x Ethnic relations.
17   651  0      Unterfranken (Germany) $x Ethnic
relations.
```

Discussion: Some catalogers will want to qualify Oxford as noted in Rule 1.4C3. Rule 1.4D5 describes how to record an item if two publishers are listed. The first one is always recorded with its place. If the first-named publisher is not in the country of the cataloging agency, and a subsequently named publisher is in that country, the subsequently named publisher is also recorded with its place. Only the British publisher is listed on the title page; the U.S. publisher is listed on the verso of the title page. The Library of Congress has decided to record the name of a U.S. publisher appearing anywhere in the item when a non–U.S. publisher appears on the chief source (*Cataloging Service Bulletin* no. 50, p. 20). In this case, "Oxford University Press" and "New York" need to be added. In the same interpretation, LC has decided to list all publishers appearing on the chief source of information. See figure 7.9 for two publishers in the United States.

As listed, the prescribed punctuation, indicators, and subfield codes are correct. Additional punctuation and subfield codes will be needed for the second place and publisher.

Fig. 7.8d. Edited OCLC bibliographic record.

```
OCLC: 20670549        Rec stat:   c
Entered: 19891103    Replaced: 19901222    Used: 19910508
Type: a  Bib lvl:  m  Source:        Lang:    eng
Repr:       Enc lvl:  8  Conf pub:  0   Ctry:    enk
Indx: 1  Mod rec:     Govt pub:       Cont:    b
Desc: a  Int lvl:     Festschr:  0   Illus:   b
         F/B:       0  Dat tp:    s   Dates:   1990,
1    010          89-26534
2    040          DLC $c DLC [Modified by author]
3    020          0198228694 : $c $48.00 (U.S.)
4    043          e-gx--- $a e-gw---
5    050 00       DS135.G3315 $b G45 1990
6    082 00       943/.004924 $2 20
7    049          KHNN
8    100 1        Gellately, Robert, $d 1943-
9    245 14       The Gestapo and German society : $b
enforcing racial policy 1933-1945 / $c Robert Gellately.
10   260          Oxford [England] : $b Clarendon Press ; $a
New York : $b Oxford University Press, $c 1990
11   300          xiv, 297 p. : $b maps ; $c 25 cm.
12   504          Includes bibliographical references.
13   650 0        Jews $z Germany $x History $y 1933-1945.
14   610 10       Germany. $b Geheime Staatspolizei.
15   650 0        Jews $Z Germany (West) $z Unterfranken $x
Persecutions.
16   651 0        Germany $x Ethnic relations.
17   651 0        Unterfranken (Germany) $x Ethnic
relations.
```

Fig. 7.9a. Title page.

Advances in Database Programming Languages

Edited by

François Bancilhon
Altaïr

Peter Buneman
University of Pennsylvania

ACM PRESS
New York, New York

Addison-Wesley Publishing Company

Reading, Massachusetts · Menlo Park, California · New York
Don Mills, Ontario · Wokingham, England · Amsterdam · Bonn
Sydney · Singapore · Tokyo · Madrid · San Juan

Fig. 7.9b. Verso of title page.

Chapter 18: Copyright, 1987, Incremental Systems Corporation. This work was supported in part by the Department of Defense, Defense Advanced Research Projects Agency, Order No. 5057, monitored by the Department of the Navy, Space and Naval Warfare Systems Command, under contract No. N00039-85-C-0126. Approved for Public Release, Distribution Unlimited.

Chapter 19: The lines from "since feeling is first", the line from "Take for example this:", and the line from the Introduction to *New Poems* are reprinted from COMPLETE POEMS, 1913–1962, by e. e. cummings, by permission of Liveright Publishing Corporation. Copyright © 1923, 1925, 1931, 1935, 1938, 1939, 1940, 1944, 1945, 1946, 1947, 1948, 1949, 1950, 1951, 1952, 1953, 1954, 1955, 1956, 1957, 1958, 1959, 1960, 1961, 1962 by the Trustees for the E. E. Cummings Trust. Copyright © 1961, 1963, 1968 by Marion Morehouse Cummings.

Also reprinted with permission of Grafton Books, a Division of the Collier Publishing Group, London.

Many of the designations used by manufacturers and sellers to distinguish their products are claimed as trademarks. Where those designations appear in this book, and Addison-Wesley was aware of a trademark claim, the designations have been printed in caps or initial caps.

The programs and applications presented in this book have been included for their instructional value. They have been tested with care, but are not guaranteed for any particular purpose. The publisher does not offer any warranties or representations, nor does it accept any liabilities with respect to the programs or applications.

Library of Congress Cataloging-in-Publication Data

Advances in database programming languages / edited by François
    Bancilhon, Peter Buneman.
        p.   cm. — (Frontier series)
    Includes bibliographical references.
    ISBN 0-201-50257-7
    1. Data base management. I. Bancilhon, François. II. Buneman,
Peter, 1943– . III. Series: Frontier series (New York, N.Y.)
QA76.9.D3A348 1990
005.74—dc20   89–37181
                                                              CIP

ACM Press Frontier Series
Instrumentation for Future Parallel Computer Systems

First printed 1990

ABCDEFGHIJ-MA-943210

Fig. 7.9c. Unedited OCLC bibliographic record.

```
OCLC: 20055716        Rec stat: c
Entered: 19890630   Replaced: 19891020    Used: 19910504
Type: a  Bib lvl:  m  Source:          Lang:   eng
Repr:    Enc lvl:  8  Conf pub:  0     Ctry:   nyu
Indx: 0  Mod rec:     Govt pub:        Cont:   b
Desc: a  Int lvl:     Festschr:  0     Illus:  a
         F/B:      0  Dat tp:    s     Dates:  1989,
1    010         89-37181
2    040         DLC $c DLC [Modified by author]
3    020         0201502577
4    050  0      QA76.9.D3 $b A348 1989
5    082 00      005.74 $2 20
6    049         KHNN
7    245 00      Advances in database programming languages
/ $c edited by Francois Bancilhon, Peter Buneman.
8    260         New York, N.Y. : $b ACM Press ; $a
Reading, Mass.  : $b Addison-Wesley Pub. Co., $c 1989.
9    263         8912
10   300         xvii, 457 p. : $b ill. ; $c 25 cm.
11   490 1       Frontier series
12   504         Includes bibliographical references.
13   650  0      Data base management.
14   700 1       Bancilhon, Francois.
15   700 1       Buneman, Peter, $d 1943-
16   830  0      Frontier series (New York, N.Y.)
```

Discussion: Rule 1.4C1 requires the transcription of the place of publication as it appears on the prescribed source. Rule 1.4C3 states that the country, state, province, or similar qualifier should follow the place if necessary for identification or to distinguish the place from others with the same name. One wonders why "New York" is qualified with "N.Y.," because it is not necessary under either of these circumstances. The Library of Congress has decided to list the state and even "U.S.A." if it is listed with the place in the prescribed source of information (*Cataloging Service Bulletin* no. 44, p. 12). The second place and publisher are in accordance with LC's interpretations (*Cataloging Service Bulletin* no. 50, p. 20). In accordance with Rule 1.4D2, "Pub. Co." should be omitted. Rules 1.4D1 and 1.4D2 state that the publishers should follow the place in the shortest form in which it can be understood and identified internationally. However, in LC's *Cataloging Service Bulletin* no. 47, page 11, catalogers are instructed to use their judgment as to whether or not to shorten a name, whatever is more efficient and effective. Catalogers are not to consider how well known the name is. The copy cataloger might note that the publisher has qualified the less well known places listed on the chief source of information for the second publisher, but not the well-known places.

The date on the verso of the title page is 1990 rather than 1989. Although previously a different date of publication was listed as a criteria for creating a new record, a new record is not needed in this case. The "8" in the encoding level in the fixed field indicates that this is prepublication cataloging (CIP). Field 263 also lists the projected publication date as December 1989. This is a case where publication was later than projected.

Because of this later publication date, the date in the fixed field will change. The date in the call number will also change to 1990. Some libraries will move the call number to an 090 field if it is being adjusted. Because the CIP on the verso of the title page has 1990 in the call number, the author does not feel this is necessary.

Prescribed punctuation, indicators, and subfield codes are correct.

Fig. 7.9d. Edited OCLC bibliographic record.

```
OCLC: 20055716        Rec stat: c
Entered: 19890630     Replaced: 19891020     Used: 19910504
Type: a  Bib lvl:  m  Source:          Lang:    eng
Repr:       Enc lvl:  8  Conf pub:  0    Ctry:    nyu
Indx: 0  Mod rec:      Govt pub:       Cont:    b
Desc: a  Int lvl:      Festschr:  0    Illus:   a
         F/B:       0  Dat tp:    s    Dates:   1990,
1     010          89-37181
2     040          DLC $c DLC [Modified by author]
3     020          0201502577
4     050  0       QA76.9.D3 $b A348 1990
5     082 00       005.74 $2 20
6     049          KHNN
7     245 00       Advances in database programming languages
/ $c edited by Francois Bancilhon, Peter Buneman.
8     260          New York, N.Y. : $b ACM Press ; $a
Reading, Mass.  : $b Addison-Wesley, $c 1990.
9     263          8912
10    300          xvii, 457 p. : $b ill. ; $c 25 cm.
11    490 1        Frontier series
12    504          Includes bibliographical references.
13    650  0       Data base management.
14    700 1        Bancilhon, Francois.
15    700 1        Buneman, Peter, $d 1943-
16    830  0       Frontier series (New York, N.Y.)
```

Fig. 7.10a. Title page. (Verso only has a picture.)

BACK HOME
BY JOE CLARK HBSS

Privately printed for the Tennessee Squire Association

Copyright 1965 By The Tennessee Squire Association

Printed in the United States of America by

Kingsport Press, Inc., Kingsport, Tennessee

Fig. 7.10b. Unedited OCLC bibliographic record.

```
OCLC: 1841748        Rec stat:   n
Entered: 19751118    Replaced: 19900424    Used: 19910109
Type: a  Bib lvl:  m  Source:       Lang:    eng
Repr:    Enc lvl:  I  Conf pub:  0  Ctry:    tnu
Indx: 0  Mod rec:     Govt pub:     Cont:
Desc:    Int lvl:     Festschr:  0  Illus:   ac
         F/B:      0  Dat tp:    s  Dates:   1965,
1    010        66-6552
2    040        DLC $c FQG $d m/c [Modified by author]
3    050  0     F437 $b .C55
4    082 00     811.54
5    049        KHNN
6    100 1      Clark, Joe.
7    245 10     Back home.
8    260        Kingsport, $b privately printed for the
Tennessee Squire Association by Kingsport Press $c
c1965.
9    300        1 v. (unpaged) $b illus., port. $c 27 x 29
cm.
10   651  0     Tennessee $x Description and travel $x
Views.
11   650  0     Poetry of places $z Tennessee.
12   651  0     Tennessee $x Description and travel $x
Poetry.
13   710 2      Tennessee Squire Association.
```

Discussion: Even though Kingsport is not well known, it does not have to be qualified by "Tenn." because Tennessee is listed in subfield b. Rule 1.4D3 instructs to retain words indicating the function performed by the person or body. In Rule A.7B1, one is told to capitalize the first word of the element if it is not an integral part of the publisher.

Rule 1.4F6 states that one should give the copyright date if the publication and distribution dates are unknown.

This record will require editing in many of the fields to bring it into accordance with *AACR2*. (The cataloging on pre-*AACR2* records is likely to be correct according to the rules under which it was cataloged.) The copy cataloger will need to consult with a supervisor for a policy on editing pre-*AACR2* cataloging. Many libraries do not see a need to update pre-*AACR2* cataloging. However, this record has been converted to *AACR2* for purposes of comparison.

Fig. 7.10c. Edited OCLC bibliographic record.

```
OCLC: 1841748        Rec stat:   n
Entered: 19751118    Replaced: 1990 0424    Used: 19910109
Type: a   Bib lvl:  m   Source:         Lang:     eng
Repr:     Enc lvl:  I   Conf pub:  0    Ctry:     tnu
Indx: 0   Mod rec:      Govt pub:       Cont:
Desc: a   Int lvl:      Festschr:  0    Illus:    ac
          F/B:       0  Dat tp:    s    Dates: 1965,
1    010           66-6552
2    040           DLC $c FQG $d m/c [Modified by author]
3    050  0        F437 $b .C55
4    082 00        811.54
5    049           KHNN
6    100 1         Clark, Joe.
7    245 10        Back home / $c by Joe Clark.
8    260           Kingsport : $b Privately printed for the
Tennessee Squire Association by Kingsport Press, $c
c1965.
9    300           1 v. (unpaged) : $b ill., port. ; $c 27 x
29 cm.
10   651  0        Tennessee $x Description and travel $x
Views.
11   650  0        Poetry of places $z Tennessee.
12   651  0        Tennessee $x Description and travel $x
Poetry.
13   710 2         Tennessee Squire Association.
```

If desired, the reader may now practice the exercises in chapter 10 for the 260 field for monographs. Figures 10.1–10.3 and 10.5 need editing in the 260 fields. Consult chapter 11 for the answers.

Physical Description Area
(Rule 2.5; Field 300)

Fig. 7.11a. Title page of volume 1.

Handbook of Industrial
and Organizational Psychology

SECOND EDITION

Volume 1

Marvin D. Dunnette and Leaetta M. Hough
Editors

Consulting Psychologists Press, Inc.
Palo Alto, California

Fig. 7.11b. Verso of title page of volume 1.

Library of Congress Cataloging-in-Publication Data

Handbook of industrial and organizational psychology / Marvin D. Dunnette, Leaetta M. Hough, editors. – 2nd ed.
    p. cm.
    Includes bibliographical references and index.
    ISBN 0–89106–041–3 (v. 1)
    1. Psychology, Industrial. 2. Organizational behavior.
    I. Dunnette, Marvin D. II. Hough, Leaetta M.
    HF5548.8.H265 1990
    158.7–dc20   90–2294
                                              CIP
Printed in the United States of America

ADDITIONAL INFORMATION. Volume 1: The pagination is viii–xxvii, followed by two unnumbered pages, followed by 2–755. All illustrations are black-and-white. The height is 24 centimeters. On page xxiv of volume 1 it is stated that this edition will be published in four volumes.

Fig. 7.11c. Title page of volume 2.

Handbook of Industrial and Organizational Psychology

SECOND EDITION

Volume 2

Marvin D. Dunnette and Leaetta M. Hough
Editors

Consulting Psychologists Press, Inc.
Palo Alto, California

Fig. 7.11d. Verso of title page of volume 2.

Library of Congress Cataloging-in-Publication Data
(Revised for vol. 2)

Handbook of industrial and organizational
    psychology

        Includes bibliographical references and index.
    1. Psychology, Industrial. 2. Organizational
behavior. I. Dunnette, Marvin D. II. Hough,
Leaetta M.
HF 5548.8.H265   1990   158.7   90-2294
ISBN 0-89106-041-3 (v. 1)
ISBN 0-89106-042-1 (v. 2)

Printed in the United States of America

ADDITIONAL INFORMATION. Volume 2: The pagination is viii–xxv, followed by two unnumbered pages, followed by 2–957. All illustrations are black-and-white. The height is 24 centimeters.

Fig. 7.11e. Unedited OCLC bibliographic record.

```
OCLC: 21909396        Rec stat:   c
Entered: 19900605    Replaced: 19910330     Used: 19910603
Type: a  Bib lvl:  m  Source:         Lang:    eng
Repr:    Enc lvl:  8  Conf pub:  0    Ctry:    cau
Indx: 1  Mod rec:     Govt pub:       Cont:    b
Desc: a  Int lvl:     Festschr:  0    Illus:   a
         F/B:       0 Dat tp:    m    Dates:   1990,9999
1    010          90-2294
2    040          DLC $c DLC [Modified by author]
3    020          0891060413 (v. 1) : $c $55.00
4    050 00       HF5548.8 $b .H265 1990
5    082 00       158.7 $2 20
6    049          KHNN
7    245 00       Handbook of industrial and organizational
psychology / $c Marvin D. Dunnette, Leaetta M. Hough,
editors.
9    250          2nd ed.
10   260          Palo Alto, Calif. : $b Consulting
Psychologists Press, $c 1990-
11   263          9011
12   300          2 v. $b ill. ; $c 24 cm.
13   504          Includes bibliographical references.
14   650  0       Psychology, Industrial.
15   650  0       Organizational behavior.
16   700  1       Dunnette, Marvin D.
17   700  1       Hough, Leaetta M.
```

Discussion: For a volume set, the volumes are recorded (Rule 2.5B17). Two volumes are listed, but page xxiv of the preface of volume 1 states that the set is being published in four volumes. In some libraries, the total number of volumes in the set would be listed, even if the library does not have the entire set. The volumes contained in the library's collection are listed on item records or penciled on the card set. Because of the lack of time, some libraries make the penciled notation only on certain cards (i.e., shelflist and main entry). When the library receives another volume, a new item record will be generated or the penciled notation will be updated on the cards. In an automated environment, the volumes in hand at the time of cataloging are sometimes listed in angular brackets and then updated as additional volumes are received.

The illustrative matter is recorded as stated in Rule 2.5C. The height is recorded as instructed in Rule 2.5D1.

The prescribed punctuation to precede the illustrative matter has been omitted. It should be a colon. The semicolon before the dimensions is correct (Rule 2.5A1).

The indicators and subfield codes are correct.

Fig. 7.11f. Edited OCLC bibliographic record.

```
OCLC: 21909396       Rec stat:   c
Entered: 19900605   Replaced: 19910330      Used: 19910603
Type: a  Bib lvl:  m  Source:        Lang:     eng
Repr:       Enc lvl:  8  Conf pub:  0   Ctry:     cau
Indx: 1  Mod rec:     Govt pub:      Cont:     b
Desc: a  Int lvl:      Festschr:  0   Illus:    a
         F/B:       0  Dat tp:    m   Dates:    1990,9999
1    010        90-2294
2    040        DLC $c DLC [Modified by author]
3    020        0891060413 (v. 1) : $c $55.00
4    050 00     HF5548.8 $b .H265 1990
5    082 00     158.7 $2 20
6    049        KHNN
7    245 00     Handbook of industrial and organizational
psychology / $c Marvin D. Dunnette, Leaetta M. Hough,
editors.
9    250        2nd ed.
10   260        Palo Alto, Calif. : $b Consulting
Psychologists Press, $c 1990-
11   263        9011
12   300        4 v. : $b ill. ; $c 24 cm.
13   504        Includes bibliographical references and
indexes.
14   650  0     Psychology, Industrial.
15   650  0     Organizational behavior.
16   700  1     Dunnette, Marvin D.
17   700  1     Hough, Leaetta M.
```

Fig. 7.12a. Title page.

THE REDISCOVERY OF NORTH AMERICA

Barry Lopez

THE UNIVERSITY PRESS OF KENTUCKY

Fig. 7.12b. Verso of title page.

Publication of this book was assisted by a grant
from the Gaines Center for the Humanities, which
initiated and supports the Thomas D. Clark
Lectureship Series.

The author would like to express his appreciation to
Robley Wilson for his help with the manuscript.

Published by The University Press of Kentucky

Scholarly publisher for the Commonwealth,
serving Bellarmine College, Berea College, Centre
College of Kentucky, Eastern Kentucky University,
The Filson Club, Georgetown College, Kentucky
Historical Society, Kentucky State University,
Morehead State University, Murray State University,
Northern Kentucky University, Transylvania University,
University of Kentucky, University of Louisville,
and Western Kentucky University

Editorial and Sales Offices: Lexington, Kentucky 40508-4008

Library of Congress Cataloging-in-Publication Data

Lopez, Barry Holstun, 1945–
    The rediscovery of North America / Barry Lopez
      p   cm. — (The Thomas D. Clark lectures 1990)
    ISBN 0-8131-1742-9
    1. North America—Description and travel—1981– 2. Man—Influence
on nature—North America 3. America—Discovery and exploration
—Spanish—Influence I. Title II. Series
E27.5.L67 1990
970.01'6—dc20   90-24487

This book is printed on acid-free recycled paper meeting
the requirements of the American National Standard
for Permanence of Paper for Printed Library Materials ⊖

ADDITIONAL INFORMATION: The pages are not numbered. There are no illustrations. The height is 21.3 centimeters.

Fig. 7.12c. Unedited OCLC bibliographic record.

```
OCLC: 22810996        Rec stat:  p
Entered: 19901107   Replaced: 19910810    Used: 19910926
Type: a  Bib lvl:  m  Source:        Lang:    eng
Repr:      Enc lvl:     Conf pub:  0  Ctry:    kyu
Indx: 0  Mod rec:     Govt pub:  s  Cont:
Desc: a  Int lvl:     Festschr:  0  Illus:
          F/B:       0  Dat tp:    s  Dates:   1990,
1    010        90-24487
2    040        DLC $c DLC [Modified by author]
3    020        0813117429
4    043        n---   $a s       $a e sp
5    050 00     E27.5 $b .L67 1990
6    082 00     970.01/6 $2 20
7    049        KHNN
8    100 1      Lopez, Barry Holstun, $d 1945-
9    245 14     The rediscovery of North America / $c
Barry Lopez.
10   260        Lexington, Ky. : $b University Press of
Kentucky, $c c1990.
11   300        1 v. (unpaged) : $b 21 cm.
12   440  4     The Thomas D. Clark lectures ; $v 1990
13   651  0     North America $x Description and travel $y
1981-
14   650  0     Man $x Influence on nature $z North
America.
15   651  0     America $x Discovery and exploration $x
Spanish $x Influence.
```

Discussion: Subfield a of the 300 field appears to be incorrect. Rule 2.5B7 gives three options for recording the number of pages if the pages are unnumbered; however, the Library of Congress does not follow this rule except for rare books. LC will be using "1 v. (unpaged)" for books with unnumbered pages (*Cataloging Service Bulletin* no. 52, p. 15). Rule 2.5D1 instructs to give the height in centimeters, always rounding up to the next whole centimeter; thus, the size in field 300 should be 22 cm. The prescribed punctuation for preceding the dimensions is a semicolon.

The indicators are correct for this field. The subfield code is incorrect. It should be "c."

Fig. 7.12d. Edited OCLC bibliographic record.

```
OCLC: 22810996        Rec stat:  p
Entered: 19901107    Replaced: 19910810     Used: 19910926
Type: a  Bib lvl:  m  Source:          Lang:    eng
Repr:       Enc lvl:     Conf pub:  0   Ctry:    kyu
Indx: 0  Mod rec:        Govt pub:  s   Cont:
Desc: a  Int lvl:        Festschr:  0   Illus:
         F/B:        0  Dat tp:    s   Dates:   1990,
1    010         90-24487
2    040         DLC $c DLC [Modified by author]
3    020         0813117429
4    043         n------ $a s------ $a e-sp---
5    050 00      E27.5 $b .L67 1990
6    082 00      970.01/6 $2 20
7    049         KHNN
8    100 1       Lopez, Barry Holstun, $d 1945-
9    245 14      The rediscovery of North America / $c
Barry Lopez.
10   260         Lexington, Ky. : $b University Press of
Kentucky, $c c1990.
11   300         1 v. (unpaged) ; $c 22 cm.
12   440  4      The Thomas D. Clark lectures ; $v 1990
13   651  0      North America $x Description and travel $y
1981-
14   650  0      Man $x Influence on nature $z North
America.
15   651  0      America $x Discovery and exploration $x
Spanish $x Influence.
```

Fig. 7.13a. Title page.

FICHTE'S THEORY OF SUBJECTIVITY

FREDERICK NEUHOUSER

Harvard University

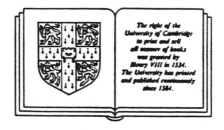

The right of the
University of Cambridge
to print and sell
all manner of books
was granted by
Henry VIII in 1534.
The University has printed
and published continuously
since 1584.

CAMBRIDGE UNIVERSITY PRESS

CAMBRIDGE

NEW YORK   PORT CHESTER   MELBOURNE   SYDNEY

Fig. 7.13b. Verso of title page.

Published by the Press Syndicate of the University of Cambridge
The Pitt Building, Trumpington Street, Cambridge CB2 1RP
40 West 20th Street, New York, NY 10011, USA
10 Stamford Road, Oakleigh, Melbourne 3166, Australia

© Cambridge University Press 1990

First published 1990

Printed in the United States of America

Library of Congress Cataloging-in-Publication Data
Neuhouser, Frederick.
Fichte's theory of subjectivity / Frederick Neuhouser.
p.   cm. – (Modern European philosophy)
Includes bibliographical references.
ISBN 0-521-37433-2. – ISBN 0-521-39938-6 (pbk.)
1. Fichte, Johann Gottlieb, 1762–1814 – Contributions in concept of
subjectivity.   2. Subjectivity.   I. Title.   II. Series.
B2849.S92N48   1990

126 – dc20   89-49731
                                                             CIP

British Library Cataloguing in Publication Data
Neuhouser, Frederick
Fichte's theory of subjectivity. – (Modern European
philosophy).
1. German philosphy. Fichte, Johann Gottlieb
I. Title   II. Series
193

ISBN 0-521-37433-2 hardback
ISBN 0-521-39938-6 paperback

ADDITIONAL INFORMATION: The pagination is vii–x, followed by 1–180.
There are no illustrations. The height is 22.2 centimeters.

Fig. 7.13c. Unedited OCLC bibliographic record.

```
OCLC: 20824432        Rec stat:  n
Entered:  19891201  Replaced: 19891228    Used: 19910425
Type: a  Bib lvl:  m  Source:        Lang:    eng
Repr:    Enc lvl:  8  Conf pub:  0   Ctry:    enk
Indx: 1  Mod rec:     Govt pub:      Cont:    b
Desc: a  Int lvl:     Festschr:  0   Illus:
         F/B:      0  Dat tp:    s   Dates:   1990,
1    010          89-49731
2    040          DLC $c DLC [Modified by author]
3    020          0521374332
4    020          0521399386 (pbk.)
5    050 00       B2849.S92 $b N48 1990
6    082 00       126 $2 20
7    049          KHNN
8    100 1        Neuhouser, Frederick.
9    245 10       Fichte's theory of subjectivity / $c
Frederick Neuhouser.
10   260          Cambridge [England] ; $a New York : $b
Cambridge University Press, $c 1990.
11   263          9008
12   300          p. cm.
13   440  0       Modern European philosophy
14   504          Includes bibliographical references and
index.
15   600 10       Fichte, Johann Gottlieb, $d 1762-1814 $x
Contributions in concept of subjectivity.
16   650  0       Subjectivity.
```

Discussion: The copy cataloger will experience this situation frequently. The "8" in the encoding level in the fixed field indicates that this is CIP. Because the cataloging was done from galley proofs, the pagination and other physical characteristics may not have been in their final forms at that time. CIP usually does not include the physical description. Upon examining the book, one finds the preliminary information numbered in Roman numerals, vii-x. The text is in Arabic numerals, 1-180. There are no illustrations. The height of the book is 22.2 centimeters.

The indicators are correct. A subfield code for dimensions will be needed when the record is edited.

Fig. 7.13d. Edited OCLC bibliographic record.

```
OCLC: 20824432       Rec stat:  n
Entered:  19891201   Replaced: 19891228    Used: 19910425
Type: a  Bib lvl:  m  Source:        Lang:   eng
Repr:      Enc lvl:  8  Conf pub:  0    Ctry:   enk
Indx: 1  Mod rec:     Govt pub:      Cont:   b
Desc: a  Int lvl:     Festschr:  0    Illus:
            F/B:      0  Dat tp:    s    Dates:  1990,
1     010          89-49731
2     040          DLC $c DLC [Modified by author]
3     020          0521374332
4     020          0521399386 (pbk.)
5     050 00       B2849.S92 $b N48 1990
6     082 00       126 $2 20
7     049          KHNN
8     100 1        Neuhouser, Frederick.
9     245 10       Fichte's theory of subjectivity / $c
Frederick Neuhouser.
10   260          Cambridge [England] ; $a New York : $b
Cambridge University Press, $c 1990.
11   263          9008
12   300          x, 180 p. ; $c 23 cm.
13   440   0      Modern European philosophy
14   504          Includes bibliographical references and
index.
15   600 10       Fichte, Johann Gottlieb, $d 1762-1814 $x
Contributions in concept of subjectivity.
16   650   0      Subjectivity.
```

Fig. 7.14a. Title page.

The
Diversity
of Life

THE BELKNAP PRESS OF
HARVARD UNIVERSITY PRESS
CAMBRIDGE, MASSACHUSETTS
1992

Fig. 7.14b. Verso of title page.

ADDITIONAL INFORMATION: The pagination is 3–424. There are black-and-white and color illustrations; the latter are on glossy paper. Most of the color illustrations are on 16 unnumbered pages between pp. 280 and 281, with some on two unnumbered pages between pp. 350 and 351. There are black-and-white maps. The height is 24.2 centimeters.

Fig. 7.14c. Unedited OCLC bibliographic record.

```
OCLC: 25508994        Rec stat:   c
Entered: 19920228     Replaced: 19930129     Used: 19930407
Type: a  Bib lvl:  m  Source:          Lang:    eng
Repr:    Enc lvl:     Conf pub:  0     Ctry:    mau
Indx: 1  Mod rec:     Govt pub:        Cont:    b
Desc: a  Int lvl:     Festschr:  0     Illus:   ab
         F/B:      0  Dat tp:    s     Dates:   1992,
1    010       92-018
2    040       DLC $c DLC $d AGL [Modified by author]
3    020       0674212983 $c 29.95
4    050 00    QH313 $b .W55 1992
5    070 0     QH313.W55 $b 1992
6    072       x300
7    082 00    333.95 $2 20
8    049       KHNN
9    100 1     Wilson, Edward Osborne, $d 1929-
10   245 14    The diversity of life / $c Edward O.
Wilson.
11   260       Cambridge, Mass. : $b Belknap Press of
Harvard University Press, $c 1992.
12   300       424 p. : $b ill., maps ; $c 25 cm.
13   440 0     Questions of science
14   504       Includes bibliographical references (p.
355-390)and index.
15   650 0     Biological diversity.
16   650 0     Biological diversity conservation.
```

Discussion: Upon comparing the book, the 300 field, and Rule 2.5, everything is correct except that some of the illustrations are in color, so "(some col.)" should follow "ill." Pages of plates could be included in this record. See figure 7.15b for an explanation of plates.

Fig. 7.14d. Edited OCLC bibliographic record.

```
OCLC: 25508994        Rec stat:   c
Entered: 19920228     Replaced: 19930129    Used: 19930407
Type: a  Bib lvl:  m  Source:         Lang:    eng
Repr:    Enc lvl:     Conf pub:  0    Ctry:    mau
Indx: 1  Mod rec:     Govt pub:       Cont:    b
Desc: a  Int lvl:     Festschr:  0    Illus:   ab
         F/B:      0  Dat tp:    s    Dates:   1992,
1    010          92-9018
2    040          DLC $c DLC $d AGL [Modified by author]
3    020          0674212983 $c 29.95
4    050 00       QH313 $b .W55 1992
5    070 0        QH313.W55 $b 1992
6    072          x300
7    082 00       333.95 $2 20
8    049          KHNN
9    100 1        Wilson, Edward Osborne, $d 1929-
10   245 14       The diversity of life / $c Edward O.
Wilson.
11   260          Cambridge, Mass. : $b Belknap Press of
Harvard University Press, $c 1992.
12   300          424 p. : $b ill. (some col.), maps ; $c 25
cm.
13   440 0        Questions of science
14   504          Includes bibliographical references (p.
355-390)and index.
15   650 0        Biological diversity.
16   650 0        Biological diversity conservation.
```

Fig. 7.15a. Title page.

Sisters and Workers in the Middle Ages

E D I T E D   B Y
Judith M. Bennett, Elizabeth A. Clark,
Jean F. O'Barr, B. Anne Vilen,
and Sarah Westphal-Wihl

The University of Chicago Press
Chicago and London

Fig. 7.15b. Verso of title page.

On the cover: Silk women collecting cocoons and weaving cloth, MS Royal 16GV fol. 542. By permission of the British Library.

The essays in this volume originally appeared in various issues of SIGNS: JOURNAL OF WOMEN IN CULTURE AND SOCIETY. Acknowledgment of the original publication date can be found on the first page of each essay.

The University of Chicago Press, Chicago 60637
The University of Chicago Press, Ltd., London
© 1976, 1980, 1982, 1987, 1989 by The University of Chicago
All rights reserved. Published 1989
Printed in the United States of America
93 92 91 90 89 5 4 3 2 1

Library of Congress Cataloging-in-Publication Data

Sisters and workers in the Middle Ages / edited by Judith M. Bennett . . . [et al.].

    p.   cm.

    Includes bibliographies and indexes.
    ISBN 0-226-04247-2 (alk. paper) : $30.00 (est.). —ISBN
    0-226-04248-0 (pbk. : alk. paper) : $15.00 (est.)
    1. Women—History—Middle Ages, 500–1500. 2. Monastic and religious life of women—History—Middle Ages, 600–1500. 3. Women—Employment—Europe—History. 4. Sex role—Europe—History.
    I. Bennett, Judith M.
    HD1143.S55 1989
    305.4'09'02—dc20

                                       89-9137
                                         CIP

The paper used in this publication meets the minimum requirements of American National Standard for Information Sciences—Permanence of Paper for Printed Library Materials, ANSI Z39.48-1984.

ADDITIONAL INFORMATION: The pagination is 2–299. The only illustrations are on eight pages inserted between pp. 160 and 161. The illustrations are black-and-white on glossy paper. They are numbered, but the pages they are on are not numbered. Some pages have more than one illustration. The height is 22.7 centimeters.

Fig. 7.15c. Unedited OCLC bibliographic record.

```
OCLC: 19739987        Rec stat:  p
Entered: 19890502     Replaced: 19900414     Used: 19910517
Type: a  Bib lvl:  m  Source:          Lang:    eng
Repr:    Enc lvl:     Conf pub:  0     Ctry:    ilu
Indx: 1  Mod rec:     Govt pub:        Cont:    b
Desc: a  Int lvl:     Festschr:  0     Illus:   af
         F/B:      0  Dat tp:    s     Dates:   1989,
1    010        89-9137
2    040        DLC $c DLC   [Modified by author]
3    020        0226042472 (alk. paper) : $c $30.00 (est.)
4    020        0226042480 (pbk. : alk. paper) : $c $15.00
(est.)
5    043        e------
6    050 00     HD1143 $b .S55 1989
7    082 00     305.4/09/02 $2 20
8    049        KHNN
9    245 00     Sisters and workers in the Middle Ages /
$c edited by Judith M. Bennett ... [et al.].
10   260        Chicago : $b University of Chicago Press,
$c 1989.
11   300        299 p., [8] p. of plates : $b ill. ; $c 24
cm.
12   504        Includes bibliographical references and
indexes.
13   650   0    Women $x Employment $y Middle Ages, 500-
1500.
14   650   0    Monastic and religious life of women $x
History $y Middle Ages, 600-1500.
15   650   0    Women $x Employment $z Europe $x History.
16   650   0    Sex role $z Europe $x History.
17   700 1      Bennett, Judith M.
```

Discussion: Except for size, the 300 field is correct according to Rule 2.5. The Library of Congress will only give the number of pages of plates when they are numbered or when they represent an important feature of the book (*Cataloging Service Bulletin* no. 51, p. 29).

This record will be edited in figure 7.15d as LC copy might now appear. However, most libraries would not change it.

Fig. 7.15d. Edited OCLC bibliographic record.

```
OCLC: 19739987       Rec stat:  p
Entered: 1980502     Replaced: 19900414     Used: 19910517
Type: a  Bib lvl:  m  Source:         Lang:    eng
Repr:    Enc lvl:     Conf pub:  0    Ctry:    ilu
Indx: 1  Mod rec:     Govt pub:       Cont:    b
Desc: a  Int lvl:     Festschr:  0    Illus:   a
         F/B:      0  Dat tp:    s    Dates:   1989,
1    010          89-9137
2    040          DLC $c DLC [Modified by author]
3    020          0226042472 (alk. paper) : $c $30.00 (est.)
4    020          0226042480 (pbk. : alk. paper) : $c $15.00
(est.)
5    043          e------
6    050 00       HD1143 $b .S55 1989
7    082 00       305.4/09/02 $2 20
8    049          KHNN
9    245 00       Sisters and workers in the Middle Ages /
$c edited by Judith M. Bennett ... [et al.].
10   260          Chicago : $b University of Chicago Press,
$c 1989.
11   300          299 p. : $b ill. ; $c 23 cm.
12   504          Includes bibliographical references and
indexes.
13   650  0       Women $x Employment $y Middle Ages, 500-
1500.
14   650  0       Monastic and religious life of women $x
History $y Middle Ages, 600-1500.
15   650  0       Women $x Employment $z Europe $x History.
16   650  0       Sex role $z Europe $x History.
17   700 1        Bennett, Judith M.
```

If desired, the reader may now practice the exercises in chapter 10 for the 300 field for monographs. Figures 10.1-10.3 and 10.5 need editing in the 300 fields. Consult chapter 11 for the answers.

Series Area (Rules 1.6 and 2.6; Field 4xx)

Fig. 7.16a. Title page.

Operations Analysis in the U.S. Army Eighth Air Force in World War II

Charles W. McArthur

HISTORY OF MATHEMATICS

Volume 4

AMERICAN MATHEMATICAL SOCIETY
LONDON MATHEMATICAL SOCIETY

Fig. 7.16b. Verso of title page.

1980 *Mathematics Subject Classification* (1985 *Revision*). Primary 01A60.

Library of Congress Cataloging-in-Publication Data

McArthur, Charles W., 1921–
    Operations analysis in the United States Army Eighth Air Force in World War II/Charles W. McArthur.
    p. cm.—(History of mathematics, ISSN 0899-2428; v. 4)
    ISBN 0-8218-0158-9
    1. World War, 1939–1945—Aerial operations, America. 2. United States. Army Air Forces. Air Force, 8th—History. 3. Strategy. I. Title. II. Series.
D790.M226   1990   90-829
940.54'4973—dc20   CIP

From *Europe: From Argument to V-E Day, January 1944 to May 1945*, vol. 3 of *The Army Air Forces in World War II*. Copyright ©1951. Reprinted by permission of The University of Chicago Press.

A General's Life. An Autobiography. Copyright ©1983 by the Estate of General of the Army Omar N. Bradley and Clay Blair. Reprinted by permission of Simon & Schuster, Inc.

My Three Years with Eisenhower. Copyright ©1946 by Harry C. Butcher, renewed ©1973 by Harry C. Butcher. Reprinted by permission of Simon & Schuster, Inc.

From *The First and the Last* by Adolf Galland. Copyright 1954, ©1982 by Holt, Rinehart and Winston. Reprinted by permission of Henry Holt and Company, Inc.

From *Brave Men* by Ernie Pyle. Copyright ©1943, 1944 by Scripps-Howard Newspaper Alliance. Copyright ©1944 by Henry Holt and Co., Inc., copyright ©1971, 1972 by Holt, Rinehart and Winston. Reprinted by permission of Henry Holt and Co., Inc.

Fig. 7.16c. Unedited OCLC bibliographic record.

```
OCLC: 21592879        Rec stat:  p
Entered: 19900509     Replaced: 19910223     Used: 19910531
Type: a  Bib lvl:  m  Source:          Lang:    eng
Repr:    Enc lvl:     Conf pub:  0     Ctry:    riu
Indx: 1  Mod rec:     Govt pub:        Cont:    b
Desc: a  Int lvl:     Festschr:  0     Illus:   af
         F/B:     0   Dat tp:    s     Dates:   1990,
1    010          90-829
2    040          DLC $c DLC [Modified by author]
3    020          0821801589
4    043          n-us---
5    050 00       D790 $b .M226 1990
6    082 00       940.54/4973 $2 20
7    049          KHNN
8    100 1        McArthur, Charles W., $d 1921-
9    245 10       Operations analysis in the U.S. Army
Eighth Air Force in World War II / $c Charles W.
McArthur.
10   260          Providence, R.I. : $b American
Mathematical Society ; $a [London] : $b London
Mathematical Society $c c1990.
11   300          xxiv, 349 p., [16] p. of plates : $b ill.
; $c 27 cm.
12   440  0       History of Mathematics, $x 0899-2428 ; $v
vol. 4
13   504          Includes bibliographical references and
index.
14   650  0       World War, 1939-1945 $x Aerial operations,
American.
15   610 10       United States. $b Army Air Forces. $b Air
Force,8th $x History.
16   650  0       Strategy.
17   740 01       Operations analysis in the United States
Army eighth Air Force in World War II.
```

Discussion: The title of the series should be recorded as the title proper (Rule 1.6B1). Thus, "Mathematics" should not be capitalized. Rule 1.6F1 states that one should list the ISSN of the series in the standard manner (i.e., "ISSN" followed by a space and two groups of four digits separated by a hyphen). ISSN is missing before the number. Rule 1.6G1, using Appendices B and C for abbreviations and numerals, instructs to give the number in the terms as they appear in the item. In Appendix B, "v." and "vol." are listed as abbreviations for volume. In footnote 10 following "vols.," one discovers that "vol." is to be used only at the beginning of a statement and before a roman numeral. Thus the correct abbreviation for volume is "v." Sometimes LC uses "vol."; therefore, some libraries may have exceptions to this abbreviation. The copy cataloger needs to consult with a supervisor on exceptions and their notation.

The punctuation is correct according to Rule 1.6A, except that the entire series should be enclosed in parentheses. Upon reading the series section in *Bibliographic Formats*, one discovers that ISSN is a print constant and should not be input into the field. Parentheses around the series are also a print constant and should not be input into the field. The indicator and subfield codes are correct.

Fig. 7.16d. Edited OCLC bibliographic record.

```
OCLC: 21592879        Rec stat:   p
Entered: 19900509     Replaced: 19910223    Used: 19910531
Type: a  Bib lvl:  m  Source:          Lang:    eng
Repr:    Enc lvl:     Conf pub:  0     Ctry:    riu
Indx: 1  Mod rec:     Govt pub:        Cont:    b
Desc: a  Int lvl:     Festschr:  0     Illus:   af
         F/B:      0  Dat tp:    s     Dates:   1990,
1   010          90-829
2   040          DLC $c DLC [Modified by author]
3   020          0821801589
4   043          n-us---
5   050 00       D790 $b .M226 1990
6   082 00       940.54/4973 $2 20
7   049          KHNN
8   100 1        McArthur, Charles W., $d 1921-
9   245 10       Operations analysis in the U.S. Army
Eighth Air Force in World War II / $c Charles W.
McArthur.
10  260          Providence, R.I. : $b American
Mathematical Society ; $a [London] : $b London
Mathematical Society $c c1990.
11  246 3        Operations in the United States Army Eight
Air Force in World War II.
12  300          xxiv, 349 p., [16] p. of plates : $b ill.
; $c 27 cm.
13  440  0       History of mathematics, $x 0899-2428 ; $v
v. 4
14  504          Includes bibliographical references and
index.
15  650  0       World War, 1939-1945 $x Aerial operations,
American.
16  610 10       United States. $b Army Air Forces. $b Air
Force,8th $x History.
17  650  0       Strategy.
```

Fig. 7.17a. Series title page.

Politics today
Series editor: Bill Jones

American politics today
   R. A. Maidment and M. Tappin
West European politics today
   G. K. Roberts and J. Lovecy
Political issues in America today
   P. J. Davies and F. Waldstein (eds.)
Political issues in Britain today
   Bill Jones (ed.)
British politics today
   Bill Jones and Dennis Kavanagh
Trade unions in Britain today
   John McIlroy

Forthcoming, to include:

General elections today
   F. Conley
Government and the economy today
   G. Thomas
Party politics today
   R. N. Kelly and R. W. Garner
Soviet politics today
   C. A. P. Binns
Local government today
   J. A. Chandler

Of related interest

The financial system today
   E. Rowley

Fig. 7.17b. Title page.

Parliament today

Andrew Adonis

Manchester University Press

Manchester and New York

Distributed exclusively in the USA and Canada by St. Martin's Press

Fig. 7.17c. Verso of title page.

Copyright © Andrew Adonis 1990

Published by Manchester University Press
Oxford Road, Manchester M13 9PL, UK
and Room 400, 175 Fifth Avenue,
New York, NY 10010, USA

Distributed exclusively in the USA and Canada
by St. Martin's Press, Inc.,
175 Fifth Avenue, New York, NY 10010, USA

British Library cataloguing in publication data
Adonis, Andrew
  Parliament today.
  1. Great Britain. Parliament
  I. Title
  328.41

Library of Congress cataloging in publication data
Adonis, Andrew, 1963–
    Parliament today / Andrew Adonis.
     p. cm. – (Politics today)
    Includes bibliographical references.
    ISBN 0-7190-3082-X. – ISBN 0-7190-3083-8 (pbk.)
    1. Great Britain. Parliament. I. Title. II. Series: Politics
today (Manchester, England)
JN550 1990
328.41'072 – dc20   90-5563

ISBN 0 7190 3082 X *hardback*
    0 7190 3083 8 *paperback*

Phototypeset in Great Britain
by Williams Graphics, Llanddulas, North Wales

Printed in Great Britain
by Biddles Ltd, Guildford and King's Lynn

Fig. 7.17d. Unedited OCLC bibliographic record.

```
OCLC: 21118872      Rec stat:  p
Entered: 19900206   Replaced: 19901112    Used: 19910426
Type: a  Bib lvl:  m  Source:        Lang:    eng
Repr:    Enc lvl:     Conf pub:  0    Ctry:    enk
Indx: 1  Mod rec:     Govt pub:      Cont:    b
Desc: a  Int lvl:     Festschr:  0    Illus:   a
         F/B:      0  Dat tp:    s    Dates:   1990,
1    010        90-5563
2    040        DLC $c DLC [Modified by author]
3    020        071903082X
4    020        0719030838 (pbk.)
5    043        e-uk---
6    050 00     JN550 $b 1990
7    082 00     328.41/072 $2 20
8    049        KHNN
9    100 1      Adonis, Andrew, $d 1963-
10   245 10     Parliament today / $c Andrew Adonis.
11   260        Manchester ; $a New York : $b Manchester
University Press ; $a New York : $b Distributed
exclusively in the USA and Canada by St. Martin's Press,
$c c1990.
12   300        viii, 194 p. : $b ill. ; $c 21 cm.
13   490 0      Politics today / Bill Jones, special
editor
14   504        Includes bibliographical references (p.
[186]-189).
15   610 10     Great Britain. $b Parliament.
```

Discussion: According to Rule 1.6E1, the statement of responsibility for a series should not be recorded unless it is considered necessary for identification. "Bill Jones" is not necessary for identifying this series; therefore, the name should not be recorded. On the series title page no series number is listed. The item also does not contain an ISSN for the series.

The tag of 490 indicates that the series is either not traced or it is traced in a different way. Upon consulting the local series authority file, one finds this series is to be traced as "Politics today (Manchester, England)." The first indicator is not correct. The first indicator should be "1" if the series is to be traced differently. The different form should be recorded in an 8xx field. There will not be any subfields because there is no ISSN or series number. The 8xx field will be: "830 0 Politics today (Manchester, England)."

Fig. 7.17e. Edited OCLC bibliographic record.

```
OCLC: 21118872        Rec stat:  p            Entered:
19900206
Replaced: 19901112   Used: 19910426
Type: a  Bib lvl:  m  Source:          Lang:    eng
Repr:    Enc lvl:     Conf pub:  0     Ctry:    enk
Indx: 1  Mod rec:     Govt pub:        Cont:    b
Desc: a  Int lvl:     Festschr:  0     Illus:   a
         F/B:      0  Dat tp:    s     Dates:   1990,
1    010       90-5563
2    040       DLC $c DLC [Modified by author]
3    020       071903082X
4    020       0719030838 (pbk.)
5    043       e-uk---
6    050 00    JN550 $b 1990
7    082 00    328.41/072 $2 20
8    049       KHNN
9    100 1     Adonis, Andrew, $d 1963-
10   245 10    Parliament today / $c Andrew Adonis.
11   260       Manchester ; $a New York : $b Manchester
University Press ; $a New York : $b Distributed
exclusively in the USA and Canada by St. Martin's Press,
$c c1990.
12   300       viii, 194 p. : $b ill. ; $c 21 cm.
13   490 1     Politics today
14   504       Includes bibliographical references (p.
[186]-189).
15   610 10    Great Britain. $b Parliament.
16   830  0    Politics today (Manchester, England)
```

Fig. 7.18a. Series title page.

NATO ASI Series

Advanced Science Institutes Series

A series presenting the results of activities sponsored by the NATO Science Committee, which aims at the dissemination of advanced scientific and technological knowledge, with a view to strengthening links between scientific communities.

The series is published by an international board of publishers in conjunction with the NATO Scientific Affairs Division

A	Life Sciences	Plenum Publishing Corporation
B	Physics	New York and London
C	Mathematical and Physical Sciences	Kluwer Academic Publishers Dordrecht, Boston, and London
D	Behavioral and Social Sciences	
E	Applied Sciences	
F	Computer and Systems Sciences	Springer-Verlag
G	Ecological Sciences	Berlin, Heidelberg, New York, London,
H	Cell Biology	Paris, and Tokyo

Recent Volumes in this Series

Volume 211—Phase Transitions in Soft Condensed Matter
edited by Tormod Riste and David Sherrington

Volume 212—Atoms in Strong Fields
edited by Cleanthes A. Nicolaides, Charles W. Clark, and Munir H. Nayfeh

Volume 213—Interacting Electrons in Reduced Dimensions
edited by Dionys Baeriswyl and David K. Campbell

Volume 214—Science and Engineering of One- and Zero-Dimensional Semiconductors
edited by Steven P. Beaumont, and Clivia M. Sotomayor Torres

Volume 215—Soil Colloids and their Associations in Aggregates
edited by Marcel F. De Boodt, Michael H. B. Hayes, and Adrien Herbillon

Volume 216A—The Nuclear Equation of State, Part A:
Discovery of Nuclear Shock Waves and the EOS
edited by Walter Greiner and Horst Stöcker

Volume 216B—The Nuclear Equation of State, Part B:
QCD and the Formation of the Quark-Gluon Plasma
edited by Walter Greiner and Horst Stöcker

Volume 217—Solid State Microbatteries
edited by James R. Akridge and Minko Balkanski

Series B: Physics

Fig. 7.18b. Title page.

Solid State Microbatteries

Edited by

James R. Akridge

Eveready Battery Co., Inc.
Westlake, Ohio

and

Minko Balkanski

Université Pierre et Marie Curie
Paris, France

Plenum Press
New York and London
Published in cooperation with NATO Scientific Affairs Division

Fig. 7.18c. Verso of title page.

Proceedings of the NATO Advanced Study Institute and
International School of Materials Science and Technology
Fifteenth Course on
Solid State Microbatteries,
held July 3-15, 1988,
in Erice, Trapani, Sicily, Italy

Library of Congress Cataloging-in-Publication Data

International School of Materials Science and Technology (1988
   Erice, Italy)
    Solid state microbatteries / edited by James R. Akridge and Minko
Balkanski.
        p.   cm. -- (NATO ASI series. Series B, Physics ; vol. 217)
     "Published in cooperation with NATO Scientific Affairs Division."
     "Proceedings of the NATO Advanced Study Institute and
International School of Materials Science and Technology fifteenth
course on solid state microbatteries, held July 3-15, 1988, in
Erice, Trapani, Sicily, Italy"--T.p. verso.
    Includes bibliographical references.
    ISBN 0-306-43505-5
    1. Solid state batteries--Congresses. 2. Microelectronics-
-Congresses.   I. Akridge, J. R. II. Balkanski, Minko, 1927-
III. North Atlantic Treaty Organization. Scientific Affairs
Division. IV. Title. V. Series: NATO ASI series. Series B,
Physics ; v. 217.
TK2942.I57 1988
621.31'242--dc20

                                                       90-6769
                                                          CIP

© 1990 Plenum Press, New York
A Division of Plenum Publishing Corporation
233 Spring Street, New York, N.Y. 10013

Printed in the United States of America

Fig. 7.18d. Unedited OCLC bibliographic record.

```
OCLC: 21037383        Rec stat:  p
Entered: 19900117    Replaced 19901124      Used: 19910502
Type: a  Bib lvl:  m  Source:        Lang:    eng
Repr:     Enc lvl:     Conf pub:  1  Ctry:    nyu
Indx: 1  Mod rec:     Govt pub:     Cont:    b
Desc: a  Int lvl:     Festschr:  0  Illus:   a
         F/B:       0  Dat tp:    s  Dates:   1990,
1    010         90-6769
2    040         DLC $c DLC [Modified by author]
3    020         0306435055
4    050 00      TK2942 $b .I57 1988
5    082 00      621.32/242 $2 20
6    049         KHNN
7    111 1       International School of Materials Science
and Technology $d (1988 : $c Erice, Italy)
8    245 10      Solid state microbatteries / $c edited by
James R. Akridge and Minko Balkanski.
9    260         New York : $b Plenum Press, $c c1990.
10   300         x, 439 p. : $b ill. ; $c 26 cm.
11   440   0     NATO ASI series. $n Series B. Physics $v
v. 217
12   500         "Proceedings of the NATO Advanced Study
Institute and International School of Materials Science
and Technology fifteenth course on solid state
microbatteries, held July 3-15, 1988, in Erice, Trapani,
Sicily, Italy"-- T.p. verso.
13   504         Includes bibliographical references and
index.
14   650   0     Solid state batteries $x Congresses.
15   650   0     Microelectronics $x Congresses.
16   700 1       Akridge, J. R.
17   700 1       Balkanski, Minko, $d 1927-
18   710 2       North Atlantic Treaty Organization. $b
Scientific Affairs Division.
```

Discussion: An analysis of the series title page reveals that this series has a subseries with an alphabetic designation and a title. An ISSN is not listed for the series. Reviewing Rules 1.6A1, 1.6B1, 1.6H2, and 1.6H5, one concludes that the series is recorded correctly, except for the punctuation preceding the number. The local series authority file indicates that the series is traced in this form.

The 440 tag indicates that the series is traced in the form listed. The indicators are correct. Subfield code "n" is the correct subfield code for a subseries number. The subfield code is missing for the subseries name; it should be "p." The subfield code is correct for the number of the series.

Fig. 7.18e. Edited OCLC bibliographic record.

```
OCLC: 21037383      Rec stat:  p
Entered: 19900117    Replaced 19901124      Used: 19910502
Type: a  Bib lvl:  m  Source:         Lang:    eng
Repr:    Enc lvl:      Conf pub:  1    Ctry:    nyu
Indx: 1  Mod rec:      Govt pub:       Cont:    b
Desc: a  Int lvl:      Festschr:  0    Illus:   a
         F/B:        0 Dat tp:    s    Dates:   1990,
1    010          90-6769
2    040          DLC $c DLC [Modified by author]
3    020          0306435055
4    050 00       TK2942 $b .I57 1988
5    082 00       621.32/242 $2 20
6    049          KHNN
7    111 1        International School of Materials Science
and Technology $d (1988 : $c Erice, Italy)
8    245 10       Solid state microbatteries / $c edited by
James R. Akridge and Minko Balkanski.
9    260          New York : $b Plenum Press, $c c1990.
10   300          x, 439 p. : $b ill. ; $c 26 cm.
11   440   0      NATO ASI series. $n Series B, $p Physics ;
$v v. 217
12   500          "Proceedings of the NATO Advanced Study
Institute and International School of Materials Science
and Technology fifteenth course on solid state
microbatteries, held July 3-15, 1988, in Erice, Trapani,
Sicily, Italy"-- T.p. verso.
13   504          Includes bibliographical references and
index.
14   650   0      Solid state batteries $x Congresses.
15   650   0      Microelectronics $x Congresses.
16   700 1        Akridge, J. R.
17   700 1        Balkanski, Minko, $d 1927-
18   710 2        North Atlantic Treaty Organization. $b
Scientific Affairs Division.
```

If desired, the reader may now practice the exercises in chapter 10 for the 4xx fields for monographs. Figures 10.3–10.4 need editing in the 4xx fields. Consult chapter 11 for the answers.

Note Area (Rules 1.7 and 2.7; Field 5xx)

Fig. 7.19a. Title page.

REDEEMING MODERNITY

Contradictions in Media Criticism

Joli Jensen

SAGE PUBLICATIONS
The International Professional Publishers
Newbury Park London New Delhi

Fig. 7.19b. Verso of title page.

For information address:

SAGE Publications, Inc.
2111 West Hillcrest Drive
Newbury Park, California 91320

SAGE Publications Ltd.
28 Banner Street
London EC1Y 8QE
England

SAGE Publications India Pvt. Ltd.
M-32 Market
Greater Kailash I
New Delhi 110 048 India

Printed in the United States of America

Library of Congress Cataloging-in-Publication Data

Jensen, Joli.
  Redeeming modernity : American media criticism as social criticism
/ by Joli Jensen
      p.   cm. — (Communication and human values)
  Includes bibliographical references.
  ISBN 0-8039-3476-9. — ISBN 0-8039-3477-7 (pbk.)
  1. Mass media. 2. Popular culture. 3. Mass media—Social
aspects. 4. Mass media—United States   I. Title. II. Series :
Communication and human values (Newbury Park, Calif.)
P91.J47 1990
302.23'0973—dc20   90-8269
                                                                       CIP

FIRST PRINTING, 1990

Sage Production Editor: Astrid Virding

ADDITIONAL INFORMATION: At the top of page 202 is "References," followed by a bibliography that continues through page 206.

Fig. 7.19c. Unedited OCLC bibliographic record.

```
OCLC: 21229375        Rec stat:  p
Entered: 19900227     Replaced: 19901124     Used: 19910411
Type: a  Bib lvl:  m  Source:        Lang:    eng
Repr:    Enc lvl:     Conf pub:  0   Ctry:    cau
Indx: 1  Mod rec:     Govt pub:      Cont:    b
Desc: a  Int lvl:     Festschr:  0   Illus:
         F/B:      0  Dat tp:    s   Dates:   1990,
1    010        90-8269
2    040        DLC $c DLC [Modified by author]
3    020        0803934769
4    020        0803934777 (pbk.)
5    043        n-us---
6    050 00     P91 $b .J47 1990
7    082 00     302.23/0973 $2 20
8    049        KHNN
9    100 1      Jensen, Joli.
10   245 10     Redeeming modernity : $b contradictions in
media criticism / $c Joli Jensen.
11   260        Newbury Park, Calif. : $b Sage
Publications, $c c1990.
12   300        221 p. ; $c 23 cm.
13   490 1      Communication and human values
14   504        Bibliography: p. 202-206.
15   500        Includes index.
15   650  0     Mass media.
16   650  0     Popular culture.
17   650  0     Mass media $x Social aspects.
18   650  0     Mass media $z United States.
19   830  0     Communication and human values (Newbury,
Calif.)
```

Discussion: The bibliography/discography note is a very common one (Rule 2.7B18). The form of this note has varied. The form in this record is like an example in *AACR2R*. Since 1990 the Library of Congress has used a slightly different form. The note by LC's latest interpretations would be: "Includes bibliographical references (pp. 202–206) and index." (*Cataloging Service Bulletin* no. 47, p. 33). Notice that the index note has been combined with the bibliography note. Many libraries will not change the bibliographical note to the latest LC form. The time it takes cannot be justified, and the change does not affect the user. The copy cataloger will need to learn the policy of the library.

Sometimes the first or last page of a bibliography does not have a page number, while the rest of the pages in the bibliography are paginated. In these cases, determine the number that the page would bear and enclose it in brackets (see figure 7.17).

If the bibliographical references are not all located together in the book, the page numbers are not given (see figure 7.20e).

The bibliographical note has a tag of 504. Both indicators are blank.

Fig. 7.19d. Edited OCLC bibliographic record.

```
OCLC: 21229375        Rec stat:  p
Entered: 19900227     Replaced: 19901124     Used: 19910411
Type: a  Bib lvl:  m  Source:          Lang:    eng
Repr:    Enc lvl:      Conf pub:  0    Ctry:    cau
Indx: 1  Mod rec:      Govt pub:       Cont:    b
Desc: a  Int lvl:      Festschr:  0    Illus:
         F/B:       0  Dat tp:    s    Dates:   1990,
1    010           90-8269
2    040           DLC $c DLC [Modified by author]
3    020           0803934769
4    020           0803934777 (pbk.)
5    043           n-us---
6    050 00        P91 $b .J47 1990
7    082 00        302.23/0973 $2 20
8    049           KHNN
9    100 1         Jensen, Joli.
10   245 10        Redeeming modernity : $b contradictions in
media criticism / $c Joli Jensen.
11   260           Newbury Park, Calif. : $b Sage
Publications, $c c1990.
12   300           221 p. ; $c 23 cm.
13   490 1         Communication and human values
14   504           Includes bibliographical references (p.
202-206) and index.
15   650  0        Mass media.
16   650  0        Popular culture.
17   650  0        Mass media $x Social aspects.
18   650  0        Mass media $z United States.
19   830  0        Communication and human values (Newbury,
Calif.)
```

Fig. 7.20a. Title page.

Color Symbolism

Six Excerpts from the Eranos Yearbook 1972

Adolf Portmann Christopher Rowe
Dominique Zahan Ernst Benz
René Huyghe Toshihiko Izutsu

Spring Publications, Inc.
Dallas, Texas

Fig. 7.20b. Verso of title page.

Published by Spring Publications, Inc.; P.O. Box 222069;
Dallas, Texas 75222. Printed in the United States of America

International distributors:
Spring; Postfach; 8800 Thalwil; Switzerland.
Japan Spring Sha, Inc.;
12-10, 2-Chome, Nigawa Takamaru;
Takarazuka 665, Japan.
Element Books Ltd; Longmead Shaftesbury;
Dorset SP7 8PL; England.

Library of Congress Cataloging-in-Publication Data

Color symbolism.

"Papers ... delivered at the annual Eranos
Conference, Ascona, Switzerland, August 1972 ...
then published in the trilingual volume Eranos
41—1972, The realms of colour"—T. p. verso.
Includes bibliographies and index.
1. Color—Congresses. 2. Symbolism of colors—
Congresses. 3. Colors—Religious aspects—
Congresses. I. Portmann, Adolf, 1897- .
II. Eranos Conference (1972 : Ascona, Switzerland)
III. Eranos Jahrbuch.
BH301.C6C67 1988 306'.47   87-35614
ISBN 0-88214-400-6 (pbk.)

Fig. 7.20c. Acknowledgments page.

ACKNOWLEDGMENTS

These six papers were delivered at the annual Eranos Conference, Ascona, Switzerland, August 1972. They were then published in the trilingual volume *Eranos 41—1972, The Realms of Colour (Die Welt der Farben, Le Monde des Couleurs)*, together with papers by Gershom Scholem, Henry Corbin, Peter Dronke, S. Sambursky, and P. A. Riedel. We are grateful to the editors of the yearbook, Adolf Portmann and Rudolf Ritsema, as well as its publisher, E. J. Brill, Leiden. We especially thank the four translators for having accomplished almost impossible tasks. This volume was composed by Susan Haule, editorially aided by Robert Weening who also made the index.

Cover: The "Juno Chamber" in which Goethe received his visitors in his house at Weimar (part of a pastel by Franz Huth), adapted by Sven Doehner. The intensely contrasting yellows and blues bespeak Goethe's color theory.

Fig. 7.20d. Unedited OCLC bibliographic record.

```
OCLC: 17263623       Rec stat:  p
Entered: 19871207    Replaced: 19880430    Used: 19910506
Type: a  Bib lvl:  m  Source:        Lang:    eng
Repr:    Enc lvl:     Conf pub:  1   Ctry:    txu
Indx: 1  Mod rec:     Govt pub:      Cont:    b
Desc: a  Int lvl:     Festschr:  0   Illus:   a
         F/B:      0  Dat tp:.   c   Dates:   1988,1977
1    010          87-35614
2    040          DLC $c DLC [Modified by author]
3    020          0882144006 (pbk.)
4    050  0       BH301.C6 $b C67 1988
5    082 00       306/.47 $2 19
6    049          KHNN
7    245 00       Color symbolism : $b six excerpts from the
Eranos yearbook, 1972 / $c Adolf Portmann ... [et al.].
8    260          Dallas, Tex. : $b Spring Publications, $c
c1977 (1988 printing).
9    300          202 p. : $b ill. ; $c 21 cm.
10   500          "Papers...delivered at the annual Eranos
Conference, Ascona, Switzerland, August 1972...then
published in the trilingual volume Eranos 41-1972, The
realms of colour"--Ack.
11   504          Includes bibliographies and index.
12   650  0       Color $x Congresses.
13   650  0       Symbolism of colors $x Congresses.
14   650  0       Colors $x Religious aspects $x Congresses.
15   700  1       Portmann, Adolf, $d 1897-
16   711  2       Eranos Conference $d (1972 : $c Ascona,
Switzerland)
17   730 01       Eranos Jahrbuch.
```

Discussion: If the book is a result of a conference, symposium, or meeting that is not named in the 245 field (title), this fact is stated in a general note. A general note is also used for previous publication information. Rule 1.7A5 instructs one to combine notes when appropriate. In this case, a conference note and a publication note have been combined. Rule 1.7A3 says to enclose a quotation in quotation marks and to give its source unless it comes from the chief source of information.

The two marks of omissions are not preceded and followed by spaces as instructed in Rule 1.0C1. This note was found in the acknowledgments, but there is no abbreviation for acknowledgments in Appendix B. The CIP on the title page verso lists the source of the quoted note as "T.p. verso." The publisher probably changed the location after the CIP was prepared from the galley proofs.

Rule 2.7B states that the order of the notes should be as discussed in Rules 2.7B1 through 2.7B19, unless it has been decided that a specific note is of primary importance. In this record there are two notes. The first is a combined note from Rules 2.7B1 (Nature, scope, or artistic form) and 2.7B9 (Publication, distribution, etc.). The second is a selective content note based on Rule 2.7B18. This bibliographical note could be edited to the latest LC interpretation if desired. General notes have a tag of 500 with both indicators blank. The bibliography note has a tag of 504 with both indicators blank.

Fig. 7.20e. Edited OCLC bibliographic record.

```
OCLC: 17263623        Rec stat:   p
Entered: 19871207     Replaced: 19880430     Used: 19910506
Type: a   Bib lvl:   m   Source:           Lang:     eng
Repr:     Enc lvl:       Conf pub:  1      Ctry:     txu
Indx: 1   Mod rec:       Govt pub:         Cont:     b
Desc: a   Int lvl:       Festschr:  0      Illus:    a
          F/B:       0   Dat tp:    c      Dates:    1988,1977
1    010          87-35614
2    040          DLC $c DLC [Modified by author]
3    020          0882144006 (pbk.)
4    050   0      BH301.C6 $b C67 1988
5    082  00      306/.47 $2 19
6    049          KHNN
7    245  00      Color symbolism : $b six excerpts from the
Eranos yearbook, 1972 / $c Adolf Portmann ... [et al.].
8    260          Dallas, Tex. : $b Spring Publications, $c
c1977 (1988 printing).
9    300          202 p. : $b ill. ; $c 21 cm.
10   500          "Papers ... delivered at the annual Eranos
Conference, Ascona, Switzerland, August 1972 ... then
published in the trilingual volume Eranos 41-1972, The
realms of colour"--Acknowledgments.
11   504          Includes bibliographical references and
index.
12   650   0      Color $x Congresses.
13   650   0      Symbolism of colors $x Congresses.
14   650   0      Colors $x Religious aspects $x Congresses.
15   700   1      Portmann, Adolf, $d 1897-
16   711   2      Eranos Conference $d (1972 : $c Ascona,
Switzerland)
17   730  01      Eranos Jahrbuch.
```

If desired, the reader may now practice the exercises in chapter 10 for the 500 fields for monographs. Figures 10.1–10.5 need editing in the 5xx fields. Consult chapter 11 for the answers.

Standard Number and Terms of Availability Area (Rules 1.8 and 2.8; Field 020)

Fig. 7.21a. Title page.

Backyard Adventure

How to Create Outdoor Play Spaces for Kids

by

Paula Brook

Chester, Connecticut

Fig. 7.21b. Verso of title page.

To Shaw, Abby & Shira

Updated in Fall 1990

Copyright © 1988 by Paula Brook

Photographs on pages 104, 134, 138, 148, 150, 159, and 169 by Krisitn Mullally; remaining photographs provided by the author. Illustrations by Liz Mowrey.

Library of Congress Cataloging-in-Publication Data

Brook, Paula.
    Backyard adventure: how to create outdoor play spaces for kids / by Paula Brook.—1st ed.
       p. cm.
    Reprint. Originally published: Moscow, Idaho : Solstice Press, 1988.
      Includes bibliographical references and index.
    ISBN 0-87106-359-X
    1. Play—United States. 2. Creative activities and seat work.
3. Games. I. Title.
[HQ782.B76 1990]   90-39436
649'.5—dc20   CIP

Manufactured in the United States of America
First Edition/Second Printing

Fig. 7.21c. Unedited OCLC bibliographic record.

```
OCLC: 21761950        Rec stat:  p
Entered: 19900515     Replaced: 19910427     Used: 19910430
Type: a  Bib lvl:  m  Source:          Lang:    eng
Repr:    Enc lvl:     Conf pub:  0     Ctry:    ctu
Indx: 1  Mod rec:     Govt pub:        Cont:    b
Desc: a  Int lvl:     Festschr:  0     Illus:   a
         F/B:      0  Dat tp:    r     Dates:   1990,1988
1    010       90-39436
2    040       DLC $c DLC [Modified by author]
3    020       087106359X
4    043       n-us---
5    050 00    G425 $b .B76 1990
6    082 00    649/.5 $2 20
7    049       KHNN
8    100 1     Brook, Paula.
9    245 10    Backyard adventure : $b how to create
outdoor play spaces for kids / $c by Paula Brook.
10   250       1st ed.
11   260       Chester, Conn. : $b Globe Pequot Press, $c
1990.
12   300       xii, 179 p. : $b ill. ; $c 23 cm.
13   500       Reprint. Originally published: Moscow,
Idaho :   Solstice Press, 1988.
14   504       Includes bibliographical references (p.
178-179) and index.
15   650 0     Playgrounds $x Planning.
16   650 0     Playgrounds $x Equipment and supplies $x
Design and construction.
17   650 0     Playgrounds $x Design and construction.
18   650 0     Creative activities and seat work.
19   650 0     Play.
```

Discussion: According to Rule 1.8B1, and to *Bibliographic Formats*, the ISBN is entered correctly in the 020 field. This record is correct. No editing is needed.

Fig. 7.22a. Title page.

The Holocaust: An Annotated Bibliography and Resource Guide

Edited by
DAVID M. SZONYI

KTAV PUBLISHING HOUSE, INC.
for
THE NATIONAL JEWISH RESOURCE CENTER
New York

Fig. 7.22b. Verso of title page.

This work was made possible in part by a grant from the
National Endowment for the Humanities (EH-0362-79)

Library of Congress Cataloging in Publication Data

Main entry under title·

The Holocaust: an annotated bibliography and resource guide

   1. Holocaust, Jewish (1939-1945)—Bibliography.
I. Szonyi, David M. II. National Jewish Resource Center
III. B'nai B'rith. Anti-defamation League.
Z6374.H6H65   1985   [D810.J4]   016.94053'15'03924   84-26191
ISBN 0-88125-057-0
ISBN 0-88125-058-9 (pbk.)

MANUFACTURED IN THE UNITED STATES OF AMERICA

Fig. 7.22c. Unedited OCLC bibliographic record.

```
OCLC: 11497131        Rec stat:  c
Entered: 19841120   Replaced: 19870530     Used: 19910417
Type: a  Bib lvl:  m  Source:        Lang:    eng
Repr:    Enc lvl:     Conf pub:  0   Ctry:    nju
Indx: 0  Mod rec:     Govt pub:      Cont:    b
Desc: a  Int lvl:     Festschr:  0   Illus:
         F/B:      0  Dat tp:    s   Dates:   1985,
1    010        84-6191//r85
2    040        DLC $c DLC $d m/c [Modified by author]
3    020        0881250570 : $29.50
4    020        0881250589 pbk. : $c $16.95
5    050  0     Z6374.H6 $b H65 1985 $a D810.J4
6    082 00     016.94053/15/03924 $2 19
7    049        KHNN
8    245 04     The Holocaust : $b an annotated
bibliography and resource guide / $c edited by David M.
Szonyi.
9    260        [Hoboken, NJ] : $b KTAV Pub. House for the
National Jewish Resource Center, New York, $c c1985.
10   300        xiv, 396 p. ; $c 25 cm.
11   650  0     Holocaust, Jewish (1939-1945) $x
Bibliography.
12   700 1      Szonyi, David M.
13   710 2      National Jewish Resource Center (U.S.)
```

Discussion: Terms of availability are optional facts that may be added to the ISBN. Price is the most common term of availability (Rule 1.8D1). If an item bears more than one ISBN for the edition in hand and by the same publisher, more than one number may be given. If this is done, all numbers except the first need to be qualified (Rule 1.8B2). In this case, the second number is qualified, but it needs to be in parentheses (Rule 1.8A1). Also, from Rule 1.8A1 and the examples shown, it appears that both ISBNs should be in a single 020 field. However, upon reading the pertinent information in *Bibliographic Formats*, one discovers that multiple ISBNs are to be transcribed into separate 020 fields. Terms of availability is a separate subfield; therefore, it needs a subfield code of "c."

Fig. 7.22d. Edited OCLC bibliographic record.

```
OCLC: 11497131       Rec stat:   c
Entered: 19841120    Replaced: 19870530      Used: 19910417
Type: a  Bib lvl:  m  Source:          Lang:    eng
Repr:    Enc lvl:     Conf pub:  0     Ctry:    nju
Indx: 0  Mod rec:     Govt pub:        Cont:    b
Desc: a  Int lvl:     Festschr:  0     Illus:
         F/B:      0  Dat tp:    s     Dates:   1985,
1    010         84-26191//r85
2    040         DLC $c DLC $d m/c [Modified by author]
3    020         0881250570 : $c $29.50
4    020         0881250589 (pbk.) : $c $16.95
5'   050  0      Z6374.H6 $b H65 1985 $a D810.J4
6    082 00      016.94053/15/03924 $2 19
7    049         KHNN
8    245 04      The Holocaust : $b an annotated
bibliography and resource guide / $c edited by David M.
Szonyi.
9    260         [Hoboken, NJ] : $b KTAV Pub. House for the
National Jewish Resource Center, New York, $c c1985.
10   300         xiv, 396 p. ; $c 25 cm.
11   650  0      Holocaust, Jewish (1939-1945) $x
Bibliography.
12   700 1       Szonyi, David M.
13   710 2       National Jewish Resource Center (U.S.)
```

Fig. 7.23a. Title page of volume 1.

THE FIRST WORLD WAR

Volume I

Charles à Court Repington

Gregg Revivals

in association with
Department of War Studies
King's College London

Fig. 7.23b. Verso of title page of volume 1.

© Preface, Brian Bond 1991

First published in Great Britain in 1920 by
Constable

Reprinted in 1991 by
Gregg Revivals
Gower House
Croft Road
Aldershot
Hampshire GU11 3HR
England

Gregg Revivals
Distributed in the United States by
Ashgate Publishing Company
Old Post Road
Brookfield
Vermont 05036
USA

A CIP catalogue record for this book is available
from the British Library

A CIP catalogue record for this book is available
from the US Library of Congress

ISBN Volume I 0 7512 0036 0
    Set   0 7512 0038 7

Printed by Billing & Sons Ltd. Worcester

Fig. 7.23c. Title page of volume 2.

THE FIRST WORLD WAR

Volume II

Charles à Court Repington

Gregg Revivals

in association with
Department of War Studies
King's College London

Fig. 7.23d. Verso of title page of volume 2.

© Preface, Brian Bond 1991

First published in Great Britain in 1920 by
Constable

Reprinted in 1991 by
Gregg Revivals
Gower House
Croft Road
Aldershot
Hampshire GU11 3HR
England

Gregg Revivals
Distributed in the United States by
Ashgate Publishing Company
Old Post Road
Brookfield
Vermont 05036
USA

A CIP catalogue record for this book is available
from the British Library

A CIP catalogue record for this book is available
from the US Library of Congress

ISBN Volume II 0 7512 0037 9
      Set   0 7512 0038 7

Printed by Billing & Sons Ltd, Worcester

Fig.7.23e. Unedited OCLC bibliographic record.

```
OCLC: 25536707        Rec stat:   c
Entered: 19920326    Replaced: 19920326     Used: 19930131
Type: a   Bib lvl:  m  Source:    d    Lang:    eng
Repr:     Enc lvl:  I  Conf pub:  0    Ctry:    enk
Indx: 1   Mod rec:     Govt pub:       Cont:
Desc: a   Int lvl:     Festschr:  0    Illus:
          F/B:        0a Dat tp:   r    Dates:   1991,1920
1    040         TXA $c TXA [Modified by author]
3    020         0751200360 (v. 1)
4    020         0751200379 (v. 2)
2    020         0751200387 (set)
5    090         D544 $b .R43 1991
6    049         KHNN
7    100 1       Repington, Charles à Court, $d 1858-1925.
8    245 14      The first world war / $c Charles à Court
Repington.
9    260         Hampshire, England : $b Gregg Revivals ;
$a Brookfield, Vt. : $b Distributed in the United States
by Ashgate Pub. Co., $c 1991.
10   300         2 v. ; $c 22 cm.
11   440  0      Modern revivals in military history
12   500         Reprint. Originally published: The first
world war, 1914-1918. London : Constable, 1920. With a
new preface by Brian Bond.
13   600 10      Repington, Charles à Court, $d 1858-1925.
14   650  0      World War, 1914-1918 $x Personal
narratives, British.
15   700 1       Repington, Charles à Court, $d 1858-1925.
$t First world war, 1914-1918.
```

Discussion: For a volume set, Rule 2.8D1 instructs one to follow each ISBN with the designation of the volume to which it applies.

The Books Format instructs one to list the ISBN for the set first if the record is for a multivolume set. The opposite is true if the bibliographic record is only for one volume of the set. Because this record is for the set, the set ISBN needs to be listed first.

Fig. 7.23f. Edited OCLC bibliographic record.

```
OCLC: 25536707        Rec stat:   c
Entered: 19920326     Replaced: 19920326     Used: 19930131
Type: a  Bib lvl:  m  Source:    d     Lang:     eng
Repr:    Enc lvl:  I  Conf pub:  0     Ctry:     enk
Indx: 1  Mod rec:     Govt pub:        Cont:
Desc: a  Int lvl:     Festschr:  0     Illus:
         F/B:        0a Dat tp:   r     Dates:    1991,1920
1    040        TXA $c TXA [Modified by author]
2    020        0751200387 (set)
3    020        0751200360 (v. 1)
4    020        0751200379 (v. 2)
5    090        D544 $b .R43 1991
6    049        KHNN
7    100 1      Repington, Charles à Court, $d 1858-1925.
8    245 14     The first world war / $c Charles à Court
Repington.
9    260        Hampshire, England : $b Gregg Revivals ;
$a Brookfield, Vt. : $b Distributed in the United States
by Ashgate Pub. Co., $c 1991.
10   300        2 v. ; $c 22 cm.
11   440  0     Modern revivals in military history
12   500        Reprint.  Originally published: The first
world war, 1914-1918.  London : Constable, 1920.  With a
new preface by Brian Bond.
13   600 10     Repington, Charles à Court, $d 1858-1925.
14   650  0     World War, 1914-1918 $x Personal
narratives, British.
15   700 1      Repington, Charles à Court, $d  1858-1925.
$t First world war, 1914-1918.
```

Fig. 7.24a. Title page.

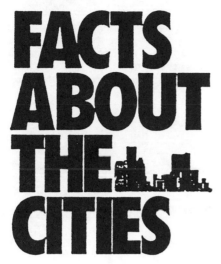

FACTS ABOUT THE CITIES

Compiled by ALLAN CARPENTER

With CARL PROVORSE

The H.W. Wilson Company
New York
1992

Fig. 7.24b. Verso of title page.

Printed in the United States of America

Library of Congress Cataloging-in-Publication Data

Carpenter, Allan, 1917–
    Facts about the cities/by Allan Carpenter.
        p. cm.
    ISBN 0-9242-0800-5
    1. Cities and towns—United States—Handbooks, manuals, etc.
    I. Title.
    HT123.C385 1991
    307.76′0973—dc20

                                                              91-19057
                                                                   CIP

Fig. 7.24c. Unedited OCLC bibliographic record.

```
OCLC:   23900621      Rec stat:  p
Entered: 19910510    Replaced: 19920509    Used: 19930105
Type: a  Bib lvl:  m  Source:        Lang:    eng
Repr:      Enc lvl:     Conf pub:  0    Ctry:    nyu
Indx: 0  Mod rec:     Govt pub:       Cont:    f
Desc: a  Int lvl:     Festschr:  0    Illus:
         F/B        0  Dat tp:    s    Dates:  1992,
1    010         91-19057
2    040         DLC $c DLC [Modified by author]
3    019         25493842
4    020         0824208005
5    043         n-us---
6    050 00      HT123 $b .C385 1991
7    082 00      307.76/0973 $2 20
8    049         KHNR
9    100 1       Carpenter, Allan, $d 1917-
10   245 10      Facts about the cities / $c compiled by
Allan Carpenter ; with Carl Provorse.
11   260         New York : $b H.W. Wilson, $c 1992.
12   300         xx, 473 p. ; $c 26 cm.
13   650  0      Cities and towns $z United States $x
Handbooks, manuals, etc.
14   700 1       Provorse, Carl.
```

Discussion: If one tries to search by ISBN on the verso of the title page to find this OCLC record, no record will be retrieved. After locating the record through another search, one quickly notices that the ISBN in the OCLC record does not match the one on the verso of the title page. It is not easy to determine which ISBN is right. If one tries to correct the ISBN in OCLC to match the one in the book, OCLC automatically places it in z subfield, which signifies that it is invalid. The computer is able to determine the ISBN's invalidity based on an algorithm. Because the ISBN on the item will be the number used if one is searching with the book in hand, one may want to include it in the OCLC record. The copy cataloger may want to include both the correct and incorrect ISBNs by using a separate field or a z subfield.

Because OCLC relegated the ISBN in the book to a z subfield, the OCLC record will be edited to include both ISBN numbers.

Fig. 7.24d. Edited OCLC bibliographic record.

```
OCLC:   23900621      Rec stat:  p
Entered: 19910510     Replaced: 19920509    Used: 19930105
Type: a  Bib lvl:  m  Source:         Lang:    eng
Repr:    Enc lvl:     Conf pub:  0    Ctry:    nyu
Indx: 0  Mod rec:     Govt pub:       Cont:    f
Desc: a  Int lvl:     Festschr:  0    Illus:
         F/B        0  Dat tp:    s    Dates:   1992,
1    010         91-19057
2    040         DLC $c DLC [Modified by author]
3    019         25493842
4    020         0824208005 $z 0924208005
5    043         n-us---
6    050 00      HT123 $b .C385 1991
7    082 00      307.76/0973 $2 20
8    049         KHNR
9    100 1       Carpenter, Allan, $d 1917-
10   245 10      Facts about the cities / $c compiled by
Allan Carpenter ; with Carl Provorse.
11   260         New York : $b H.W. Wilson, $c 1992.
12   300         xx, 473 p. ; $c 26 cm.
13   650  0      Cities and towns $z United States $x
Handbooks, manuals, etc.
14   700 1       Provorse, Carl.
```

If desired, the reader may now practice the exercise in chapter 10 for the 020 field for monographs. Figure 10.5 needs editing in the 020 field. Consult chapter 11 for the answer.

The previous examples illustrated copy cataloging with exact copy for the seven major areas of a bibliographic record for a book. (The material [or type of publication] specific details area does not apply to books). The OCLC-MARC record contains other fields. With the exception of key access points, examples of editing those fields are not shown. Some of those fields occur infrequently, some cannot be changed except by OCLC or LC, and some are hard to verify; also, the policy on editing varies widely among libraries. The copy cataloger should use *Bibliographic Formats* in conjunction with local policies for editing those fields.

8

Access for Monographs

Access to information is what the library is all about. The key to access is for the library to help the user find information from the user's point of reference (e.g., author, title, series, subject). Often the user's name or term may not be what the library uses. Authority work should provide a bridge between the user's name or term and the name or term used by the library. There are various online and manual authority lists for names, titles, and subjects that a library may use.

The OCLC authority file will be briefly discussed. The key fields are listed below.

> 1xx Correct form of name, uniform title, or subject. This form could be in a 1xx, 4xx, 6xx, 7xx, or 8xx field on the bibliographic record.

> 4xx Variant form of the name, uniform title, or subject. This form should not be on the bibliographic record. If it is on the bibliographic record, there is a conflict.

> 5xx Related form of name, title, or subject. This form is correct in some usage. It may be an earlier or later form of a name, or it may be a broader subject.

> 642 Series numbering example. Contains an example of the form of series numbering that should be used in subfield v.

645 Series tracing practice.

646 Series classification practice.

670 Source data found.

The last two digits of a tag in an authority record have similarities, just as those in a bibliographic record do. One observes the following:

00 personal name

10 corporate name

11 conference name

30 uniform title

50 topical subject heading

51 geographical name

Name, uniform title, series title, and subject access points in each bibliographic record should be verified in an authority file. Even if the form used in the bibliographic record is the incorrect form, the indexing structure will still allow the record to be retrieved as long as the variant form is listed in a 4xx field. In the bibliographic record, the form of the name, title, or subject in fields 1xx, 4xx, 6xx, 7xx, or 8xx should be the form in the 1xx of the authority record. If not, a conflict exists that must be resolved. If this is the case, the copy cataloger needs to follow library policy on resolving the conflict. In some libraries, it will mean passing the conflict to a higher-level supervisor. Elsewhere, the copy cataloger may be allowed to resolve it. Whatever the policy, care needs to be taken, as authority work is complex and detailed.

Users have for a long time requested fiction on a certain subject or a specific genre or form of literature. The catalog was of no use in this search, because fiction works received no subjects, nor were genre or form specified to any great extent. However, in the last decade there have been some projects to index fiction. The 655 field, which lists genre/form, has seen increased use in the last few years.

This chapter will discuss names, titles, subjects, and call numbers. For names, this manual will mainly concentrate on chapter 21 of *AACR2R* and *Bibliographic Formats*. The titles are covered in chapters 21 and 25 of *AACR2R* and *Bibliographic Formats*. Because *AACR2R* covers only descriptive cataloging, subject headings and call numbers are discussed only from the MARC format as found in *Bibliographic Formats*. Examples will follow the same format as used in the previous chapter.

Name and Title Entries (Chapters 21, 22, 24, and 25; Tags 100, 110, 111, 240, 700, 710, and 711)

Name and title entries provide many of the key access points that users search under when accessing a collection. Chapter 21 of *AACR2R* instructs one on what entries should be made for various situations. Chapters 22 through 25 describe the forms of these entries. Because the copy cataloger will often be able to find the correct form in an authority file, chapters 22 through 25 will not be discussed.

For users to be able to retrieve all the relevant records for a search, authority control is a must. For example, if the library has one of Keithe Saunders's books entered under Saunders, Keithe J., and another of his books entered under Saunders, K. J., the user will not necessarily retrieve both books.

The copy cataloger may or may not be involved in authority work. But even if not involved with the creation of authority records, the copy cataloger needs to be aware of how it is done in the library. The library may check names in OCLC's authority file or in a local file. If the library has an online catalog, authority work may be at the point of cataloging, or it may be delayed until the record is downloaded into the local system.

Fig. 8.1a. Title page.

ORGANIC
POLYMER CHEMISTRY

AN INTRODUCTION TO THE ORGANIC CHEMISTRY
OF ADHESIVES, FIBRES, PAINTS, PLASTICS AND
RUBBERS

Second edition

K. J. SAUNDERS

Department of Applied Chemical and Biological Sciences
Ryerson Polytechnical Institute, Toronto

LONDON   NEW YORK

CHAPMAN AND HALL

Fig. 8.1b. Verso of title page.

First published in 1973 by
Chapman and Hall Ltd.
11 New Fetter Lane, London EC4P 4EE
Second edition 1988
Published in the USA by
Chapman and Hall
29 West 35th Street, New York, NY 10001
© 1973, 1988 K. J. Saunders
Printed in Great Britain by
J. W. Arrowsmith Ltd, Bristol
ISBN 0 412 27570 8

British Library Cataloguing in Publication Data

Saunders, K. J. (Keith John)
    Organic polymer chemistry: an introduction
    to the organic chemistry of adhesives, fibres,
    paints, plastics and rubbers.—2nd ed.
    1. Polymers and polymerization.
    I. Title.
    547.7   QD381

    ISBN 0-412-27570-8

Library of Congress Cataloging in Publication Data

Saunders, K. J. (Keith J.), 1931-
    Organic polymer chemistry.

    Includes index.
    1. Polymers and polymerization. 2. Plastics.
    I. Title.
    TP1140.S32   1988   668.9   87-31974
    ISBN 0-412-27570-8

Fig. 8.1c. Unedited OCLC bibliographic record.

```
OCLC: 16985674      Rec stat:  c
Entered: 19871029    Replaced: 19891017      Used: 19910507
Type: a  Bib lvl:  m  Source:          Lang:    eng
Repr:       Enc lvl:     Conf pub:  0    Ctry:    enk
Indx: 1   Mod rec:     Govt pub:       Cont:    b
Desc: a   Int lvl:     Festschr:  0    Illus:   a
          F/B:     0  Dat tp:    s   Dates:   1988,
1    010          87-31974
2    040          DLC $c DLC $d FCU [Modified by author]
3    020          0412275708
4    050   0      TP1140 $b .S32 1988
5    082 00       668.9 $2 19
6    049          KHNN
7    100 1        Saunders, Keithe J. 1931-
8    245 10       Organic polymer chemistry : $b an
introduction  to the organic chemistry of adhesives,
fibres, paints, plastics, and rubbers / $c K.J.
Saunders.
9    250          2nd ed.
10   260          London ; $a New York : $b Chapman and
Hall, $c  1988.
11   300          502 p. : $b ill. ; $c 24 cm.
12   504          Includes bibliographical references.
13   650   7      Polym'eres. $2 ram
14   650   7      Mati'eres plastiques. $2 ram
15   650   7      Chimie organique $x Synth'ese. $2 ram
16   650   0      Polymerization.
17   650   0      Plastics.
```

Discussion: A work by one personal author is to be entered under the author (Rule 21.4A1). This means that the author will be the main entry, and the author's name will be listed in field 100. In chapter 22 of *AACR2R* one finds that the form should be the name by which the author is commonly known (Rule 22.1A). Is it Keithe J. or K. J.? Through the use of the OCLC authority file it can be determined that he uses K. J. If a fuller form of the name is known, it may be added in parentheses (Rule 22.18). Also, the author's birth and death dates may be added (Rule 22.17). A title entry should be made for the record (Rule 21.30J1).

The tag 100 is for a personal name main entry. The first indicator of "1" means the name is a single surname. The second indicator is always blank. The qualifier and dates should not be in subfield a, the qualification of the name should be in subfield q, and the dates should be in subfield d. The first indicator of "1" in the 245 will generate a title card if the library receives catalog cards.

Fig. 8.1d. Edited OCLC bibliographic record.

```
OCLC: 16985674        Rec stat:   c
Entered: 19871029     Replaced: 19891017    Used: 19910507
Type: a  Bib lvl:  m  Source:         Lang:    eng
Repr:       Enc lvl:     Conf pub:  0  Ctry:    enk
Indx: 1  Mod rec:     Govt pub:      Cont:    b
Desc: a  Int lvl:     Festschr:  0   Illus:   a
         F/B:       0  Dat tp:    s  Dates:   1988,
1    010          87-31974
2    040          DLC $c DLC $d FCU [Modified by author]
3    020          0412275708
4    050  0       TP1140 $b .S32 1988
5    082 00       668.9 $2 19
6    049          KHNN
7    100 1        Saunders, K. J. $q (Keithe J.), $d 1931-
8    245 10       Organic polymer chemistry : $b an
introduction to the organic chemistry of adhesives,
fibres, paints, plastics, and rubbers / $c K.J.
Saunders.
9    250          2nd ed.
10   260          London ; $a New York : $b Chapman and
Hall, $c 1988.
11   300          502 p. : $b ill. ; $c 24 cm.
12   504          Includes bibliographical references.
13   650  7       Polym'eres. $2 ram
14   650  7       Mati'eres plastiques. $2 ram
15   650  7       Chimie organique $x Synth'ese. $2 ram
16   650  0       Polymerization.
17   650  0       Plastics.
```

Fig. 8.2a. Title page.

HUMAN BIOLOGY

AN INTRODUCTION TO HUMAN EVOLUTION, VARIATION AND GROWTH

BY

G. A. HARRISON

Anthropology Laboratory
Department of Human Anatomy
University of Oxford

J. S. WEINER

M.R.C. Environmental Physiology Research Unit
London School of Hygiene and Tropical Medicine
University of London

J. M. TANNER

Department of Growth and Development
Institute of Child Health
University of London

N. A. BARNICOT

Department of Anthropology
University College, University of London

1964

OXFORD UNIVERSITY PRESS

NEW YORK AND OXFORD

Fig. 8.2b. Verso of title page.

© *Oxford University Press 1964*
Third printing, 1970
Printed in the United States of America

Fig. 8.2c. Unedited OCLC bibliographic record.

```
OCLC: 551254          Rec stat:   c
Entered: 19711207     Replaced: 19840909    Used: 19930316
Type: a   Bib lvl:  m  Source:        Lang:    eng
Repr:     Enc lvl:  1  Conf pub:  0   Ctry:    nyu
Indx: 0   Mod rec:     Govt pub:      Cont:    b
Desc:     Int lvl:     Festschr:  0   Illus:   a
          F/B:      0  Dat tp:    s   Dates:   1964,
1    010         64-7372//842
2    040         DLC $c DLC $d m.c. [Modified by author]
3    050  0      QH368 $b .H37
4    082 00      573
5    049         KHNN
6    100 1       Harrison, G. A. $q (Geoffrey Ainsworth),
$d 1927-
7    245 10      Human biology; $b an introduction to human
evolution, variation and growth, $c by G. A. Harrison
[and others]
8    260         New York, $b Oxford University Press, $c
1964.
9    300         xvi, 536 p. $b illus. $c 22 cm.
10   504         Includes bibliographical references.
11   650  0      Physical anthropology.
12   650  0      Human biology.
```

Discussion: From the title page, one can ascertain that four authors are responsible for the intellectual content of this book. This is a work of shared responsibility by more than three persons, with principal responsibility not attributed to any one, two, or three of them. Thus, the main entry is under title (Rule 21.6C2). The one named first will get an added entry. One readily ascertains that this record is not in accordance with *AACR2R*. Many libraries will not convert it to *AACR2R* because use is not affected. If one does convert, then one must decide if the Cutter number will be changed to correspond to the main entry. In this example, the Cutter number has been changed and the call number moved from an 050 field to an 090 field. (Because the Cutter number has changed, it is no longer an LC assigned number. Refer to the Call Numbers section later in this chapter for more information on Cutter numbers.)

For purposes of illustration, the record has been changed to *AACR2R*. Because the main entry is changing, there will be changes in the MARC 100 and 245 fields. The 100 field will become a 700 field. As the title is becoming the main entry, an added title entry will not be wanted. Therefore, the first indicator should be changed to "0."

Fig. 8.2d. Edited OCLC bibliographic record.

```
OCLC: 551254          Rec stat:   c
Entered: 19711207     Replaced: 19840909     Used: 19930316
Type: a   Bib lvl:   m   Source:          Lang:     eng
Repr:     Enc lvl:   1   Conf pub:  0     Ctry:     nyu
Indx: 0   Mod rec:       Govt pub:        Cont:     b
Desc: a   Int lvl:       Festschr:  0     Illus:    a
          F/B:       0   Dat tp:    s     Dates:    1964,
1    010          64-7372//842
2    040          DLC $c DLC $d m.c. [Modified by author]
3    090          QH368 $b .H93
4    082 00       573
5    049          KHNN
6    245 00       Human biology : $b an introduction to
human evolution, variation and growth / $c by G. A.
Harrison ... [et al.].
7    260          New York : $b Oxford University Press, $c
1964.
8    300          xvi, 536 p. : $b ill. ; $c 22 cm.
9    504          Includes bibliographical references.
10   650  0       Physical anthropology.
11   650  0       Human biology.
12   700  1       Harrison, G. A. $q (Geoffrey Ainsworth),
$d 1927-
```

Fig. 8.3a. Title page.

SLEEP AND COGNITION

**EDITED
BY
RICHARD R.
BOOTZIN,
JOHN F.
KIHLSTROM
AND
DANIEL L.
SCHACTER**

**UNIVERSITY
OF
ARIZONA**

**American Psychological Association
Washington, DC**

Fig. 8.3b. Verso of title page.

Published by
American Psychological Association
1200 Seventeenth Street, NW
Washington, DC 20036

Copies may be ordered from
APA Order Department
P.O. Box 2710
Hyattsville, MD 20784

Designed by Paul M. Levy (Cover design adapted from conference poster designed by
    Elizabeth C. Tang)
Typeset by TAPSCO, Inc., Akron, PA
Printed by Bookcrafters, Chelsea, MI
Technical editing and production coordinated by
    Susan Bedford and Mary Lynn Skutley

Library of Congress Cataloging-in-Publication Data

Sleep and cognition / edited by Richard R. Bootzin, John F. Kihlstrom, and
    Daniel L. Schacter.
        p. cm.
    Based on the Arizona Conference on Sleep and Cognition, held in Tucson,
Jan. 19–22, 1989.
    Includes index.
    ISBN 1-55798-083-7
    1. Sleep—Congresses. 2. Cognition—Congresses. I. Bootzin, Richard R.,
1940- . II. Kihlstrom, John F. III. Schacter, Daniel L. IV. Arizona
Conference on Sleep and Cognition (1989: Tucson, Ariz.)
    [DNLM: 1. Cognition—physiology—congresses. 2. Sleep—physiology—
congresses. WL 108 S612 1989]
QP425.S664   1990
154.6—dc20
DNLM/DLC   90-672

Printed in the United States of America
First edition

Fig. 8.3c. Unedited OCLC bibliographic record.

```
OCLC: 21521929      Rec stat:  p
Entered: 19900420   Replaced: 19901222    Used: 19910425
Type: a  Bib lvl:  m  Source:     c   Lang:    eng
Repr:    Enc lvl:     Conf pub:  1   Ctry:    dcu
Indx: 1  Mod rec:     Govt pub:      Cont:    b
Desc: a  Int lvl:     Festschr:  0   Illus:   a
         F/B:      0  Dat tp:    s   Dates:   1990,
1    010       90-672
2    040       DNLM/DLC $c DLC  [Modified by author]
3    020       1557980837
4    050 00    QP425 $b .B667 1990
5    060       WL 108 S612 1989
6    082 00    154.6 $2 20
7    049       KHNN
8    100 1     Bootzin, Richard R., $d 1940-
9    245 10    Sleep and cognition / $c edited by Richard
R. Bootzin, John F. Kihlstrom and Daniel L. Schacter.
10   250       1st ed.
11   260       Washington, DC : $b American Psychological
Association, $c c1990.
12   300       xvii, 205 p. : $b ill. ; $c 24 cm.
13   500       The Proceedings of the Arizona Conference
on Sleep and Cognition, held in Tucson, Jan. 19-22,
1989.
14   504       Includes bibliographical references and
index.
15   650  0    Sleep $x Congresses.
16   650  0    Cognition $x Congresses.
17   650  2    Cognition $x physiology $x congresses.
18   650  2    Sleep $x physiology $x congresses.
19   700 1     Kihlstrom, John F.
20   700 1     Schacter, Daniel L.
21   711 2     Arizona Conference on Sleep and Cognition
(1989 : Tucson, Ariz.)
```

Discussion: This book is edited by three individuals. Based on Rules 21.7A1 and 21.7B1, the main entry should be under title. Bootzin, Kihlstrom, and Schacter should have added entries. Because the conference was not prominently named, it did not qualify as the main entry. It is, however, an entry that some users might use to retrieve the item; therefore, an added entry is needed (Rule 21.29C).

As the main entry is changing, some MARC tags and indicators will need to be changed. The tag for Bootzin will become 700. The indicators for the 245 will become 00. Even though *AACR2R* lists *conference* as an example of a corporate name, conferences have their own tag of 711 in the MARC format. Two subfield codes are missing from the 711 field. The date of the conference should be in subfield d, and the place should be in subfield c.

As in the previous example, the main entry is changing; thus, one must decide whether to change the Cutter number and move the call number to an 090 field. In this example, the Cutter number was changed and the call number moved.

Fig. 8.3d. Edited OCLC bibliographic record.

```
OCLC: 21521929       Rec stat:  p
Entered: 19900420    Replaced: 19901222    Used: 19910425
Type: a  Bib lvl:  m  Source:     c    Lang:    eng
Repr:        Enc lvl:    Conf pub: 1    Ctry:    dcu
Indx: 1  Mod rec:      Govt pub:      Cont:    b
Desc: a  Int lvl:      Festschr:  0    Illus:   a
         F/B:      0  Dat tp:    s    Dates:   1990,
1    010          90-672
2    040          DNLM/DLC $c DLC [Modified by author]
3    020          1557980837
4    090          QP425 $b .S664 1990
5    060          WL 108 S612 1989
6    082 00       154.6 $2 20
7    049          KHNN
8    245 00       Sleep and cognition / $c edited by Richard
R. Bootzin, John F. Kihlstrom and Daniel L. Schacter.
9    250          1st ed.
10   260          Washington, DC : $b American Psychological
Association, $c c1990.
11   300          xvii, 205 p. : $b ill. ; $c 24 cm.
12   500          The Proceedings of the Arizona Conference
on Sleep and Cognition, held in Tucson, Jan. 19-22,
1989.
13   504          Includes bibliographical references and
index.
14   650   0      Sleep $x Congresses.
15   650   0      Cognition $x Congresses.
16   650   2      Cognition $x physiology $x congresses.
17   650   2      Sleep $x physiology $x congresses.
18   700 1        Bootzin, Richard R., $d 1940-
19   700 1        Kihlstrom, John F.
20   700 1        Schacter, Daniel L.
21   711 2        Arizona Conference on Sleep and Cognition
$d (1989 : $c Tucson, Ariz.)
```

Fig. 8.4a. Title page.

THE CORPORATION, ETHICS, AND THE ENVIRONMENT

EDITED BY

W. Michael Hoffman,
Robert Frederick, and
Edward S. Petry, Jr.

Foreword by Gregory H. Adamian

From the Eighth National Conference on Business Ethics
Sponsored by the Center for Business Ethics at Bentley College

QUORUM BOOKS
NEW YORK • WESTPORT, CONNECTICUT • LONDON

Fig. 8.4b. Verso of title page.

Library of Congress Cataloging-in-Publication Data

National Conference on Business Ethics (8th : 1990 : Bentley College)
   The corporation, ethics, and the environment / edited by W.
 Michael Hoffman, Robert Frederick, and Edward S. Petry, Jr.
     p.   cm.
     "From the Eighth National Conference on Business Ethics sponsored
 by the Center for Business Ethics at Bentley College."
   Includes bibliographical references.
   ISBN 0-89930-603-9 (lib. bdg. : alk. paper)
   1. United States—Industries—Environmental aspects—Congresses.
 2. Business ethics—United States—Congresses.   3. Industry—Social
 aspects—United States—Congresses.   I. Hoffman, W. Michael.
 II. Frederick, Robert.   III. Petry, Edward S.   IV. Bentley College.
 Center for Business Ethics.   V. Title.
 HC110.E5N32   1990a
 363.7'08'0973—dc20   90-8402

British Library Cataloguing in Publication Data is available.

Library of Congress Catalog Card Number: 90-8402
ISBN: 0-89930-603-9

First published in 1990

Quorum Books, 88 Post Road West, Westport, CT 06881
An imprint of Greenwood Publishing Group, Inc.

Printed in the United States of America

The paper used in this book complies with the
Permanent Paper Standard issued by the National
Information Standards Organization (Z39.48-1984).

10 9 8 7 6 5 4 3 2 1

Fig. 8.4c. Unedited OCLC bibliographic record.

```
OCLC: 21337866       Rec stat:  c
Entered: 19900322    Replaced: 19910316    Used: 19910607
Type: a  Bib lvl:  m  Source:        Lang:    eng
Repr:    Enc lvl:     Conf pub:  1   Ctry:    nyu
Indx: 1  Mod rec:     Govt pub:      Cont:    b
Desc: a  Int lvl:     Festschr:  0   Illus:   a
         F/B:      0  Dat tp:    s   Dates:   1990,
1    010       90-8402
2    040       DLC $c DLC [Modified by auhtor]
3    020       0899306039 (lib bdg. : alk. paper)
4    043       n-us---
5    050 00    HC110.E5 $b N32 1990a
6    082 00    363.7/08/0973 $2 20
7    049       KHNN
8    111 2     National Conference on Business Ethics
(8th : $d 1990 : $c Bentley College)
9    245 14    The corporation, ethics, and the
environment / $c edited by W. Michael Hoffman, Robert
Frederick, and Edward S. Petry, Jr. ; foreword by
Gregory H. Adamian.
10   260       New York : $b Quorum Books, $c 1990.
11   300       xxiv, 323 p. : $b ill. ; $c 25 cm.
12   500       "From the Eighth National Conference on
Business Ethics sponsored by the Center for Business
Ethics at Bentley College."
13   504       Includes bibliographical references and
index.
14   650  0    United States $x Industries $x
Environmental aspects $x Congresses.
15   650  0    Business ethics $z United States $x
Congresses.
16   650  0    Industry $x Social aspects $z United
States $x Congresses.
17   700 1     Hoffman, W. Michael.
18   700 1     Petry, Edward S.
19   700 1     Bentley College. $b Center for Business
Ethics.
```

Discussion: This is a work from a conference. The main entry should be under the conference because it is prominently named (Rule 21.1B2d). The three editors should have access points (Rules 21.30A1 and 21.30D); Frederick has not been given an access point. An individual who writes a foreword is not responsible for the intellectual content of the work; therefore, no entry is made for Adamian. An added entry is made for the Center for Business Ethics at Bentley College (Rule 21.30E).

The subfield code for the conference number has been omitted. The tag and first indicator for the Center for Business Ethics at Bentley College are incorrect. The tag should be 710 and the first indicator 2.

Fig. 8.4d. Edited OCLC bibliographic record.

```
OCLC: 21337866       Rec stat:   c
Entered: 19900322    Replaced: 19910316     Used: 19910607
Type: a  Bib lvl:  m  Source:         Lang:    eng
Repr:     Enc lvl:     Conf pub:  1   Ctry:    nyu
Indx: 1  Mod rec:     Govt pub:      Cont:    b
Desc: a  Int lvl:     Festschr:  0   Illus:   a
         F/B:      0  Dat tp:    s   Dates:   1990,
1    010         90-8402
2    040         DLC $c DLC [Modified by author]
3    020         0899306039 (lib bdg. : alk. paper)
4    043         n-us---
5    050 00      HC110.E5 $b N32 1990a
6    082 00      363.7/08/0973 $2 20
7    049         KHNN
8    111 2       National Conference on Business Ethics $n
(8th :$d 1990 : $c Bentley College)
9    245 14      The corporation, ethics, and the
environment / $c edited by W. Michael Hoffman, Robert
Frederick, and Edward S. Petry, Jr. ; foreword by
Gregory H. Adamian.
10   260         New York : $b Quorum Books, $c 1990.
11   300         xxiv, 323 p. : $b ill. ; $c 25 cm.
12   500         "From the Eighth National Conference on
Business Ethics sponsored by the Center for Business
Ethics at Bentley College."
13   504         Includes bibliographical references and
index.
14   651  0      United States $x Industries $x
Environmental aspects $x Congresses.
15   650  0      Business ethics $z United States $x
Congresses.
16   650  0      Industry $x Social aspects $z United
States $x Congresses.
17   700 1       Hoffman, W. Michael.
18   700 1       Frederick, Robert.
19   700 1       Petry, Edward S.
20   710 2       Bentley College. $b Center for Business
Ethics.
```

Fig. 8.5a. Title page.

Toward a Superconsciousness:

Meditational Theory & Practice

By Hiroshi Motoyama

Translation by:
Shigenori Nagatomo
& Clifford R. Ames

ASIAN HUMANITIES PRESS
Berkeley, California

Fig. 8.5b. Verso of title page.

ASIAN HUMANITIES PRESS

Asian Humanities Press offers to the specialist and the general reader alike, the best in new translations of major works as well as significant original contributions, to enhance our understanding of Asian literature, religions, cultures and philosophies.

"Asian Humanities Press" is a trademark of Jain Publishing Company.

Copyright © 1990 by Hiroshi Motoyama. All rights reserved. No part of this book may be reproduced, stored in a retrieval system, or transmitted, in any form or by any means, electronic, mechanical, photocopying, recording or otherwise, without the written permission of the publisher except for brief passages quoted in a review.

ISBN 0-89581-914-7

Printed in the United States of America

Fig. 8.5c. Unedited OCLC bibliographic record.

```
OCLC: 22957110        Rec stat:   c
Entered: 19891004     Replaced:   19910318   Used: 19910521
Type: a  Bib lvl:  m  Source:          Lang:    eng
Repr:    Enc lvl:  I  Conf pub:  0     Ctry:    cau
Indx: 1  Mod rec:     Govt pub:        Cont:    b
Desc: a  Int lvl:     Festschr:  0     Illus:
         F/B:      0  Dat tp:    s     Dates:   1990,
1    010         89-81298
2    040         DLC $c DLC $d DGW [Modified by author]
2    020         0895819147
3    041 1       eng $h jpn
4    090         B132.Y6 $b M6713 1990
6    049         KHNN
7    100 1       Motoyama, Hiroshi.
8    240 00      Choishiki e no Hiyaku.  English.
9    245 10      Toward a superconsciousness : $b
meditational theory & practice / $c by Hiroshi Motoyama
; translation by Shigenori Nagatomo & Clifford R. Ames.
11   260         Berkeley, Calif. ; $b Asian Humanities
Press, $c c1990.
12   300         xiii, 150 p. : $b ill. ; $c 22 cm.
13   500         Translation of: Choishiki e no Hiyaku.
14   504         Includes bibliographical references.
15   650  0      Yoga.
16   650  0      Meditation.
```

Discussion: According to Rule 25.1, a uniform title, field 240, is needed when various manifestations of a book have appeared under different titles. The uniform title should be the title in the original language (Rule 25.3). The language should be added as instructed in Rule 25.5C1. A translation note is also given based on Rule 2.7B2.

The first indicator and the library's OCLC profile determine whether the uniform title prints on cards. The only valid first indicator today in the United States is one; however, until recently zero was valid. The OCLC database contains several bibliographic records with a first indicator of zero. The copy cataloger will want to follow the library's policy on entering the uniform title. The second indicator shows the number of positions to be ignored in sorting and filing processes. A subfield code of "1" should precede the language.

Fig. 8.5d. Edited OCLC bibliographic record.

```
OCLC: 22957110        Rec stat:   c
Entered: 19891004     Replaced:   19910318    Used: 19910521
Type: a   Bib lvl:  m  Source:          Lang:    eng
Repr:     Enc lvl:  I  Conf pub:  0     Ctry:    cau
Indx: 1   Mod rec:     Govt pub:        Cont:    b
Desc: a   Int lvl:     Festschr:  0     Illus:
          F/B:      0  Dat tp:    s     Dates:   1990,
1    10              89-81298
2    040             DLC $c DLC $d DGW [Modified by author]
3    020             0895819147
4    041 1           eng $h jpn
5    090             B132.Y6 $b M6713 1990
6    049             KHNN
7    100 1           Motoyama, Hiroshi.
8    240 10          Choishiki e no Hiyaku. $1 English.
9    245 10          Toward a superconsciousness : $b
meditational theory & practice / $c by Hiroshi Motoyama
; translation by Shigenori Nagatomo & Clifford R. Ames.
11   260             Berkeley, Calif. ; $b Asian Humanities
Press, $c c1990.
12   300             xiii, 150 p. : $b ill. ; $c 22 cm.
13   500             Translation of: Choishiki e no Hiyaku.
14   504             Includes bibliographical references.
15   650  0          Yoga.
16   650  0          Meditation.
```

If desired, the reader may now practice the exercises in chapter 10 for the name and title access points (fields 100, 110, 111, 240, 700, 710, and 711) for monographs. Figures 10.1–10.2, 10.4, and 10.6–10.7 need editing in those fields. Consult chapter 11 for the answers.

Subject Entries (Fields 600, 610, 650, and 651)

Subject headings are extremely important to users. Automation has made it easier for an item to have many subject headings. The policies on subject headings for copy cataloging vary greatly among libraries. In some, new subject headings are only added if the OCLC record has no subject headings. In others, subject headings are checked to see if the heading is still valid and in the correct OCLC-MARC format. Elsewhere, the degree of checking depends on the source of cataloging. For instance, Library of Congress records may not be verified, while member records are. Very few libraries check the subjects to see if they are the best for the book. (The assumption is that the individual who originally cataloged it assigned the correct headings.)

This manual will only illustrate the MARC format for Library of Congress subject headings. Of course, *AACR2R* will not be cited, as it does not cover subject headings.

Fig. 8.6a. Title page.

The Journals of William A. Lindsay

An Ordinary Nineteenth-Century Physician's Surgical Cases

Edited by
Katherine Mandusic McDonell

Indianapolis
Indiana Historical Society
1989

Fig. 8.6b. Verso of title page.

Publications in Indiana Medical History   Number 2

© 1989 Indiana Historical Society

Library of Congress Cataloging-in-Publication Data

Lindsay, William A., 1795-1876.
  The journals of William A. Lindsay.

  (Publications in Indiana medical history; no. 2)
  Bibliography: p.
  Includes index.
1. Surgery, Operative--Case studies. 2. Surgery--Middle West--History--19th
century--Sources. 3. Lindsay, William A., 1795-1876--Diaries. 4. Surgeons--
United States--Diaries. I. McDonell, Katherine Mandusic.
II. Title. III. Series.
RD34.L49 1989   617'092'4   88-32003
ISBN 0-87195-029-4

The paper in this book meets the guidelines for permanence and durability of the Committee on
Production Guidelines for Book Longevity of the Council on Library Resources.

Fig. 8.6c. Unedited OCLC bibliographic record.

```
OCLC: 18716076        Rec stat:  p
Entered: 19881017     Replaced: 19890826     Used: 19910621
Type: a  Bib lvl:  m  Source:           Lang:    eng
Repr:    Enc lvl:     Conf pub:  0       Ctry:    inu
Indx: 1  Mod rec:     Govt pub:          Cont:    b
Desc: a  Int lvl:     Festschr:  0       Illus:   a
         F/B:        0d Dat tp:    s     Dates:   1989,
1    010        88-32003
2    040        DLC $c DLC [Modified by author]
3    020        0871950294 (alk. paper)
4    043        n-us--- $a n-usc--
5    050 0      RD34 $b .L49 1989
6    082 00     617/.092/4 $2 19
7    049        KHNN
8    100 1      Lindsay, William A., $d 1795-1876.
9    245 14     The journals of William A. Lindsay : $b an
ordinary nineteenth-century physician's surgical cases /
$c edited by Katherine Mandusic McDonell.
10   260        Indianapolis : $b Indiana Historical
Society, $c1989.
11   300        xlix, 216 p. : $b ill. (some col.) : $c 24
cm.
12   440 0      Publications in Indiana medical history ;
$v no. 2
13   504        Includes bibliographical references (p.
201-204) and index.
14   650 0      Surgery, Operative $x Case studies.
15   650 0      Surgery $z Middle West $x History $y 19th
century $x Sources.
16   600 10     Lindsay, William A., $b 1795-1876 $x
Diaries.
17   650 0      Surgeons $z United States $x Diaries.
18   700 1      McDonell, Katherine Mandusic.
```

Discussion: Subject headings are the 6xx fields. The topical subject headings 650s will be discussed in later examples. This example will discuss a single surname as a subject. The first indicator of "1" in the 600 field indicates that the name is a single surname. The second indicator of "0" indicates that it is a Library of Congress subject heading. The subfield code for the author's dates is incorrect; it should be "d." Subfield code "x" is the correct subfield code for a general subdivision.

Fig. 8.6d. Edited OCLC bibliographic record.

```
OCLC: 18716076        Rec stat:  p
Entered: 19881017   Replaced: 19890826    Used: 19910621
Type: a  Bib lvl:  m  Source:        Lang:    eng
Repr:    Enc lvl:     Conf pub:  0  Ctry:    inu
Indx: 1  Mod rec:     Govt pub:      Cont:    b
Desc: a  Int lvl:     Festschr:  0  Illus:   a
         F/B:       0d Dat tp:    s  Dates:   1989,
1    010        88-32003
2    040        DLC $c DLC [Modified by author]
3    020        0871950294 (alk. paper)
4    043        n-us--- $a n-usc--
5    050 0      RD34 $b .L49 1989
6    082 00     617/.092/4 $2 19
7    049        KHNN
8    100 1      Lindsay, William A., $d 1795-1876.
9    245 14     The journals of William A. Lindsay : $b an
ordinary nineteenth-century physician's surgical cases /
$c edited by Katherine Mandusic McDonell.
10   260        Indianapolis : $b Indiana Historical
Society, $c1989.
11   300        xlix, 216 p. : $b ill. (some col.) : $c 24
cm.
12   440 0      Publications in Indiana medical history ;
$v no. 2
13   504        Includes bibliographical references ( p.
201-204) and index.
14   650 0      Surgery, Operative $x Case studies.
15   650 0      Surgery $z Middle West $x History $y 19th
century $x Sources.
16   600 10     Lindsay, William A., $d 1795-1876 $x
Diaries.
17   650 0      Surgeons $z United States $x Diaries.
18   700 1      McDonell, Katherine Mandusic.
```

Fig. 8.7a. Title page.

Melanie A.May

BONDS OF UNITY
Women, Theology, and the
Worldwide Church

Scholars Press
Atlanta, Georgia

Fig. 8.7b. Verso of title page.

BONDS OF UNITY
Women, Theology, and the Worldwide Church

by
Melanie A. May

© 1989
The American Academy of Religion

Library of Congress Cataloging in Publication Data

May, Melanie A.
    Bonds of unity: women, theology, and the worldwide church/
Melanie A. May.
       p. cm--(American Academy of Religion academy series: no. 65)
       Bibliography: p.
       ISBN 1-55540-308-5 (alk. paper). -- ISBN 1-55540-309-3 (pbk.:
       alk. paper)
       1. Christian union--History--20th century. 2. World Council of
       Churches--History. 3. Women in Christianity--History--20th century.
       4. Church and minorities--History 20th century. 5. Theology,
       Doctrinal--History-20th century. L Title. II. Series.
       BX6.5.M39 1989   88-37682
       262'.0011--dc19   CIP

Printed in the United States of America
on acid-free paper

Fig. 8.7c. Unedited OCLC bibliographic record.

```
OCLC: 18835737        Rec stat:  p
Entered: 19881103    Replaced: 19900406      Used: 19910511
Type: a  Bib lvl:  m  Source:          Lang:    eng
Repr:       Enc lvl:     Conf pub:  0    Ctry:    gau
Indx: 0  Mod rec:      Govt pub:       Cont:    b
Desc: a  Int lvl:      Festschr:  0    Illus:
             F/B:      0  Dat tp:    s    Dates:   1989,
1    010        88-37682
2    040        DLC $c DLC [Modified by author]
3    020        1555403085 (alk. paper)
4    020        1555403093 (pbk. : alk. paper)
5    050 00     BX6.5 $b .M39 1989
6    082 00     262/.0011 $2 19
7    049        KHNN
8    100 1      May, Melanie A.
9    245 10     Bonds of unity : $b women, theology, and
the worldwide church / $c Melanie A. May.
10   260        Atlanta, Ga. : $b Scholars Press, $c 1989.
11   300        x, 196 p. ; $c 23 cm.
12   440  0     American Academy of Religion academy
series ; $v no. 65
13   504        Includes bibliographical references (p.
[177]-196).
14   650  0     Christian union $x History $y 20th
century.
15   610 10     World Council of Churches $x History.
16   650  0     Women in Christianity $x History $y 20th
century.
17   650  0     Church and minorities $x History $y 20th
century.
18   650  0     Theology, Doctrinal $x History $y 20th
century.
```

Discussion: This example will discuss corporate name subject headings. Corporate names as subjects go into a 610 field. The first indicator of "1" indicates that the name is a place or place plus name. World Council of Churches is not a geographic name; therefore, the first indicator needs to be changed to a "2" to indicate that it is a name in direct order. The second indicator of "0" denotes that it is a Library of Congress subject heading. Subfield code "x" is the correct subfield code for a general subdivision.

Fig. 8.7d. Edited OCLC bibliographic record.

```
OCLC: 18835737        Rec stat:  p
Entered: 19881103     Replaced: 19900406     Used: 19910511
Type: a   Bib lvl:  m  Source:          Lang:    eng
Repr:     Enc lvl:     Conf pub:  0    Ctry:    gau
Indx: 0   Mod rec:     Govt pub:       Cont:    b
Desc: a   Int lvl:     Festschr:  0    Illus:
          F/B:       0  Dat tp:    s    Dates:   1989,
1    010         88-37682
2    040         DLC $c DLC [Modified by author]
3    020         1555403085 (alk. paper)
4    020         1555403093 (pbk. : alk. paper)
5    050 00      BX6.5 $b .M39 1989
6    082 00      262/.0011 $2 19
7    049         KHNN
8    100 1       May, Melanie A.
9    245 10      Bonds of unity : $b women, theology, and
the worldwide church / $c Melanie A. May.
10   260         Atlanta, Ga. : $b Scholars Press, $c 1989.
11   300         x, 196 p. ; $c 23 cm.
12   440  0      American Academy of Religion academy
series ; $v no. 65
13   504         Includes bibliographical references (p.
[177]-196).
14   650  0      Christian union $x History $y 20th
century.
15   610 20      World Council of Churches $x History.
16   650  0      Women in Christianity $x History $y 20th
century.
17   650  0      Church and minorities $x History $y 20th
century.
18   650  0      Theology, Doctrinal $x History $y 20th
century.
```

Fig. 8.8a. Title page.

River towns in the

Great West

The structure of provincial urbanization in the American Midwest, 1820–1870

TIMOTHY R. MAHONEY
University of Nebraska, Lincoln

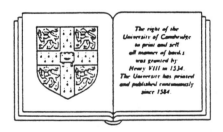

The right of the
University of Cambridge
to print and sell
all manner of books
was granted by
Henry VIII in 1534.
The University has printed
and published continuously
since 1584.

CAMBRIDGE UNIVERSITY PRESS
Cambridge
New York   Port Chester   Melbourne   Sydney

Fig. 8.8b. Verso of title page.

Published by the Press Syndicate of the University of Cambridge
The Pitt Building, Trumpington Street, Cambridge CB2 1RP
40 West 20th Street, New York, NY 10011, USA
10 Stamford Road, Oakleigh, Melbourne 3166, Australia

© Cambridge University Press 1990

First published 1990

Printed in the United States of America

Library of Congress Cataloging-in-Publication Data
Mahoney, Timothy R., 1953–
River towns in the Great West: the structure of provincial
urbanization in the American Midwest, 1820-1870 / Timothy R. Mahoney.
  p. cm.
ISBN 0–521–36130–3
1. Cities and towns – Middle West – History – 19th century.
2. Urbanization – Middle West – History – 19th century. 3. Land
settlement – Middle West – History – 19th century. I. Title.
HT123.5.M53M34 1990
307.76'0977–dc20 89–32208

British Library Cataloguing in Publication Data
Mahoney, Timothy R.
River towns in the Great West: the structure of
provincial urbanization in the American Midwest, 1820–1870.
1. United States. Midwestern states.
Urbanisation, history
I. Title
307.7'6'0977

ISBN 0–521–36130–3 hard covers

Fig. 8.8c. Unedited OCLC bibliographic record.

```
OCLC: 19554042        Rec stat:  p
Entered: 19890320    Replaced: 19910223    Used: 19910604
Type: a  Bib lvl:  m  Source:         Lang:    eng
Repr:    Enc lvl:     Conf pub:  0   Ctry:    enk
Indx: 1  Mod rec:     Govt pub:       Cont:    b
Desc: a  Int lvl:     Festschr:  0   Illus:   ab
         F/B:      0  Dat tp:    s   Dates:   1990,
1    010        89-32208
2    040        DLC $c DLC [Modified by author]
3    020        0521361303
4    043        b-usc--
5    050 00     HT123.5.M53 $b M34 1990
6    082 00     307.76/0977 $2 20
7    049        KHNN
8    100 1      Mahoney, Timothy R., $d 1953-
9    245 10     River towns in the Great West : $b the
structure of provincial urbanization in the American
Midwest, 1820-  1870 / $c Timothy R. Mahoney.
10   260        Cambridge [England] ; $a New York : $b
Cambridge University Press, $c 1990.
11   300        xi, 319 p. : $b ill., maps ; $c 24 cm.
12   500        Spine title: River towns in the Great
West.
13   504        Includes bibliographical references and
index.
14   650  0     Cities and towns $z Middle West $x History
$x 19th century.
15   650  0     Urbanization $z Middle West $x History $x
19th century.
16   650  0     Land settlement $x Middle West $z History
$x 19th century.
17   740 01     River towns of the Great West.
```

Discussion: These three topical subject headings, 650 fields, have the correct tags and indicators for Library of Congress subject headings. However, the subfield codes are incorrect. In the first three headings, the subfield code for a period subdivision should be "y." In the third subject heading, the subfield code for place should be "z," and the subfield code for the general subdivision should be "x."

Fig. 8.8d. Edited OCLC bibliographic record.

```
OCLC: 19554042        Rec stat:  p
Entered: 19890320     Replaced: 19910223     Used: 19910604
Type: a   Bib lvl:  m  Source:        Lang:    eng
Repr:     Enc lvl:     Conf pub:  0   Ctry:    enk
Indx: 1   Mod rec:     Govt pub:      Cont:    b
Desc: a   Int lvl:     Festschr:  0   Illus:   ab
          F/B:      0  Dat tp:    s   Dates:   1990,
1    010        89-32208
2    040        DLC $c DLC [Modified by author]
3    020        0521361303
4    043        b-usc--
5    050 00     HT123.5.M53 $b M34 1990
6    082 00     307.76/0977 $2 20
7    049        KHNN
8    100 1      Mahoney, Timothy R., $d 1953-
9    245 10     River towns in the Great West : $b the
structure of provincial urbanization in the American
Midwest, 1820-1870 / $c Timothy R. Mahoney.
10   246 18     River towns in the Great West.
11   260        Cambridge [England] ; $a New York : $b
Cambridge University Press, $c 1990.
12   300        xi, 319 p. : $b ill., maps ; $c 24 cm.
13   504        Includes bibliographical references and
index.
14   650  0     Cities and towns $z Middle West $x History
$y 19th century.
15   650  0     Urbanization $z Middle West $x History $y
19th century.
16   650  0     Land settlement $z Middle West $x History
$y 19th century.
```

Fig. 8.9a. Title page.

Women's Dionysian Initiation
The Villa of Mysteries in Pompeii

LINDA FIERZ-DAVID

Translated by Gladys Phelan
and with an Introduction by
M. Esther Harding

Spring Publications, Inc.
Dallas, Texas

Fig. 8.9b. Verso of title page.

Jungian Classics Series 11

Published 1988 by Spring Publications, Inc.;

P.O. Box 222069; Dallas, Texas 75222.

Printed in the United States of America

© 1988 by Spring Publications, Inc. All rights reserved

Gladys Phelan's translation is of the work *Psychologische Betrachtungen zu der Freskenfolge der Villa dei Misteri in Pompeii: Ein Versuch*, mimeographed in Zürich, Switzerland, 1957, © by the Psychological Club of Zürich.

Mimeographing of the German study was made possible in the memory of Linda Fierz-David by her sons: Markus, Heinrich, Felix and Niklaus Fierz.

International distributors:

Spring; Postfach; 8803 Ruschlikon; Switzerland.

Japan Spring Sha, Inc.; 12-10, 2-Chome, Nigawa Takamaru; Takarazuka 665, Japan.

Element Books Ltd; Longmead Shaftesbury; Dorset SP7 8PL; England.

Library of Congress Cataloging-in-Publication Data

Fierz-David, Linda.
  Women's Dionysian initiation.

  (Jungian classics series ; 11)
  Translation of: Psychologische Betrachtungen zu der Freskenfolge der Villa dei Misteri in Pompeii.
  Bibliography: p.
  1. Villa of the Mysteries frescoes (Mural painting)
  2. Mural painting and decoration – Italy – Pompeii
(Ancient city) 3. Dionysus (Greek deity) – Art. 4. Villa of the Mysteries (Pompeii) 5. Pompeii (Ancient city) – Buildings, structures, etc. 6. Dionysia in art.
7. Mysteries, Religious, in art. 8. Women – Psychology.
9. Jung, C. G. (Carl Gustav), 1875-1961 – Criticism and interpretation. 10. Italy – Antiquities. I. Title.
  II. Series.
ND2575.F513 1988   755'.9238'09377   88-4893
ISBN 0-88214-510-X (pbk.)

Fig. 8.9c. Unedited OCLC bibliographic record.

```
OCLC: 17774235       Rec stat:   c
Entered: 19880318    Replaced: 19900623    Used: 19910412
Type: a  Bib lvl:  m  Source:        Lang:    eng
Repr:      Enc lvl:     Conf pub:  0   Ctry:    txu
Indx: 0  Mod rec:     Govt pub:      Cont:    b
Desc: a  Int lvl:     Festschr:  0   Illus:   af
         F/B:       0  Dat tp:    s   Dates:   1988,
 1   010         88-4893//r902
 2   040         DLC $c DLC [Modified by author]
 3   020         088214510X
 4   041 1       eng $h ger
 5   043         e-it---
 6   050 00      ND2575 $b .F513 1988
 7   082 00      755/.9238/09377 $2 19
 8   049         KHNN
 9   100 1       Fierz-David, Linda.
10   240 10      Psychologische Betrachtungen zu der
Freskenfolge der Villa dei Misteri in Pompeii. $1
English
11   245 10      Women's Dionysian initiation : $b the
Villa of Mysteries in Pompeii / $c Linda Fierz-David ;
translated by Gladys Phelan and with an introduction by
M. Esther Harding.
12   260         Dallas, Tex. : $b Spring, $c 1988.
13   300         xvii, 149 p., [4] p. of plates : $b ill.
(some col.) ; $c 23 cm.
14   440  0      Jungian classics series ; $v 11
15   500         Translation of: Psychologische
Betrachtungen zu der Freskenfolge der Villa dei Misteri
in Pompeii.
16   504         Includes bibliographical references.
17   650  0      Villa of the Mysteries frescoes (Mural
painting)
18   650  0      Mural painting and decoration $x Italy $x
Pompeii (Ancient city)
19   600 00      Dionysus (Greek deity) $x Art.
20   610 20      Villa of the Mysteries (Pompeii)
21   650  0      Pompeii (Ancient city) $x Buildings,
structures, etc.
22   650  0      Dionysia in art.
23   650  0      Mysteries, Religious, in art.
24   650  0      Women $x Psychology.
```

Discussion: This record has lots of subject access points. The tag for "Dionysus (Greek deity) $x Art" is incorrect. It seems that it should be a personal name entry, but LC places deities in 650 fields. The tag is also incorrect for "Pompeii (Ancient city) $x Buildings, structures, etc." The tag should be 651 for a geographic heading.

The subfield codes for "Mural painting and decoration $x Italy $x Pompeii (Ancient city)" are incorrect. The subfield code for a geographic subdivision is "$z."

Fig. 8.9d. Edited OCLC bibliographic record.

```
OCLC: 17774235        Rec stat:   c
Entered: 19880318    Replaced: 19900623    Used: 19910412
Type: a   Bib lvl:  m   Source:         Lang:    eng
Repr:     Enc lvl:      Conf pub:  0    Ctry:    txu
Indx: 0   Mod rec:      Govt pub:       Cont:    b
Desc: a   Int lvl:      Festschr:  0    Illus:   af
          F/B:      0   Dat tp:    s    Dates:   1988,
1    010           88-4893//r902
2    040           DLC $c DLC [Modified by author]
3    020           088214510X
4    041 1         eng $h ger
5    043           e-it---
6    050 00        ND2575 $b .F513 1988
7    082 00        755/.9238/09377 $2 19
8    049           KHNN
9    100 2         Fierz-David, Linda.
10   240 10        Psychologische Betrachtungen zu der
Freskenfolge der Villa dei Misteri in Pompeii. $l
English
11   245 10        Women's Dionysian initiation : $b the
Villa of Mysteries in Pompeii / $c Linda Fierz-David ;
translated by Gladys Phelan and with an introduction by
M. Esther Harding.
12   260           Dallas, Tex. : $b Spring, $c 1988.
13   300           xvii, 149 p., [4] p. of plates : $b ill.
(some col.) ; $c 23 cm.
14   440  0        Jungian classics series ; $v 11
15   500           Translation of: Psychologische
Betrachtungen zu der Freskenfolge der Villa dei Misteri
in Pompeii.
16   504           Includes bibliographical references.
17   650  0        Villa of the Mysteries frescoes (Mural
painting)
18   650  0        Mural painting and decoration $z Italy $z
Pompeii (Ancient city)
19   650  0        Dionysus (Greek deity) $x Art.
20   610 20        Villa of the Mysteries (Pompeii)
21   651  0        Pompeii (Ancient city) $x Buildings,
structures, etc.
22   650  0        Dionysia in art.
23   650  0        Mysteries, Religious, in art.
24   650  0        Women $x Psychology.
```

If desired, the reader may now practice the exercises in chapter 10 for the subject access points (fields 600, 610, 650, and 651) for monographs. Figures 10.1–10.2 and 10.6 need editing in those fields. Consult chapter 11 for the answers.

Call Numbers (Fields 050, 082, 090, and 092)

Call numbers serve two functions. The first is a location function: the call number acts as an address for the item. The second is to collocate materials on the same subject. The first part of a call number is the classification number, which places the item with other items on the same subject. The second part is the Cutter number, which places items in the same classification number in alphabetical order by main entry in most cases. For biographies, the Cutter number is for the biographee. Other elements may be added to the call number, such as date or workmark.

The two main classification systems in use in the United States are Dewey Decimal Classification (DDC) and the Library of Congress Classification (LCC). If the number is assigned by the Library of Congress, the LC number goes in field 050 and the Dewey number goes in 082. If the number is assigned by another library, the LC number goes in 090 and the Dewey number goes in 092.

Many libraries compare the call number to their own shelflist. The subject content may be compared to the subject of other items with that classification number. This comparison is based on subject headings and titles of the other items. The Cutter number is checked to see if it places the item in the correct alphabetical order within that classification number. In a card shelflist, a temporary card is often inserted to hold the place for the forthcoming card for the item. This process is called *shelflisting.*

In some libraries, shelflisting is performed only by specified individuals. Other libraries accept the call number on the bibliographic record without checking the shelflist or classification schedule. Several libraries accept the call numbers assigned by the Library of Congress while verifying call numbers not assigned by LC. In all cases, the copy cataloger needs to understand some basic guidelines for inputting call numbers on OCLC. If the library uses LCC, some basic guidelines are:

1. Field 050 is used if the number is assigned by LC or another national library.

2. Field 090 is used if the number is added by agencies other than LC. Some libraries place an "x" at the end of the call number if it has been assigned by a library other than LC. This prevents having an exact conflict with a call number that LC has assigned to another title.

3. Subfield a contains the classification number and the first Cutter number if there are two Cutter numbers.

4. If there is only one Cutter number, it goes into subfield b.

5. The first Cutter number is always preceded by a decimal point.

6. A date may precede either the first or second Cutter number, but most often the date follows the last Cutter number.

7. The date following the last Cutter number usually represents the publication date, but there are exceptions. For instance, with conferences, it is the date of the conference.

8. If the bibliographic record has both an 050 and an 090 field, the 090 field will print on catalog cards.

9. If there are two "a" subfields in the 050 field, the cataloger is being given an alternative number. The first number is complete, while the second number is only the classification number. One of the numbers needs to be deleted. If the cataloger decides to use the alternative number, a Cutter number needs to be added. LC assigns alternative numbers for bibliographies and for some series, if a series call number is used.

For a call number to print correctly, spacing has to be exact according to OCLC's guidelines. *Bibliographic Formats* lists the spacing requirements for each element of the call number.

If the library uses DDC, some basic guidelines are:

1. Field 082 is used if the number is assigned by the Library of Congress or National Library of Canada (NLC).

2. Field 092 is used if the number is assigned by agencies other than LC or NLC.

3. Field 082 only contains the classification number.

4. Libraries using *DDC* must always assign the Cutter number in order to maintain correct order for each classification number. *Bibliographic Formats* lists guidelines for transferring the classifications number from the 082 field.

5. Subfield a contains the classification number, and subfield b the Cutter number, workmark, date, and so on.

6. A comma space (,) must be entered before each new line in subfield b.

7. Field 082 may contain two or more subfields listing alternative classification numbers. In DDC, the Library of Congress gives alternative numbers for biographies.

8. Subfield 2 gives the DDC edition number used in assigning the classification. This is a key subfield because the classification number may need to be changed if it is not from the latest DDC edition.

9. Library policy must be known and followed for shortening the classification number. The logical places to shorten a classification number are represented with slashes in the 082 field.

Because the process of verifying the call number is unique to each library, only one example will be used to illustrate call numbers. Figure 7.9 represents a situation that occurs frequently: The publication was delayed, so the date in the CIP call number is off by year. Figures 8.2 and 8.3 illustrate the Cutter number changing when the main entry changes.

Fig. 8.10a. Title page.

CONTEMPORARY LEGEND

A Folklore Bibliography

Gillian Bennett
Paul Smith

GARLAND PUBLISHING, INC. • NEW YORK & LONDON
1993

Fig. 8.10b. Verso of title page.

Library of Congress Cataloging-in-Publication Data

Bennett, Gillian.
    Contemporary legend : a folklore bibliography / Gillian Bennett, Paul
Smith.
        p.   cm. — (Garland folklore bibliographies : vol. 18) (Garland
reference library of the humanities ; vol. 1307)
    Includes indexes.
    ISBN 0-8240-6103-9 (alk. paper)
    1. Urban folklore—Bibliography. 2. Legends—Bibliography. I. Smith,
Paul, 1947 Mar. 6. II. Title. III. Series. IV. Series: Garland folklore
bibliographies ; vol. 18.
    Z5981.B46   1993
    [GR78]
    016.398'091732—dc20   93-15549
                                                                         CIP

Printed on acid-free, 250-year-life paper
Manufactured in the United States of America

Fig. 8.10c. Unedited OCLC bibliographic record.

```
OCLC: 27926490       Rec stat:  p
Entered: 19930325    Replaced: 19940115    Used: 19940318
Type: a  Bib lvl:  m  Source:          Lang:    eng
Repr:     Enc lvl:     Conf pub:  0    Ctry:    nyu
Indx: 1  Mod rec:      Govt pub:       Cont:    b
Desc: a  Int lvl:      Festschr:  0    Illus:
         F/B:       0  Dat tp:    s    Dates:   1993,
1    010          93-15549
2    040          DLC $c DLC $d UKM [Modified by author]
3    015          GB94-206
4    020          0824061039 (alk. Paper)
5    050 00       Z5981 $b .B46 1993 $a GR78
6    082 00       016.398/09173/2 $2 20
7    049          KHNN
8    100 1        Bennett, Gillian.
9    245 10       Contemporary legend : $b a folklore
bibliography/ $c Gillian Bennett, Paul Smith.
10   260          New York : $b Garland, $c 1993.
11   300          xxv, 340 p. ; $c 23 cm.
12   440   0      Garland folklore bibliographies ; $v v. 18
13   440   0      Garland reference library of the
humanities ; $v v. 1307
14   500          Includes indexes.
15   650   0      Urban folklore $d Bibliography.
16   650   0      Legends $x Bibliography.
17   653          Tales
18   700 1        Smith, Paul, $d 1947 Mar. 6-
```

Discussion: The Library of Congress gives a choice of call numbers for bibliographies. Bibliographies may be classed together in the Zs or 016s, or bibliographies may be classed with other materials on that subject. In this example, this item could be classed in the Zs or the Gs if using LCC. Even though an alternative number is not shown in field 082, DDC does allow the option of it being placed into 398. Library of Congress gives the complete call number for Z, but only the classification number for G. This field cannot be accepted as is. The "$a GR78" must be deleted if the Z number is going to be used. If the GR78 number is going to be used, "Z5981 $b .B46 1993" must be deleted and a Cutter number or a Cutter number and date added to GR78. This record has been edited to illustrate the use of the GR78 number. It will go into an 090 field because LC has not assigned the Cutter number.

For the Dewey number, LC shows with a slash where the classification number can legitimately be shortened. A small or even a medium-size library would probably shorten this number to 016.398. Subfield 2 shows which edition of DDC was used in determining this number. For the DDC number, this record will be edited by shortening the classification number and adding a Cutter number based on *C. A. Cutter's Three-Figure Author Table*.

Libraries will use either LCC or DDC. The field representing the classification system not used will either be deleted or left unedited. If both fields are left in the bibliographic record, the library's profile at OCLC will determine which field is used.

Fig. 8.10d. Edited OCLC bibliographic record.

```
OCLC: 27926490      Rec stat:  p
Entered: 19930325   Replaced: 19940115    Used: 19940318
Type: a  Bib lvl:  m  Source:       Lang:    eng
Repr:    Enc lvl:     Conf pub:  0   Ctry:    nyu
Indx: 1  Mod rec:     Govt pub:      Cont:    b
Desc: a  Int lvl:     Festschr:  0   Illus:
         F/B:       0  Dat tp:    s   Dates:   1993,
1    010           93-15549
2    040           DLC $c DLC $d UKM [Modified by author]
3    015           GB94-206
4    020           0824061039 (alk. Paper)
5    090 00        GR78 $b .B46 1993x
6    092 00        016.398 $b B439
7    049           KHNN
8    100 1         Bennett, Gillian.
9    245 10        Contemporary legend : $b a folklore
bibliography/ $c Gillian Bennett, Paul Smith.
10   260           New York : $b Garland, $c 1993.
11   300           xxv, 340 p. ; $c 23 cm.
12   440 0         Garland folklore bibliographies ; $v v. 18
13   440 0         Garland reference library of the
humanities ; $v v. 1307
14   500           Includes indexes.
15   650 0         Urban folklore $d Bibliography.
16   650 0         Legends $x Bibliography.
17   653           Tales
18   700 1         Smith, Paul, $d 1947 Mar. 6-
```

If desired, the reader may now practice the exercises in chapter 10 for the call numbers. Figures 10.4–10.5 for *LCC* need to be edited. Figures 10.1–10.2 for *DDC* need to be edited. Consult chapter 11 for the answers.

9

Other Types of Materials

If one can catalog monographs, it is easy to move to other types of materials. (In the computer and MARC realm, the word *format* is often used instead of "other type of materials." *Format* refers to the physical presentation of an item.) Many of the rules and fields are the same. *AACR2R* has a chapter on each type of material. As with monographs, one is referred back to chapter 1 when the general rules cover treatment of that element (i.e., for information on the title element one is referred to chapter 1).

Around 1980, several books appeared that described and illustrated *AACR2*. These were used heavily in the early 1980s. Now, use of these books has decreased significantly because catalogers have become familiar with *AACR2* (now *AACR2R*). This is not the case for other types of materials, which individuals do not feel as comfortable cataloging. Until recently, many libraries did not catalog them in depth. In fact, little attention was given to cataloging rules for materials other than monographs before *AACR2*. Also, there are few LC examples; therefore, there is no leader to follow. Inconsistencies abound in the cataloging copy available for use. Individuals seek help in interpreting *AACR2R* for these materials. If a copy cataloger needs help in cataloging materials other than monographs, confer with a supervisor for sources to consult.

This chapter will provide a few selected examples of copy cataloging for materials other than monographs. The procedures used in the previous chapters will be followed.

Cartographic Materials
(Chapters 1 and 3)

Fig. 9.1a. Part of the map showing title.

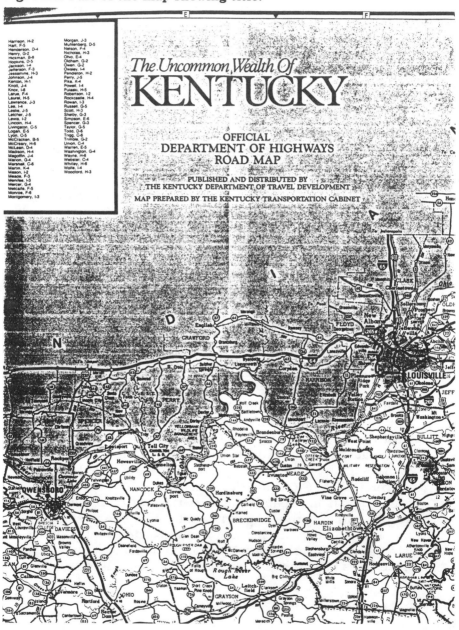

Fig. 9.1b. Part of the map showing legend.

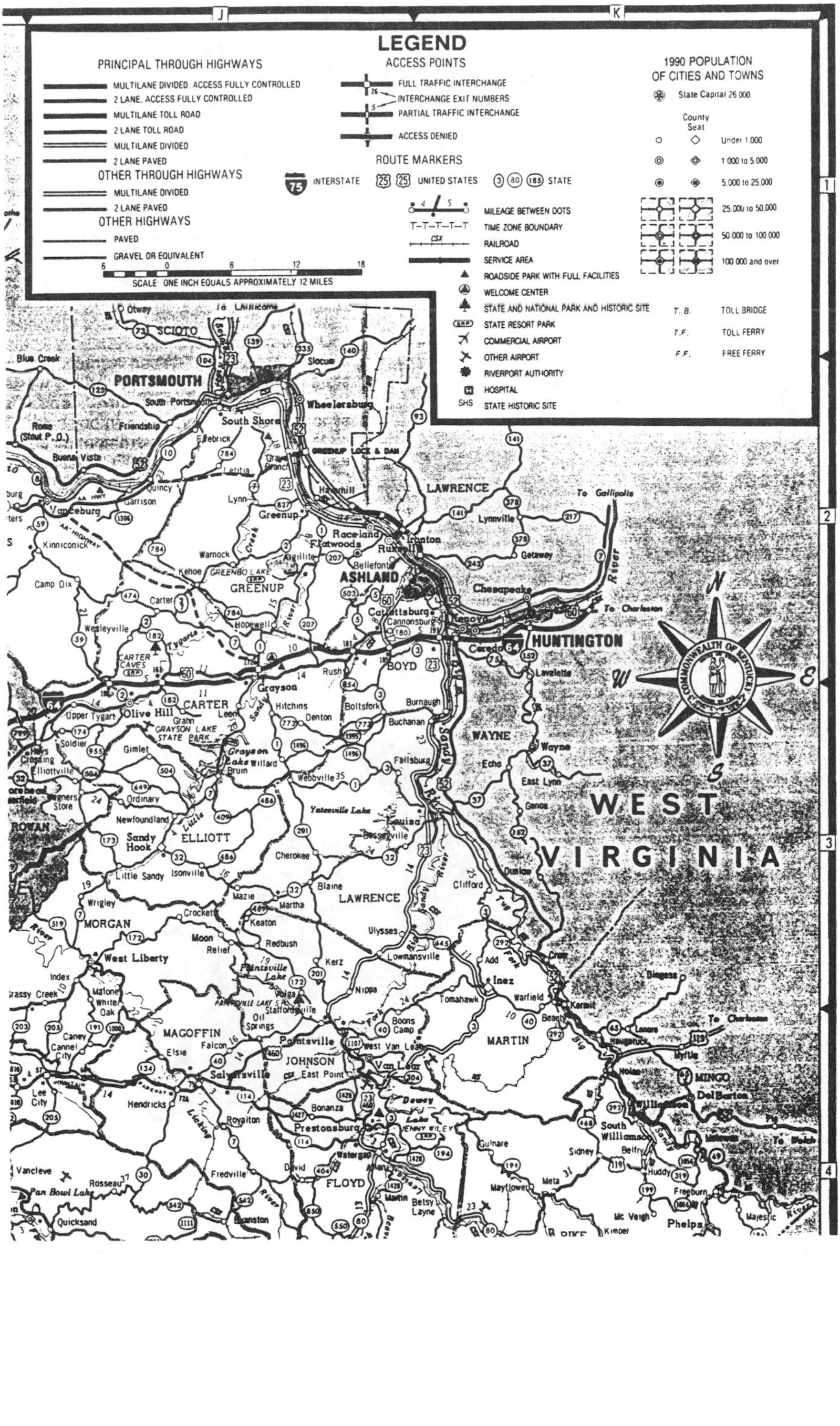

Fig. 9.1c. Front map panel.

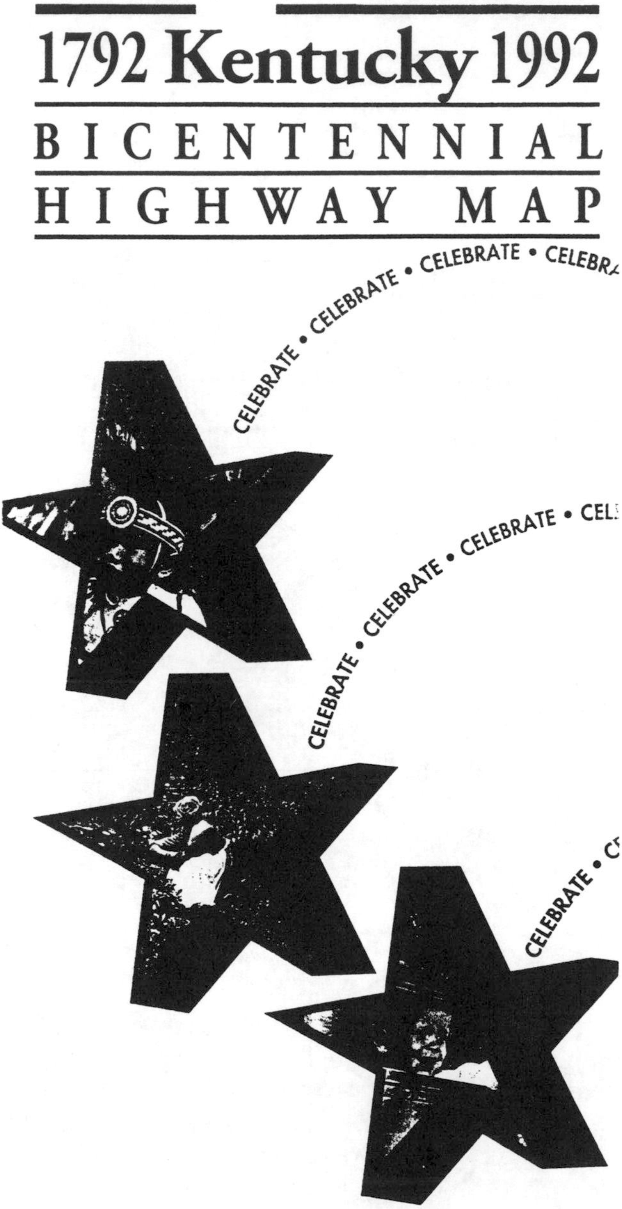

1792 Kentucky 1992

BICENTENNIAL
HIGHWAY MAP

ADDITIONAL INFORMATION: The map is in color. It is 39 x 85 centimeters on a sheet that is 56 x 88 centimeters. The sheet also contains an index, a mileage chart, and eight insets of cities. The verso contains text on Kentucky, a list of attractions, and color illustrations.

Fig. 9.1d. Unedited OCLC bibliographic record.

```
OCLC: 26382544        Rec stat:   n
Entered: 19920812    Replaced: 19920812      Used: 19931020
Type:    e    Bib lvl: m   Source:    d    Lang:    eng
RecG:    a    Enc lvl: I   Govt pub: s     Ctry:    kyu
Relief:       Mod rec:     Base:      ^^^  Form:
Desc:    a    Indx:    1   Dat tp:    s    Dates:   1992,
1    040         GZN $c GZN [Modified by author]
2    007         a $b j $d c $e a $f n $g z $h n
3    034 1       a $b 760320
4    052         3951
6    049         KHNN
7    245 14      The uncommon wealth of Kentucky official
Department of Highways road map / $c published and
distributed by the Kentucky Department of Travel
Development ; prepared by the Kentucky Transportation
Cabinet.
8    255         Scale [ca. 1:760,320]. 1 in = approx. 12
mi.
9    260         Frankfort : $b Kentucky Dept. of Travel
Development, $c 1992.
10   300         1 map : $b col. ; $c 39 x 85 cm. on sheet
56 x 88 cm.
11   500         Panel title: Kentucky bicentennial highway
map, 1792-1992.
12   500         Includes index, mileage chart, and 8 local
routemaps.
13   500         Text, list of attractions, and col. ill.
on verso.
14   651  0      Kentucky $x Road maps.
15   710  1      Kentucky. $b Dept. of Travel Development.
16   740  01     Kentucky bicentennial highway map, 1792-
1992.
```

Discussion: Cartographic materials include maps, atlases, globes, charts, and the like that represent the whole or part of the Earth or any celestial body. The chief source of information for a map is the map itself. Maps often have different forms of the title in various places. Rule 3.1B3 gives guidance on solving this dilemma. In this example, the title on the map is "The Uncommon Wealth of Kentucky Official Department of Highways Road Map." If the map is folded, the title on the outside of the fold is "1792 Kentucky 1992 Bicentennial Highway Map." In a library collection, maps are usually stored flat or rolled to prevent wear and tear. When unfolded, "1792 Kentucky 1992 Bicentennial Highway Map" is on the reverse side of the map.

The tile proper should be "The Uncommon Wealth of Kentucky"; however, the title showing when the map is folded should be given access through a 246 field. Field 246 with a first indicator of "1" and a blank in the second indicator position will generate an access point and a note. The information in subfield i, which comes before subfield a tells the user what kind of title is listed in subfield a. "Official Department of Highways Road Map" would be other title information.

The general material designation (GMD) is an optional element in the 245 field. The Library of Congress uses it with selected formats. LC does not use it with cartographic materials; however, individual libraries may choose to use it. A copy cataloger should check with a supervisor to determine the library's policy. If used, it would be in subfield h as [map]. Since 1993, OCLC guidelines instruct one to enclose the GMD in brackets. If the brackets are missing, the print program will supply them (*Bibliographic Formats* 245 $h).

Bibliographic records for cartographic items always have a mathematical data area (Rule 3.3B). This area gives the scale of the map as a representative fraction expressed as a ratio "1:_____" preceded by the word *scale*. The scale on the map is only given as one inch equals approximately 12 miles; it is not given as a representative fraction, so one calculates it and places it in square brackets. This area will also have a statement of projection if found on the item. Optionally, coordinates and equinox may be given.

The date of publication is not on the map; therefore, it should be in brackets (Rule 3.4F1). The map is printed so that it can be folded to have an outside panel; thus, the dimensions of the folded form should be given (Rule 3.5D1).

This map was prepared by the Kentucky Transportation Cabinet and published and distributed by the Kentucky Department of Travel Development. According to Rule 21.1B2, the main entry for this map would be "Kentucky. Transportation Cabinet." Some libraries create an added entry for a publisher if it is an association, institution, government agency, or religious organization. On these grounds and its prominent location, the added entry for "Kentucky. Department of Travel Development" may be retained. (As a title main entry, there is an error in the 245 field. The first indicator should be "0." Also, until recently, "uncommon" would also have been capitalized because it was a title main entry beginning with an article according to Rule A.4D1. This rule was deleted in the 1993 amendments.)

This bibliographic record does not have a call number. Libraries may give maps DDC or LCC call numbers or use some special classification scheme for maps. The author has assigned a call number by using the 049 and 099 fields. The last character of the 049 field, based on the library's profile, places the item in a specific collection. The 099 field is a local free-text call number. A number is assigned to each map as it is cataloged. The scheme places the maps in numerical order without regard to subject content.

Fields 034 and 052 are fields used with cartographic materials. Field 034 is used for coded mathematical data—in this case, a single horizontal scale. Field 052 lists a geographic classification code based on the LCC number from the G schedule.

Many formats contain an 007 field that physically describes the item in coded form. In this example:

"a" in subfield a means that the item is a map

"j" in subfield b means that the specific material designation is "map"

"c" in subfield d means that the item is in multicolor

"a" in subfield e means that the physical medium is paper

"n" in subfield f means that the field is not applicable

"z" in subfield g means that production is other than those types listed

"n" in subfield h means that the field is not applicable

Fig. 9.1e. Edited OCLC bibliographic record.

```
OCLC: 26382544          Rec stat:    n
Entered: 19920812     Replaced: 19920812      Used: 19931020
Type:    e      Bib lvl: m  Source:    d     Lang:     eng
RecG:    a      Enc lvl: I  Govt pub: s      Ctry:     kyu
Relief:         Mod rec:    Base:      ^^^   Form:
Desc:    a      Indx:    1  Dat tp:    s     Dates:    1992,
1     040          GZN $c GZN [Modified by author]
2     007          a $b j $d c $e a $f n $g z $h n
3     034 1        a $b 760320
4     052          3951
5     099          8789
6     049          KHNG
7     110 1        Kentucky. $b Transportation Cabinet.
8     245 14       The uncommon wealth of Kentucky : $b
official Department of Highways road map / $c published
and distributed by the Kentucky Department of Travel
Development ; prepared by the Kentucky Transportation
Cabinet.
9     246 1        $i Panel title: $a Kentucky bicentennial
highway map, 1772-1992.
10    255          Scale [ca. 1:760,320]. 1 in = approx. 12
mi.
11    260          Frankfort : $b Kentucky Dept. of Travel
Development, $c [1992].
12    300          1 map : $b col. ; $c 39 x 85 cm. on sheet
56 x 88 cm. folded to 19 x 10 cm.
13    500          Includes index, mileage chart, and 8 local
routemaps.
14    500          Text, list of attractions, and col. ill.
on verso.
15    651  0       Kentucky $x Road maps.
16    710 1        Kentucky. $b Dept. of Travel Development.
```

Music (Chapters 1, 5, and 25)

Fig. 9.2a. Cover.

No. 4707b

KABALEWSKI

THEME & VARIATIONS in A minor

for Piano

Opus 40 No. 2

moderately difficult

Duration: 4 minutes

Fig. 9.2b. Title page.

DIMITRI KABALEWSKI

Opus 40

Piano

1. VARIATIONS in D
Twelve easy variations
on a nursery theme
Edition Peters No. 4707a

2. THEME AND VARIATIONS in A minor
Moderate Difficulty
Edition Peters No. 4707b

Piano Duet

3. VARIATIONS in D
Twelve easy variations
on a nursery theme
arranged for piano duet
by
Thomas A. Johnson
Edition Peters No. 4707c

EDITION PETERS & HINRICHSEN EDITION

New York   Frankfurt   London   Zürich

Fig. 9.2c. First page of music.

THEME and VARIATIONS in A minor

Duration: 4 mins. approx.

DIMITRI KABALEWSKI
Op. 40, No. 2

Edition Peters No. 4707b

Fig. 9.2d. Unedited OCLC bibliographic record.

```
OCLC: 15314767        Rec stat:   n
Entered: 19870313    Replace: 19870710      Used: 19911223
Type:    c      Bib lvl: m  Source:    d    Lang:    N/A
Repr:           Enc lvl: I  Format:    a    Ctry:    nyu
Accomp:         Mod rec:    Comp:      vr   Ltxt:    n
Desc:    a      Int lvl:    Dat tp:    a    Dates:   1969,
1    040          OWS $c OWS [Modified by author]
2    090          M1380 $b .K3 op.40, no.2
3    049          KHNN
4    100 1        Kabalevsky, Dmitry Borisovich, $d 1904-
5    240 10       Variations, $m piano, $n op. 40, no. 2, $r
A minor
6    245 10       Theme and variations in A minor : $b for
piano, opus 40, no. 2 / $c Dimitri Kabalewski.
7    260          New York : $b Edition Peters & Hinrichsen
Edition, $c c1960.
8    300          7 p. of music ; $c 31 cm.
9    490 0        Edition Peters ; $v 4707b
10   650 0        Piano music, Juvenile.
```

Discussion: For many, music is one of the most difficult types of materials to catalog, especially for nonmusicians. Music brings two new challenges. First, it is like a foreign language to a nonmusician, and second, any text included with the music is often in a foreign language.

Sometimes the title page of a piece of music consists of a list of titles, of which one is the piece being cataloged. In this case, for the chief source of information one is to use the cover or caption if more information is provided (Rule 5.0B1). In this example, the cover does provide more information. There will be a note indicating the cover was used as the title page substitute. When using the cover as the chief source of information, the 245 field requires two changes: "and" needs to be changed to an ampersand, and "Dimitri" needs to be deleted.

The uniform title and publisher (plate) number are important in music. The uniform title allows all the titles by one composer that are generic (e.g., Symphony No. ____) to be pulled together in a systematic way. The uniform title is composed correctly according to rules in chapter 25; it is in the 240 field in a MARC record. Using Rule 25.28A, "variations" is the initial element. Then, as instructed in Rules 25.30A1 through 25.30D1, "piano" is added as the medium, "op. 40, no. 2" as the opus number, and "A minor" as the key.

For printed music, the publisher number field contains the plate number or the publisher number. The plate number is printed on each page of the music. The publisher number is found on the title page, cover, or first page of music. The publisher number goes in field 028, and the indicators show whether it is a publisher or plate number. In this record, the plate number has been entered in a series field. When it is entered in the 028 field, the first indicator of "2" denotes that the number is a plate number.

The publication information is taken from the title page and first page of music, which fall within the prescribed source of information for publication distribution elements.

Two notes have been added to enhance this record. The first states the source of title, and the second indicates the duration.

Because this work is listed on the title page with the word "and," a 246 field has been added to provide access for users who use "and" rather than an ampersand.

Upon checking Kabalewski's name in OCLC's online authority file, one discovers that both forename and surname are different from what appears on the piece of music. This is a typical occurrence with many composers' names because of differences in transliteration tables used to romanize names.

One could disagree that the subject heading should have the qualifier "juvenile," because on the cover it states, "moderately difficult."

Fig. 9.2e. Edited OCLC bibliographic record.

```
OCLC: 15314767      Rec stat:  n
Entered: 19870313    Replace: 19870710      Used: 19911223
Type:    c   Bib lvl: m  Source:   d    Lang:   N/A
Repr:        Enc lvl: I  Format:   a    Ctry:   nyu
Accomp:      Mod rec:    Comp:     vr   Ltxt:   n
Desc:    a   Int lvl:    Dat tp:   a    Dates:  1969,
1    040         OWS $c OWS [Modified by author]
2    028 22      4707b $b Editions Peters
2    090         M1380 $b .K3 op.40, no.2
3    049         KHNN
4    100 1       Kabalevsky, Dmitry Borisovich, $d 1904-
5    240 10      Variations, $m piano, $n op. 40, no. 2, $r
A minor
6    245 10      Theme & variations in A minor : $b for
piano, opus 40, no. 2 / $c Kabalewski.
7    246 3       Theme and variations in A minor
8    260         New York : $b Edition Peters & Hinrichsen
Edition, $c c1960.
9    300         7 p. of music ; $c 31 cm.
10   500         Cover title.
11   500         Duration: 4 min.
12   650  0      Piano music.
```

Sound Recordings (Chapters 1 and 6)

Fig. 9.3a. Disc.

ROGER WHITTAKER
Greatest Hits

09026-61986-2

© 1994, BMG Music
TMK(s) ® G.E. Co., USA
& BMG Music.
Made in U.S.A.

1. New World in the Morning   2. Durham Town
3. I Don't Believe in IF Anymore   4. Mexican Whistler
5. The Last Farewell   6. I Am But a Small Voice
7. River Lady   8. You Are My Miracle
9. Albany   10. The Wind Beneath My Wings
11. The Skye Boat Song (with Des O'Conner)

Fig. 9.3b. Back of CD case.

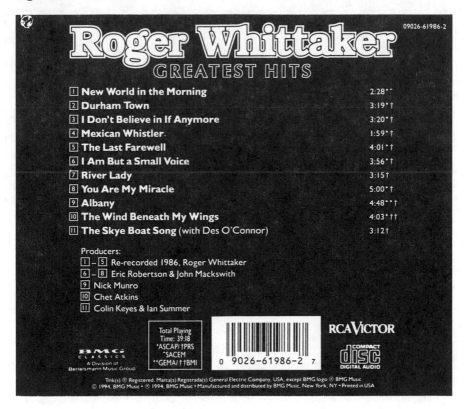

ADDITIONAL INFORMATION: The disc is 4 3/4 inches in diameter. The insert in the CD case has a short biographical sketch of Roger Whittaker. According to the local authority file, "BMG Classics" is not traced.

Fig. 9.3c. Unedited OCLC bibliographic record.

```
OCLC: 30340054        Rec stat:   n
Entered: 19940427     Replaced: 19940427      Used: 19940609
Type:    j     Bib lvl: m  Source:    d     Lang:     eng
Repr:          Enc lvl: K  Format:    n     Ctry:     nyu
Accomp:        Mod rec:    Comp:      pp    LTxt:
Desc:    a     Int lvl:    Dat tp:    s     Dates:    1994,
1    040         KCP $c KCP [Modified by author]
2    007         s $b d $d f $e s $f n $g g $h n $i n $m e
$n u
3    028 02      09026-61986-2 $b BMG
4    049         KHNN
5    100 1       Whittaker, Roger.
6    245 10      Greatest hits $h [sound recording] / $c
Roger Whittaker.
7    260         New York, NY : $b BMG Music, $c p1994.
8    300         1 sound disc : $b digital, stereo. ; $c 4
3/4 in.
9    500         Compact disc.
10   650  0      Popular music.
11   650  0      Compact discs.
```

Discussion: An initial factor to note is that this bibliographic record has an encoding level of K. (Level K means less than full-level cataloging.) This may mean that key components are missing; however, it may be a very good bibliographic record, as some libraries always enter certain formats at K level. (Some libraries use the K level when they feel uncomfortable with such a format or when they do not want to supply all of the needed information for I level, which is full-level cataloging input by OCLC participants.)

The first question to ask is whether this bibliographic record is for this compact disc. Because this is a level-K record, the question is compounded. The artist and title are the same. The publisher is different, but the publisher number is the same. The publisher listed on the bibliographic record is listed as the distributor on the back of the container. The copy cataloger will want to consult with the supervisor on how situations like this are treated in the library. In this case, the author is going to assume that the bibliographic record is for this disc.

LC uses the GMD for the sound recording format. The GMD goes immediately after the title proper in subfield h. Since 1993, OCLC guidelines require that one enclose the GMD in brackets. Earlier OCLC guidelines stated that one should not use brackets, as brackets were computer generated. If the brackets are missing, the print program will supply them (*Bibliographic Formats* 245 $h).

There has been confusion over whether a "c" or "p" should precede the copyright date. The "p" stands for "pressing." *Anglo-American Cataloging Rules* Revised Chapter 14 had required that a "p" precede the copyright date. Based on examples in *AACR2R*, the "p" is still being used.

Field 300 contains the number and type of sound recording in subfield a. Rule 6.5B2 states that the playing time should be given as instructed in Rule 1.5B4. On the back of the CD case, the playing time of each piece and the total playing time are listed. The author has chosen to give the playing time of each piece in the contents note. One could have chosen to list the total playing time in the 300 field after "disc." In subfield b, the method of recording is listed. Rules 6.5C2 and 6.5C7 state that one should list the type of recording, and to give the number of sound channels if the information is readily available. The bibliographic record states that the disc is a stereo recording. The author was unable to determine from the disc, container, or insert whether this is true. Some libraries may remove the word "stereo" to be in strict compliance with the rule, while others may leave it in. The author believes that this is a stereo recording, but has removed the word to be in compliance with the rule. The dimensions of the disc are recorded in subfield c.

On the back of the CD case is a series statement. This needs to be added as a 490 field, because in the additional information one learns that the library does not trace this series.

As the 300 field does not indicate that this is a compact disc, the fact appears in a note (Rule 6.7B10). One is instructed in Rule 6.7B11 to make a note about accompanying material not mentioned in the physical description or given in a separate description. Thus, a note needs to be made about the insert in the CD case.

Notice that no call number is given. Many libraries use a unique call number scheme for their sound recording collection. It may be something simple, such as "CD" for compact disc and a number. The CD may be generated through the 049 field and the library's specific profile. In this case, the author has changed the 049 field and added a number in an 099 field. (Field 099 is for a local free-text call number.)

The bibliographic record has the subject heading "compact disc." This is not the subject of the disc; the inputting library is probably using this field to search by format and retrieve all compact discs.

The 007 field is used for sound recordings. This field describes in coded form the physical description of the item. In this instance:

"s" in subfield a means that the item is a sound recording

"d" in subfield b means that the item is a sound disc

"f" in subfield d means that the speed is 1.4 m. per sec.

"u" in subfield e means that the configuration of playback channels is unknown

"n" in subfield f means that the groove width is not applicable

"g" in subfield g means that the disc is 4 3/4 inches in diameter

"n" in subfield h means that the tape width is not applicable

"n" in subfield i means that the tape configuration is not applicable

"e" in subfield m means that the item requires digital playback

"d" in subfield n means that the item was recorded using digital techniques

The 028 field contains the publisher number in subfield a and the label name in subfield b. The first indicator of "0" means that it is an issue number, and the second indicator of "2" means that a note will be printed on the card, but that no added entry will be generated.

Fig. 9.3d. Edited OCLC bibliographic record.

```
OCLC: 30340054        Rec stat:   n
Entered: 19940427    Replaced: 19940427     Used: 19940609
Type:    j    Bib lvl: m  Source:    d    Lang:    eng
Repr:         Enc lvl: K  Format:    n    Ctry:    nyu
Accomp:       Mod rec:    Comp:     pp    LTxt:
Desc:    a    Int lvl:    Dat tp:    s    Dates:   1994,
1    040        KCP $c KCP [Modified by author]
2    007        s $b d $d f $e u $f n $g g $h n $i n $m e
$n u
3    028 02     09026-61986-2 $b RCA Victor
4    049        KHNM
5    099        647
6    100 1      Whittaker, Roger.
7    245 10     Greatest hits $h [sound recording] / $c
Roger Whittaker.
8    260        [S.l.] : $b RCA Victor ; $a New York, NY :
$b Manufactured and distributed by BMG Music, $c p1994.
9    300        1 sound disc : $b digital ; $c 4 3/4 in.
10   490 0      BMG classics
11   500        Compact disc.
12   500        Insert in container has a short
biographical sketch of Roger Whittaker.
13   505 0      New world in the morning (2:28)--Durham
town (3:19)--I don't believe in if anymore (3:20)--
Mexican whistler (1:59)--The last farewell (4:01)--I am
but a small voice (3:56)--River lady (3:15)--You are my
miracle (5:00)--Albany (4:48)--The wind beneath my wings
(4:03)--The skye boat song with Des O'Connor (3:12).
14   650  0     Popular music.
```

Videorecordings (Chapters 1 and 7)

Fig. 9.4a. Videocassette.

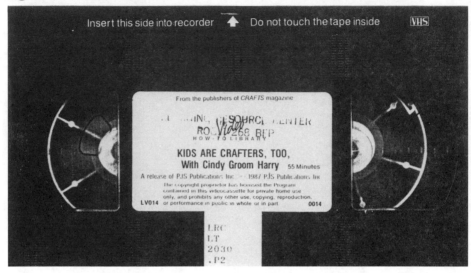

ADDITIONAL INFORMATION: A pattern guide with tips on working with children is inserted in the container. The gauge (width) of the videocassette is 1/2 inch. The cassette has sound and is in color. The title screen contains the same title as on the cassette and container. The credits screens listing the executive producer, Judith Brossart, and the producer/director, William Baker, are at the end of the recording. The copyright date is the same as the one on the cassette. The series screen contains the series in the same form as is stated on the cassette and the front of the container.

Fig. 9.4b. Part of front of container.

Fig. 9.4c. Part of back of container.

Crafts Videos
HOW-TO LIBRARY

FROM THE PUBLISHERS OF **Crafts** MAGAZINE

KIDS ARE CRAFTERS, TOO
WITH CINDY GROOM HARRY

Cindy Groom Harry, a member of the Society of Craft Designers and author of the popular column "Kids' Korner" in *Crafts* Magazine, shares her kid-tested craft projects with you. Using common household and craft items, you can confidently teach children the joys of crafting. Cindy covers stenciling on a variety of surfaces, painting by drizzling, dotting and spraying, flat and round weaving, and basic crafts. Children complete projects including a stenciled felt pencil caddy, woven heart sachet and basket, painted clothing, and a pin cushion panda and teddy bear. Cindy also provides instructions for adults in how to prepare the materials, surfaces and children for the fun of crafting. Patterns included.

Running Time: 55 Minutes   FS014

PJS Publications Inc. • P.O. Box 1790 • Peoria, IL 61656
(309) 682-6626

Fig. 9.4d. Unedited OCLC bibliographic record.

```
OCLC: 17608739        Rec stat:  n
Entered: 19880310   Replaced: 19930607    Used: 19931108
Type:      g  Bib lvl: m  Source:    d   Lang:    eng
Type mat: v   Enc lvl: I  Govt pub:       Ctry:    ilu
Int lvl:  e   Mod rec:    Tech:      1   Leng:    055
Desc:     a   Accomp:  r  Dat tp:    s   Dates:   1987,
1    040        CXP $c CXP [Modified by author]
2    007        v $b f $d c $e b $f a $g h $h o
3    092        745.5088054 $b K541 $2 19
4    049        KHNN
5    245 00     Kids are crafters, too, with Cindy Groom
Harry $h videorecording / $c from the publishers of
Crafts magazine ; producer director, William Baker ;
executive producer, Judith Brossart.
6    260        Peoria, Ill. : $b PJS Publications, $c
c1987.
7    300        1 videocassette  : $b sd., col. ; $c 1/2
in. + $e 1 pattern guide.
8    440  0     Crafts video how-to library
9    500        VHS.
10   520        Cindy Groom Harry shares her kid-tested
craft projects using common household and craft items.
Instructions are also provided in how to prepare the
materials, surfaces, and children for the projects.
11   650  0     Handicraft.
12   700  1     Harry, Cindy Groom.
13   710  2     PJS Publications.
14   730  01    Crafts (Peoria, Ill.)
```

Discussion: Videorecordings are similar to other formats; often the bibliographic information is scattered and stated in varying forms. In this case, the producer/director and executive producer are only listed at the end of the videorecording. They do not need to be in brackets because the entire item is used for the chief source of information.

LC uses the GMD for videorecordings. By present OCLC guidelines, the GMD would be in brackets. On the back of the container and on the pattern guide, the postal abbreviation "IL" is listed after Peoria. The Library of Congress has decided to use the postal abbreviation if it is used on the item (*Cataloging Service Bulletin* no. 51, p. 50).

According to Rule 7.5B2, the playing time should be given as instructed in Rule 1.5B4. The playing time is listed on the cassette and the container. In analyzing the two notes, one discovers that the 500 field tells the user which videorecording system the tape is compatible with; however, it should be in a 538 note. The 520 field gives a summary of the videorecording.

The prescribed punctuation, indicators, and subfield codes are correct. The 007 field is used for videorecordings. This field describes in coded form the physical description of the item. In this instance:

"v" in subfield a means that the item is a videorecording

"f" in subfield b means that the item is a videocassette

"c" in subfield d means that the item is in color

"b" in subfield e means that the videorecording is VHS format

"a" in subfield f means that the medium for sound is videotape

"h" in subfield g means that the item is a videotape

"o" in subfield h means that the tape is 1/2 inch

Fig. 9.4e. Edited OCLC bibliographic record.

```
OCLC: 17608739        Rec stat:   n
Entered: 19880310    Replaced: 19930607    Used: 19931108
Type:        g  Bib lvl: m  Source:    d    Lang:    eng
Type mat: v  Enc lvl: I  Govt pub:       Ctry:    ilu
Int lvl:   e  Mod rec:     Tech:     1    Leng:    055
Desc:        a  Accomp:   r  Dat tp:    s    Dates:   1987,
1    040        CXP $c CXP [Modified by author]
2    007        v $b f $d c $e b $f a $g h $h o
3    092        745.5088054 $b K541 $2 19
4    049        KHNN
5    245 00     Kids are crafters, too, with Cindy Groom
Harry $h [videorecording] / $c from the publishers of
Crafts magazine ; producer director, William Baker ;
executive producer, Judith Brossart.
6    260        Peoria, IL : $b PJS Publications, $c
c1987.
7    300        1 videocassette (55 min.) : $b sd., col. ;
$c 1/2 in.  + $e 1 pattern guide.
8    440  0     Crafts video how-to library
9    538        VHS.
10   520        Cindy Groom Harry shares her kid-tested
craft projects using common household and craft items.
Instructions are also provided in how to prepare the
materials, surfaces, and children for the projects.
11   650  0     Handicraft.
12   700  1     Harry, Cindy Groom.
13   710  2     PJS Publications.
14   730  0     Crafts (Peoria, Ill.)
```

Computer Files (Chapters 1 and 9)

Fig. 9.5a. Five disks.

(Figure continues on page 210.)

Fig. 9.5a. *(continued)*

Microsoft.Works

Disk 5

MS-DOS® Series
Disk format: Low-density (720K)
Version 3.0

Disk Assy 070-095-548
© 1987-1992 Microsoft Corporation. All rights reserved

Fig. 9.5b. Container front.

Fig. 9.5c. Unedited OCLC bibliographic record.

```
OCLC: 28465002        Rec stat:   n
Entered: 19930218     Replaced: 19930717    Used: 19931014
Type:      m  Bib lvl: m  Source:         Lang:   N/A
File:      b  Enc lvl:    Gov pub:        Ctry:   wau
Audience:     Mod rec:    Frequn:    n    Regulr:
Desc:      a              Dat tp:    s    Dates:  1992
1    010          93-790135
2    040          DLC $c DLC [Modified by author]
3    041 0        $g eng
4    050 00       QA76.76 $b .I57
5    082 10       005.369 $2 12
6    049          KHNN
7    245 00       Microsoft works $h [computer file].
8    250          Version 3.0.
9    256          Computer program.
10   260          Redmond, WA : $b Microsoft, $c c1992.
11   300          5 computer disks ; $c 3 1/2 in.
12   440 0        MS-DOS series
13   538          System requirements: IBM-compatible PC
with 8086 or higher microprocessor; 640K RAM; MS-DOS 3.0
or later (3.1 or later for network workstations); one
720K 3 1/2 floppy disk drive; MDA, CGA, EGA, VGA, XGA,
MCGA, Tandy 1000, or Hercules graphics adapter;
Microsoft mouse (preferred) or compatible pointing
device and Hayes or compatible modem optional.  Networks
supported.
14   500          Title from disk label.
15   520          Integrated software package including word
processing, database management, an electronic
spreadsheet,communications software, and utilities.
Compatible with Microsoft Word, dBASE, WordPerfect, RTF
files, and Lotus 1-2-3.
16   650  0       Integrated software $x Software.
17   650  0       Data base management $x Software.
18   650  0       Electronic spreadsheets $x Software.
19   650  0       Communications software $x Software.
20   650  0       Word processing $x Software.
21   710 2        Microsoft Corporation.
22   753          IBM PC $c DOS 3.0
```

Discussion: Computer files are relatively new in the cataloging arena. Microcomputers were introduced to the general public at about the same time as *AACR2* was introduced to the library world. Because of the rapid influx of microcomputer programs into library collections, chapter 9 of *AACR2* was rewritten in 1987. One of the biggest problems one confronts in cataloging computer files is having the equipment and knowledge to run the program in order to determine its bibliographic content.

The chief source of information is the title screen of the file; however, various alternatives are provided in case there is no title screen. The title and statement of responsibility may be taken from information issued by the publisher or creator without being enclosed in brackets. Because the title often comes from a source other than the title screen, Rule 9.1B2 states to always give the source of the title proper in a note.

With this example, a title screen flashed across the terminal screen for about one second. The author was unable to stop the screen long enough to print it; therefore, she readily accepts the note that the title was taken from the disk label. The word "Works" in the title is part of the name of the software and should be capitalized.

LC uses the GMD computer file for computer files. As the name of chapter 9 changed from "Machine-Readable Data Files" in *AACR2* to "Computer Files" in *AACR2R*, so did the GMD.

The edition area also presents new challenges. First, one must know that the word *version* is often used instead of *edition* (e.g., version 3.0 or 3.1). Second, one may see statements such as "Apple Macintosh version" or "for MS-DOS machines." These statements may go into a note describing the system requirements, or in the series area, depending on how they are worded. In this example, version 3.0 is in the edition area. "MS-DOS series" is in the series area.

Because the accompanying material is significant, one would probably want to include the physical description for it. One should note the 256 field, which contains the computer file characteristics. The 538 field contains the system requirements, and the 753 field has the system details access.

Fig. 9.5d. Edited OCLC bibliographic record.

```
OCLC: 28465002      Rec stat:  n
Entered: 19930218    Replaced: 19930717    Used: 19931014
Type:      m  Bib lvl: m  Source:       Lang:   N/A
File:      b  Enc lvl:    Gov pub:      Ctry:   wau
Audience:     Mod rec:    Frequn:    n  Regulr:
Desc:      a              Dat tp:    s  Dates:  1992
1    010         93-790135
2    040         DLC $c DLC [Modified by author]
3    041 0       $g eng
4    050 00      QA76.76 $b .I57
5    082 10      005.369 $2 12
6    049         KHNN
7    245 00      Microsoft Works $h [computer file].
8    250         Version 3.0.
9    256         Computer program.
10   260         Redmond, WA : $b Microsoft, $c c1992.
11   300         5 computer disks ; $c 3 1/2 in. + $e 1
user's guide (560 p. : ill. ; 23cm.)
12   440 0       MS-DOS series
13   538         System requirements: IBM-compatible PC
with 8086 or higher microprocessor; 640K RAM; MS-DOS 3.0
or later (3.1 or later for network workstations); one
720K 3 1/2 floppy disk drive; MDA, CGA, EGA, VGA, XGA,
MCGA, Tandy 1000, or Hercules graphics adapter;
Microsoft mouse (preferred) or compatible pointing
device and Hayes or compatible modem optional. Networks
supported.
14   500         Title from disk label.
15   520         Integrated software package including word
processing, database management, an electronic
spreadsheet,communications software, and utilities.
Compatible with Microsoft Word, dBASE, WordPerfect, RTF
files, and Lotus 1-2-3.
16   650 0       Integrated software $x Software.
17   650 0       Data base management $x Software.
18   650 0       Electronic spreadsheets $x Software.
19   650 0       Communications software $x Software.
20   650 0       Word processing $x Software.
21   710 2       Microsoft Corporation.
22   753         IBM PC $c DOS 3.0
```

Three-Dimensional Artifacts and Realia (Chapters 1 and 10)

Fig. 9.6a. Picture with joey in pocket.

Fig. 9.6b. Picture with joey out of pocket.

Fig. 9.6c. Both sides of label on kangaroo.

ADDITIONAL INFORMATION: This hand puppet is made with a brown and tan synthetic fabric. It is 42 centimeters tall. A joey finger puppet is attached with a string to the inside of the pouch. Even though many would not agree that Folktails is a series, according to the local authority file it is a traced series.

Fig. 9.6d. Unedited OCLC bibliographic record.

```
OCLC: 25755058       Rec stat:  n
Entered: 19920504    Replaced: 19920504    Used: 19930215
Type:       r  Bib lvl: m  Source:   d   Lang:   N/A
Type mat: w  Enc lvl: I  Govt pub:      Ctry:   cau
Int lvl:      Mod rec:    Tech:    n   Leng:   nnn
Desc:       a  Accomp:  z  Date tp:  q   Dates,  1900,1992
1    040         KHN $c KHN [Modified by author]
2    090         LT7000.F574 $b F3
3    049         KHNN
4    245 00      Kangaroo puppet $h toy
5    260         Emeryville, Calif. : $b Folkmanis, $c [19-
-]
6    300         1 hand puppet : $b synthetic fabric, brown
and  tan ; $c 42 cm. + $e 1 joey finger puppet.
7    440  0      Folktails
8    500         Information taken from manufacturer's tag.
9    500         Finger puppet is designed to fit into
kangaroo's pouch.
10   500         Includes the Australian aborigine legend:
"How the kangaroo learned to hop."
11   650  0      Hand puppets.
12   650  1      Hand puppets.
13   650  0      Puppets.
14   650  1      Puppets.
15   710  2      Folkmanis, Inc.
```

Discussion: Three-dimensional artifacts and realia often have little or no accompanying written information. The only written information with this puppet is a little manufacturer's label similar to one found in an article of clothing. The only bibliographic information listed on the label is "(c) Folkmanis, Inc. makers of Furry Folk Puppets, Emeryville, CA." Sometimes the catalog department may be able to obtain additional information from the acquisitions department, such as a brochure or company catalog.

Because the title "Kangaroo puppet" is not found on the item, it should be in brackets. LC uses the GMD for three-dimensional artifacts and realia. From the list on page 21 of *AACR2R*, one has to decide on the correct term to use. Is it *realia* or *toy*? The author defines realia as an artifact or a naturally occurring object. A toy is something a child would play with. There is room for debate in favor of each term. The copy cataloger should try to determine which term the library has used before. This author prefers *toy*. The manufacturer's label lists the publisher and place. The postal abbreviation was used for California; thus, Calif. should be changed to CA (*Cataloging Service Bulletin* no. 51, p. 50). No date is given, but from the looks of the puppet one can safely assume it was manufactured in the twentieth century.

The 300 field can be determined from the item. The series "Folktails" is listed on the manufacturer's label.

The first 500 note tells where the bibliographic information was found. The second is informational. The third indicates that a legend accompanies the puppet, but this was not listed in the 300 field. At the time of this cataloging, no legend was present; thus, the third 500 field should be deleted. This is a problem with some nonprint materials; even at the time of cataloging, parts may be missing. Sometimes it is hard even to determine if one has the correct bibliographic record when parts are missing. Rather than delete the note, some libraries indicate that the part is missing.

The prescribed punctuation, indicators, and subfield codes are correct. The subject headings seem to be duplicated. Upon examination of the second indicator, one discovers that one set is regular LC subject headings and the other set is children's.

Fig. 9.6e. Edited OCLC bibliographic record.

```
OCLC: 25755058        Rec stat:   n
Entered: 19920504     Replaced: 19920504     Used: 19930215
Type:        r  Bib lvl: m  Source:    d    Lang:    N/A
Type mat: w  Enc lvl: I  Govt pub:        Ctry:    cau
Int lvl:        Mod rec:      Tech:    n    Leng:    nnn
Desc:        a  Accomp:   z  Date tp:   q    Dates,   1900,1992
1    040        KHN $c KHN [Modified by author]
2    090        LT7000.F574 $b F3
3    049        KHNN
4    245 00     [Kangaroo puppet] $h [toy]
5    260        Emeryville, CA : $b Folkmanis, $c [19--]
6    300        1 hand puppet : $b synthetic fabric, brown
and   tan ; $c 42 cm. + $e 1 joey finger puppet.
7    440  0     Folktails
8    500        Information taken from manufacturer's tag.
9    500        Finger puppet is designed to fit into
kangaroo's pouch.
11   650  0     Hand puppets.
12   650  1     Hand puppets.
13   650  0     Puppets.
14   650  1     Puppets.
15   710 2      Folkmanis, Inc.
```

Fig. 9.7a. Part of top of container.

Fig. 9.7b. Part of sides of container.

ADDITIONAL INFORMATION: The place of publication, Ann Arbor, MI, is listed on the bottom of the container. The game is in color. The dimensions of the container are 24 x 47 x 4 centimeters. Game pieces include one instructional sheet, one game board, 60 landmake cards, four plastic stands, one spinner arrow, four boy and four girl playing pieces, and one black "wipe off" crayon.

Fig. 9.7c. Unedited OCLC bibliographic record.

```
OCLC: 23010817        Rec stat:   c
Entered: 19910125    Replaced: 19910125     Used: 19930329
Type:      r  Bib lvl: m  Source:    d   Lang:     eng
Type mat: g  End lvl: I  Govt pub:       Ctry:     miu
Int lvl:      Mod rec:     Tech:      n   Leng:     nnn
Desc:      a  Accomp:      Dat tp:    s   Dates:    1989,
1    040          ANO $c ANO [Modified by author]
2    007          a $b z $d c $e c
3    090          LT3600.A63 $b 08
4    049          KHNN
5    245 00       Our town $h game : $b your town / $c game
creator: Jan Parker.
6    260          Ann Arbor, Mich. : $b Aristoplay, $c 1989.
7    300          1 game (1 instruction sheet, 60 landmake
cards, 1 game board, 4 plastic stands, 1 spinner arrow,
4 boy and 4 girl playing pieces, 1 black "Wipe Off"
crayon): $b col. ; $c in box 24 x 47 x 4 cm.
8    500          "There are two levels of play, one for
non-readers ... and one for readers."
9    521          "Our Town is appropriate for use with all
children."
10   650  0       Community life.
11   650  0       Neighborhood.
12   650  0       Educational games.
13   710 2        Aristoplay, Ltd.
```

Discussion: With this game, as with many games, the accompanying material and the container contain most of the bibliographic information. The chief source of information is the object, accompanying materials, and container. One's eye goes to the top of the box for the title: *Our Town*. The playing board also has the title *Our Town*. However, when one looks at the sides and ends of the box and the instruction sheet, one sees *Our Town/Your Town*.

One could debate whether "Your Town" is part of the title proper or other title information. It seems logical to make it other title information, as it is on the OCLC record. Rules 1.1B and 1.1E state that one should transcribe exactly as to wording, but not necessarily as to punctuation and capitalization. *AACR2R* does not address what to do when the data includes a colon, slash, or equals sign, as is found on the side of the container where the creator is listed. *Cataloging Service Bulletin* (no. 44, p. 9) instructs not to transcribe unless the space may be closed up on both sides. The comma is usually substituted for the colon.

In 1991, when this record was entered into the OCLC system, brackets were not required to be placed around the GMD (*Bibliographic Formats* 245 $h).

The place of publication listed is on the bottom of the container. "Ann Arbor" is followed by "MI"; Library of Congress interpretations instructs one to use postal abbreviations if they are used on the item from where the place of publication is being transcribed (*Cataloging Service Bulletin* no. 51, p. 50). The date also appears on the bottom of the container, as "c1989." The OCLC bibliographic record should be edited to show that this is a copyright date.

Note how all the pieces are listed after "1 game" in the 300 field.

The institution that input this record included an 007 field, but according to current OCLC guidelines an 007 field is not used for games.

Fig. 9.7d. Edited OCLC bibliographic record.

```
OCLC: 23010817       Rec stat:   c
Entered: 19910125    Replaced: 19910125     Used: 19930329
Type:       r  Bib lvl: m  Source:     d   Lang:      eng
Type mat: g    End lvl: I  Govt pub:       Ctry:      miu
Int lvl:       Mod rec:    Tech:       n   Leng:      nnn
Desc:       a  Accomp:     Dat tp:     s   Dates:     1989,
1    040       ANO $c ANO [Modified by author]
3    090       LT3600.A63 $b O8
4    049       KHNN
5    245 00    Our town $h [game] : $b your town / $c
game creator, Jan Parker.
6    260       Ann Arbor, MI : $b Aristoplay, $c c1989.
7    300       1 game (1 instruction sheet, 60 landmake
cards, 1 game board, 4 plastic stands, 1 spinner arrow,
4 boy and 4 girl playing pieces, 1 black "Wipe Off"
crayon): $b col. ; $c in box 24 x 47 x 4 cm.
8    500       "There are two levels of play, one for
non-readers ... and one for readers."
9    521       "Our Town is appropriate for use with all
children."
10   650  0    Community life.
11   650  0    Neighborhood.
12   650  0    Educational games.
13   710  2    Aristoplay, Ltd.
```

Serials (Chapters 1 and 12)

Fig. 9.8a. Cover of January 1994 issue.

ADDITIONAL INFORMATION: Page four contains the ISSN number 0149-337X and information that the serial is published monthly (except semimonthly in March) by Argus Business, a division of Argus, Inc. The copyright is 1994, Atlanta, Ga. After researching in back issues of the journal, one determines that Argus took over publication of *American City & County* in September 1993. Communication Channels published it from May 1991 to August 1993. One also discovers it was published monthly (except semimonthly in March and November) through February 1993.

Fig. 9.8b. Contents page of January 1994 issue.

AMERICAN CITY & COUNTY

January 1994   Vol. 109, No. 1

22 Public Fleets

PUBLIC
FLEETS

22 **The Greening of Local Fleets**
Environmental issues are changing the way fleet administrators operate. Those who fail to address citizen and government concerns are destined to be left in the dust. □ **26** NYNJPA Fueling Operation Is Flowing More Smoothly □ **28** Computer System Eases Record Keeping □ **30** Computer System Gets Vermont Fleet Under Control

32 Solid Waste Management

COVER
STORY

32 **C&D Waste Recycling: Razing Consciousness**
With decreasing landfill space and increasing tipping fees, construction waste and demolition debris recycling is becoming an attractive alternative for municipalities and businesses alike. □ **34** Clifton Cleans Up with Clean Communities Committee □ **37** Executives Call Green Regulations Unfair □ **41** Generating Goodwill (and Energy) at City's WTE Plant □ **42** Design-Build Parnterships Save Money and Time for Municipalities

44 Disaster Reponse

DISASTER
RESPONSE AND
RECOVERY

44 **Weathering a Crisis**
Natural disasters can be predicted, but how much of the damage can be prevented? Who shoulders the responsibility when catastrophe strikes? □ **47** Grinders Hasten Tree Cleanup □ **51** Des Moines 'Rents' Power To Restore Water □ **54** GIS Guides Efforts To Contain Oil Spill □ **55** Technology 'Maps' Path for Flood Recovery

Cover photograph by Marsh Starks.

Fig. 9.8c. Unedited OCLC bibliographic record.

```
OCLC: 2243821          Rec stat:  c
Entered: 19760127   Replaced: 19930729    Used: 19940203
Type:       a Bib lvl: s  Source:        Lang:    eng
Repr:         Enc lvl:     Govt pub:      Ctry:    gau
Phys med:     Mod rec:     Conf pub: 0    Cont:
S/L ent:  0 Ser tp:  p  Frequn:    m    Alphabt: a
Desc:       a                Regulr:    n    ISDS:    1
                             Pub st:    c    Dates:   1975-999
1    010        75-647619//r91
2    040        DLC $c DLC $d OCL $d NSD [Modified by
author]
3    019        1982994 $a 1928043
4    022        0149-337X $z 1059-3659
5    030        ACCOD3
6    032        018000 $b USPS
7    042        lc $a nsdp
8    043        n-us---
9    050 00     HT101 $b .A5
10   049        KHNJ
11   210        Am. city cty.
12   222   4    The American city & county
13   245 14     The American city & county.
14   246 10     American city and county
15   260        Pittsfield, MA : $b Morgan-Grampian Pub.
Co., $c c1975-
16   300        v. : $b ill. ; $c 29 cm.
17   310        Monthly (except semimonthly in March)
18   362 0      Vol. 90, no. 9 (Sept. 1975)-
19   500        Published: Atlanta, GA : Communication
Channels, May 1991-
20   510 1      Applied science & technology $x 0003-6986
21   530        Available in microform from Xerox
University Microfilms.
22   580        March issue of each year is the Municipal
Index.
23   650   0    Cities and towns $z United States $x
Periodicals.
24   650   0    Municipal government $z United States $x
Periodicals.
25   730 0      Municipal index.
26   780 00     $t American city $x 0002-7936 $w (DLC)
11000194 $w (OCoLC)1479665
27   770 1      $t Municipal index $x 0077-2151 $w
(DLC)sc79002674 $w (OCoLC)1623690
28   850        CaAEU $a DLC $a FU $a ICRL $a In $a InU $a
KyLoU29 936 Unknown $a May 1991
```

Discussion: A serial is an item published in any medium in successive parts at intervals and intended to continue indefinitely. Some serials are hard to distinguish from monographs. In some cases, one may find a record for a specific issue of a serial in a book format and a record for all the issues of the item in a serial format. Serials pose unique challenges to copy catalogers, mainly because they are published in intervals. Often one does not have all the issues at the time of cataloging. The title and publisher may have changed one or more times during the life of the serial. Publishers can also merge two titles or split one title into two titles.

In this case, the title has changed as noted in the 780 field. The 780 field indicates that this title continues *American City*. It also has a special issue, as noted in the 580 and 770 fields. The 500 field needs to be edited to show when Argus took over publication. The first indicator in the 245 field should be "0," as it is a title main entry.

A serial record often has several title fields. In this case, there are abbreviated key title (210 field), key title (222 field), title (245 field), and varying form of title (246 field) fields. Other fields often found in serials records are current publication frequency (310 field), numeric, alphabetic, chronological designation area (field 362), citation/reference note (510 field), additional physical form available note (530 field), and succeeding entry (785 field).

Fig. 9.8d. Edited OCLC bibliographic record.

```
OCLC: 2243821          Rec stat:  c
Entered: 19760127    Replaced: 19930729    Used: 19940203
Type:      a  Bib lvl: s  Source:        Lang:    eng
Repr:         Enc lvl:    Govt pub:      Ctry:    gau
Phys med:     Mod rec:    Conf pub: 0    Cont:
S/L ent:  0  Ser tp:  p  Frequn:    m    Alphabt: a
Desc:      a             Regulr:    n    ISDS:    1
                         Pub st:    c    Dates:   1975-999
1    010        75-647619//r91
2    040        DLC $c DLC $d OCL $d NSD [Modified by
author]
3    019        1982994 $a 1928043
4    022        0149-337X $z 1059-3659
5    030        ACCOD3
6    032        018000 $b USPS
7    042        lc $a nsdp
8    043        n-us---
9    050 00     HT101 $b .A5
10   049        KHNJ
11   210        Am. city cty.
12   222  4     The American city & county
13   245 04     The American city & county.
14   246 10     American city and county
15   260        Pittsfield, MA : $b Morgan-Grampian Pub.
Co., $c c1975-
16.  300        v. : $b ill. ; $c 29 cm.
17   310        Monthly (except semi-monthly in Mar.) $b
1993-
18   321        Monthly $b 1975-1991
19   321        Monthly (except semi-monthly in Mar, and
Nov.) $b 1992-
20   362 0      Vol. 90, no. 9 (Sept. 1975)-
21   500        Published: Atlanta, GA : Communication
Channels, May 1991-Aug. 1993; Argus Business, Sept.
1993-
22   510 1      Applied science & technology $x 0003-6986
23   530        Available in microform from Xerox
University Microfilms.
24   580        One March issue of each year is the
Municipal Index.
25   650  0     Cities and towns $z United States $x
Periodicals.
26   650  0     Municipal government $z United States $x
Periodicals.
27   730 00     Municipal index.
28   780 00     $t American city $x 0002-7936 $w (DLC)
11000194 $w (OCoLC)1479665
29   770 1      $t Municipal index $x 0077-2151 $w
(DLC)sc79002674 $w (OCoLC)1623690
30   850        CaAEU $a DLC $a FU $a ICRL $a In $a InU $a
KyLoU
31   936        Unknown $a May 1991
```

Part

Practice in Copy Cataloging

10

Exercises in
Copy Cataloging

Some exercises in copy cataloging for the reader to perform are given in this chapter. The title page, part of the title page verso, and other relevant information about an item are provided. These are followed by an unedited, simulated OCLC record prepared by the author. One or more fields in each record needs to be edited. The reader will need to use *Anglo-American Cataloguing Rules*, 2d edition, 1988 revision and the 1993 amendments and OCLC's *Bibliographic Formats and Standards* while doing the exercises.

Answers in the form of edited records and comments appear in the next chapter. A rule number will be given if editing is based on an *AACR2R* rule. If editing is based on *Bibliographic Formats* requirements, the field, tag, indicator, or subfield code will be listed. The number and page will be given if the editing is based on interpretations found in *Cataloging Service Bulletin*. For these exercises, the reader will not have to consult an authority file unless directed to do so by a supervisor. Some series authority information has been given.

Fig. 10.1a. Title page.

REEF

A SAFARI THROUGH THE CORAL WORLD

Photographs and text by

JEREMY STAFFORD-DEITSCH

SIERRA CLUB BOOKS   SAN FRANCISCO

Fig. 10.1b. Verso of title page.

The photograph on the half-title page shows the shapes and colours of the reef reflected in the sinuous undersurface of the Red Sea.

The photograph opposite the title page shows a roving grouper *Plectropomus maculatus* in the Red Sea, with a grey reef shark *Carcharhinus amblyrhynchos* in the background.

The Sierra Club, founded in 1892 by John Muir, has devoted itself to the study and protection of the earth's scenic and ecological resources – mountains, wetlands, woodlands, wild shores and rivers, deserts and plains. The publishing program of the Sierra Club offers books to the public as a nonprofit educational service in the hope that they may enlarge the public's understanding of the Club's basic concerns. The point of view expressed in each book, however, does not necessarily represent that of the Club. The Sierra Club has some sixty chapters coast to coast, in Canada, Hawaii, and Alaska. For information about how you may participate in its programs to preserve wilderness and the quality of life, please address inquiries to Sierra Club, 730 Polk Street, San Francisco, CA 94109.

Library of Congress Cataloging-in-Publication Data

Stafford-Deitsch, Jeremy
   Reef: a safari through the coral world / by Jeremy Stafford-Deitsch.
     p. cm.
   Includes index.
   ISBN 0-87156-649-4
   1. Coral reef biology. 2. Coral reefs and islands – Pictorial works.
3. Coral reef fauna – Pictorial works. 4. Coral reef biology – Pictorial
works. I. Title.
QH95.B.S73 1991
574.5'2637 – dc20   90-25432
                                        CIP

AN EDDISON · SADD EDITION

Edited, designed and produced by
Eddison Sadd Editions Limited
St Chad's Court
146B King's Cross Road
London WC1X 9DH

Phototypeset in Meridien by Ampersand Typesetting
(Bournemouth) Limited, England
Origination by Scantrans, Singapore
Printing and binding in Hong Kong
Produced by Mandarin Offset

ADDITIONAL INFORMATION: The pagination is 6–200. There are many color illustrations. The height is 28.2 centimeters. A bibliography starts on page 194 and goes through page 195. The heading at the top of page 194 is: "Further Reading & Useful Addresses." There is an index.

Fig. 10.1c. Unedited OCLC bibliographic record.

```
OCLC: 22887888        Rec stat:  p
Entered: 19901120    Replaced: 19920307      Used: 19930310
Type: a  Bib lvl:  m  Source:         Lang:    eng
Repr:     Enc lvl:     Conf pub:  0   Ctry:    cau
Indx: 1  Mod rec:     Govt pub:       Cont:    b
Desc: a  Int lvl:     Festschr:  0    Illus:   a
          F/B         0  Dat tp:    s    Dates:   1991,
1    010          90-25432
2    040          DLC $c DLC [Modified by author]
3    020          0871566494 : $c $25.00
4    050 00       QH95.8 $b .S73 1991
5    082 00       574.5/2637 $2 20
6    049          KHNN
7    100 1        Stafford-Deitsch, Jeremy.
8    245 10       Reef $b a safari through the coral world /
$c photographs and text by Jeremy Stafford-Deitsch.
9    260          San Francisco $b Sierra Club Books $c
c1991.
10   300          200 p. $b col. ill. $c 28 cm.
11   504          Includes bibliographical references and
index.
12   650  0       Coral reef biology.
13   650  0       Coral reefs and islands $x Pictorial
works.
14   650          Coral reef fauna $x Pictorial works.
15   650          Coral reef biology $x Pictorial works.
```

Rewrite the fields that need editing.

Fig. 10.2a. Title page.

A NATION OF CHANGE AND NOVELTY

Radical politics, religion and literature in seventeenth-century England

'England, that Nation of Change and Novelty'

- La Nuche, a 'Spanish courtesan' in *The Rovers: Or, The Banished Cavaliers*, by Aphra Behn

CHRISTOPHER HILL

London and New York

Fig. 10.2b. Verso of title page.

First published 1990 by Routledge
11 New Fetter Lane, London EC4P 4EE

Simultaneously published in the USA and Canada
by Routledge
a division of Routledge, Chapman and Hall, Inc.
29 West 35th Street, New York, NY 10001

© 1990 Christopher Hill

Typeset in 10/12 pt Baskerville by
Colset Private Limited, Singapore
Printed in Great Britain by
T. J. Press (Padstow) Ltd, Padstow, Cornwall

British Library Cataloguing in Publication Data

Hill, Christopher *1912-*
A nation of change and novelty: Radical politics,
religion and literature in seventeenth-century England.
1. England, 1603-1714
I. Title
942.06

ISBN 0-415-04833-8

Library of Congress Cataloging in Publication Data

Also available

ADDITIONAL INFORMATION: The pagination is vi–xii, followed by 1–272. There are no illustrations. The height is 22.3 centimeters. On many pages there are bibliographical references at the bottom of the page. There is an index.

Fig 10.2c. Unedited OCLC bibliographic record.

```
OCLC: 23771145        Rec stat:  p
Entered: 19900530    Replaced: 19920131    Used: 19930330
Type: a  Bib lvl:  m  Source:          Lang:    eng
Repr:    Enc lvl:     Conf pub:  0  Ctry:    enk
Indx: 1  Mod rec:     Govt pub:      Cont:
Desc: a  Int lvl:     Festschr:  0  Illus:
         F/B:      0  Dat tp:    s  Dates:   1990,
1    010         90-38362
2    040         DLC $c DLC $d UKM [Modified by author]
3    015         GB90-638
4    019         20415246
5    020         0415048338
6    043         e-uk-en $a e-uk---
7    050 00      DA380 $b .H49 1990
8    082 00      942.06 $2 20
9    049         KHNN
10   100 1       Hill, Christopher, 1912-
11   245 10      A nation of change and novelty : $b
radical politics, religion, and literature in
seventeenth century England / $c Christopher Hill.
12   260         London : $b Routledge, $c 1990.
13   300         xii, 272 p. : $b 23 cm.
14   500         Includes bibliographical references and
index.
15   650  0      England $x Civilization $z 17th century.
16   650  0      England $x Church history $z 17th century.
17   650  0      Great Britain $x Politics and government
$z History and criticism.
18   650  0      English literature $y Early modern, 1500-
1700 $x History and criticism.
19   651  4      Great Britain $x History $y Stuarts, 1603-
1714.
20   653         England, 1603-1714.
```

Rewrite the fields that need editing.

Fig. 10.3a. Title Page.

OXFORD STUDIES IN PROBABILITY · 2

Poisson Approximation

A. D. BARBOUR

Department of Applied Mathematics
University of Zurich

LARS HOLST

Department of Mathematics
Royal Institute of Technology
Stockholm

SVANTE JANSON

Department of Mathematics
Uppsala University

CLARENDON PRESS · OXFORD
1992

Fig. 10.3b. Verso of title page.

Oxford University Press, Walton Street, Oxford OX2 6DP

Oxford New York Toronto
Delhi Bombay Calcutta Madras Karachi
Petaling Jaya Singapore Hong Kong Tokyo
Nairobi Dar es Salaam Cape Town
Melbourne Auckland
and associated companies in
Berlin Ibadan

Oxford is a trade mark of Oxford University Press

Published in the United States
by Oxford University Press, New York

© A. D. Barbour, Lars Holst, Svante Janson, 1992

A catalogue record for this book is available from the British Library

Library of Congress Cataloging in Publication Data
(Data available)

ISBN 0–19–852235–5

Text typeset by the authors using Lam S-TEX
Printed and bound in Great Britain
by Biddles Ltd, Guildford and King's Lynn

ADDITIONAL INFORMATION: The pagination is x, followed by one unnumbered page, followed by 2–277. There are no illustrations. The height is 24 centimeters. There is an index. At the top of the bibliography is the heading "References." The bibliography would start on page 264 if it were numbered, and it extends through page 272. On the front cover, two series are listed: Oxford Studies in Probability at the top and Oxford Science Publications at the bottom. There is also a series title page for Oxford Studies in Probability. According to the local series authority file, the series Oxford Studies in Probability is traced in that form and is numbered. The series Oxford Science Publications is not traced.

Fig. 10.3c. Unedited OCLC bibliographic record.

```
OCLC: 24953861        Rec stat:  c
Entered: 19911113     Replaced: 19921117    Used: 19930305
Type: a  Bib lvl:  m  Source:         Lang:    eng
Repr:    Enc lvl:     Conf pub:  0    Ctry:    enk
Indx: 1  Mod rec:     Govt pub:       Cont:    b
Desc: a  Int lvl:     Festschr:  0    Illus:
         F/B:      0  Dat tp:    s    Dates:   1992,
1    010         91-43589
2    040         DLC $c DLC $d UKM $d FPU [Modified by
author]
3    015         GB92-13922
4    019         26363363
5    020         0198522355 (cloth) : $c 30.00 (est.)
($47.50 U.S.)
6    050 00      QA273.6 $b .B377 1992
7    082 00      519.2/4 $2 20
8    049         KHNN
9    100 1       Barbour, A. D.
10   245 10      Poisson approximation / $c A.D. Barbour,
Lars Holst, and Svante Janson.
11   260         Oxford [England] ; $b Clarendon Press, $c
1992.
12   300         x, 277 p. : $c 24 cm.
13   440  0      Oxford studies in probability  $v 2
14   440  0      Oxford science publications
15   504         Includes bibliographical references (p.
264-272) and index.
16   650  7      Poisson, distribution de. $2 ram
17   650  7      Approximation, theorie de l'. $2 ram
18   650  0      Poisson distribution.
19   650  0      Approximation theory.
20   653  0      Approximation
21   700  1      Holst, Lars.
22   700  1      Janson, Svante.
```

Rewrite the fields that need editing.

Fig. 10.4a. Series title page.

DUNQUIN SERIES

Rare monographs and translations, symbolism, and depth psychology

- 2: The Logos of the Soul, Evangelos Christou
- 3: Psyche: On the Development of the Soul (Part One), Carl Gustav Carus
- 4: Pan and the Nightmare, Wilhelm Roscher-James Hillman
- 7: Hermes: Guide of Souls, Karl Kerényi
- 8: Suicide and the Soul, James Hillman
- 9: Athene: Virgin and Mother, Karl Kerényi
- 10: The Homeric Hymns, tr. Charles Boer
- 11: Goddesses of Sun and Moon, Karl Kerényi
- 12: The Book of Life, Marsilio Ficino, tr. Charles Boer
- 14: Dionysus: Myth and Cult, Walter F. Otto
- 15: An Anthology of Greek Tragedy, ed. A. Cook and E. Dolin
- 16: Apollo: The Wind, the Spirit, and the God, Karl Kerényi
- 17: Ovid's Metamorphoses, tr. Charles Boer

Fig. 10.4b. Title page.

Ovid's Metamorphoses

translated by
CHARLES BOER

Spring Publications, Inc.
Dallas, Texas

Fig. 10.4c. Verso of title page.

Cover painting: "The Haitian God Damballah Turning Spirits out of His Body,"
by Levoy Exil, 1986, private collection. Cover photograph by Julia Hillman.
Cover design and production by Bharati Bhatia. Interior art by Mary Vernon.

International distributors:
Spring; Postfach; 8803 Rüschlikon; Switzerland.
Japan Spring Sha, Inc.; 12-10, 2-Chome,
    Nigawa Takamaru; Takarazuka 665, Japan.
Element Books Ltd; Longmead Shaftesbury; Dorset SP7 8PL; England.
Astam Books Pty. Ltd.; 27B Llewellyn St.;
    Balmain, Sydney, N.S.W. 2041; Australia.
Libros e Imagenes; Apdo. Post 40-085; México D.F. 06140; México.

Library of Congress Cataloging-in-Publication Data
Ovid, 43 B.C.-17 or 18 A.D.
    [Metamorphoses. English]
    Ovid's Metamorphoses / translated by Charles Boer.
        p. cm. – (Dunquin series ; 17)
    Translation of: Metamorphoses.
    ISBN 0-88214-217-8
        1. Metamorphosis – Poetry. 2. Mythology, Classical – Poetry.
I. Boer, Charles, 1939-   II. Title.
PA6522.M2B6 1989
873'.01 – dc19   89-4223
                                                             CIP

ADDITIONAL INFORMATION: The pagination is viii–xxi, followed by four
unnumbered pages, followed by 4–359. An identical small decoration is on
the first page of each chapter. The height is 22.8 centimeters. The bibliography is on page xxi without any heading. There is no index. There is a
series title page for Dunquin Series. According to the local series file,
Dunquin Series is traced and numbered.

Fig. 10.4d. Unedited OCLC bibliographic record.

```
OCLC: 19269647        Rec stat:   c
Entered: 19890130     Replaced: 19921024     Used: 19930405
Type: a  Bib lvl:  m  Source:          Lang:     eng
Repr:    Enc lvl:     Conf pub:  0     Ctry:     txu
Indx: 1  Mod rec:     Govt pub:        Cont:
Desc: a  Int lvl:     Festschr:  0     Illus:
         F/B:      0  Dat tp:    s     Dates:    1989,
1    010          89-4223//r92
2    040          DLC $c DLC [Modified by author]
3    020          0882142178
4    041 1        eng$h lat
5    050 00       PA6522 $b .M2 B6 1989
6    082 00       873/.01 $2 19
7    049          KHNN
8    100 1        Ovid, $d 43 B.C.-17 or 18 A.D.
9    240 00       Metamorphoses. $1 English.
10   245 10       Ovid's Metamorphoses / $c translated by
Charles Boer.
11   260          Dallas, Tex. : $b Spring Publications, $c
c1989.
12   300          xxi, 359 p. ; $c 23 cm.
13   490 0        Dunquin series : $v 17
14   500          Translation of: Metamorphoses.
15   650  0       Metamorphosis $x Mythology $x Poetry.
16   650  0       Mythology, Classical $x Poetry.
17   700 1        Boer, Charles, $d 1939-
```

Rewrite the fields that need editing.

Fig. 10.5a. Title page.

Federal Regulatory Directory

Sixth Edition

With a revised introduction by
Cornelius M. Kerwin
The American University

Congressional Quarterly
Washington, D.C.

Fig. 10.5b. Page following title verso page.

Congressional Quarterly

Congressional Quarterly, an editorial research service and publishing company, serves clients in the fields of news, education, business and government. It combines Congressional Quarterly's specific coverage of Congress, government and politics with the more general subject range of an affiliated service, Editorial Research Reports.

Congressional Quarterly publishes the *Congressional Quarterly Weekly Report* and a variety of books, including college political science textbooks under the CQ Press imprint and public affairs paperbacks on developing issues and events. CQ also publishes information directories and reference books on the federal government, national elections and politics, including the *Guide to the Presidency*, the *Guide to Congress*, the *Guide to the U.S. Supreme Court*, the *Guide to U.S. Elections*, *Politics in America* and *Congress A to Z: CQ's Ready Reference Encyclopedia*. The *CQ Almanac*, a compendium of legislation for one session of Congress, is published each year. *Congress and the Nation*, a record of government for a presidential term, is published every four years.

CQ publishes *The Congressional Monitor*, a daily report on current and future activities of congressional committees, and several newsletters including *Congressional Insight*, a weekly analysis of congressional action, and *Campaign Practices Reports*, a semimonthly update on campaign laws.

An electronic online information system, Washington Alert, provides immediate access to CQ's databases of legislative action, votes, schedules, profiles and analyses.

The Library of Congress cataloged the first edition of this title as follows:

Federal regulatory directory.   1979/80—
Washington. Congressional Quarterly Inc.

KF5406.A15F4   0195-749X   79-644368

ISBN 0-87187-553-5
ISSN 0195-749X

Printed in the United States of America

ADDITIONAL INFORMATION: The pagination is ix–xiii, followed by one unnumbered page, followed by xv–xvi, followed by 1–986. There are black-and-white illustrations. The height is 23.6 centimeters. There are bibliographies throughout the book. The title page verso is blank, but the following page has information usually found on the title page verso.

Fig. 10.5c. Unedited OCLC bibliographic record.

```
OCLC: 22400239       Rec stat:  c
Entered: 19900918    Replaced: 19910130     Used: 19910521
Type: a  Bib lvl:  m  Source:      d    Lang:    eng
Repr:    Enc lvl:  I  Conf pub:   0    Ctry:    dcu
Indx: 1  Mod rec:     Govt pub:        Cont:    r
Desc: a  Int lvl:     Festschr:   0    Illus:   a
         F/B:      0  Dat tp:      s    Dates:   1990,
1    040        APT $c APT $d AEV [Modified by author]
2    020        $z 0871875533
3    090        JK610 $b F29
4    049        KHNR
5    245 10     Federal regulatory directory.
6    250        Sixth edition.
7    260        Washington, D.C. : $b Congressional
Quarterly, inc., $c c1990.
8    300        xiii, 986 p. : $b ill.; $c 24 cm.
9    500        Cover title: Congressional Quarterly's
Federal regulatory directory.
10   651  0     United States $x Executive departments $x
Directories.
11   650  0     Administrative procedure $z United States.
12   710  2     Congressional Quarterly, inc.
```

Rewrite the fields that need editing.

Fig. 10.6a. Title Page.

Terry McMillan

——

WAITING TO

E X H A L E

——

VIKING

Fig. 10.6b. Verso of title page.

VIKING
Published by the Penguin Group
Viking Penguin, a division of Penguin Books USA Inc.,
375 Hudson Street, New York, New York 10014, U.S.A.
Penguin Books Ltd, 27 Wrights Lane,
London W8 5TZ, England
Penguin Books Australia Ltd, Ringwood,
Victoria, Australia
Penguin Books Canada Ltd, 10 Alcorn Avenue, Suite 300,
Toronto, Ontario, Canada M4V 3B2
Penguin Books (N.Z.) Ltd, 182–190 Wairau Road,
Auckland 10, New Zealand

Penguin Books Ltd, Registered Offices:
Harmondsworth, Middlesex, England

First published in 1992 by Viking Penguin,
a division of Penguin Books USA Inc.

22   23   24   25   26   27   28

Copyright © Terry McMillan, 1992
All rights reserved

This is a work of fiction. It is not meant to depict, portray, or represent any
particular gender, real persons, or group of people. All the characters, incidents,
and dialogues are products of the author's imagination and are not to be construed
as real. Any resemblance to actual events or persons, living or dead, is purely
coincidental.

Grateful acknowledgment is made for permission to reprint an excerpt from "(If
There Was) Any Other Way" by Paul Bliss. © 1990 Paul Bliss Music. All rights
controlled and administered by EMI April Music Inc. All rights reserved. International copyright secured. Used by permission.

LIBRARY OF CONGRESS CATALOGING IN PUBLICATION DATA
McMillan, Terry.
Waiting to exhale / by Terry McMillan.
p.   cm.
ISBN 0–670–83980–9
I. Title.
PS3563.C3868W35   1992
813'.54—dc20   91–46564

Printed in the United States of America
Set in Caslon 540
Designed by Kathryn Parise

Without limiting the rights under copyright
reserved above, no part of this publication
may be reproduced, stored in or introduced into a
retrieval system, or transmitted, in any form,
or by any means (electronic, mechanical, photocopying,
recording or otherwise), without the prior written
permission of both the copyright owner and
the above publisher of this book.

ADDITIONAL INFORMATION: The pagination is ix–xiv, followed by two
unnumbered pages, followed by 1–409. There are no illustrations. The
height is 23.4 centimeters. Because this is a fiction book, there are no
bibliographical references or index.

Fig. 10.6c. Unedited OCLC Bibliographic record.

```
OCLC: 25048160        Rec stat:  c
Entered: 19911211    Replaced: 19931113    Used: 19950314
Type:      a  Bib lvl: m  Source:       Lang:    eng
Repr:         Enc lvl:    Conf pub: 0   Ctry:    nyu
Indx:      0  Mod rec:    Govt pub:     Cont:
Desc:      a  Int lvl:    Festschr: 0   Illus:
              F/B:     0  Dat tp:   s   Dates:  1992,
1    010       91-46564//r932
2    040       DLC $c DLC $d OCL [Modified by author]
3    020       0670839809 : $c $22.00 ($27.90 Can.)
4    043       n-us-az
5    050 00    PS3563.C3868 $b W35 1992
6    082 00    813/.54 $2 20
7    049       KHNN
8    100 2     McMillan, Terry.
9    245 10    Waiting to exhale / $c Terry McMillan.
10   260       New York, N.Y., U.S.A. : $b Viking, $c
1992.
11   300       xiv, 409 p. : $c 24 cm.
12   651 0     Afro-American women $x Fiction.
13   651 0     Afro-American men $x Fiction.
14   650 0     Friendship $x Fiction.
15   650 0     Phoenix (Ariz.) $x Fiction.
16   655 7     Love stories. $2 gsafd
```

Rewrite the fields that need editing.

Fig. 10.7a. Series title page.

Lecture Notes in Computer Science   602

Edited by G. Goos and J. Hartmanis

Advisory Board: W. Brauer   D. Gries   J. Stoer

Figures 10.7a–10.7c. Reprinted with permission of Springer-Verlag from *Computer Assisted Learning* edited by Ivan Tometk. Berlin: Springer-Verlag. Copyright © Springer-Verlag Berlin Heidelberg, 1992.

Fig. 10.7b. Title page.

I. Tomek (Ed.)

Computer Assisted Learning

4th International Conference, ICCAL '92
Wolfville, Nova Scotia, Canada, June 17-20, 1992
Proceedings

Springer-Verlag
Berlin Heidelberg New York
London Paris Tokyo
Hong Kong Barcelona
Budapest

Fig. 10.7c. Verso of title page.

Series Editors

Gerhard Goos
Universität Karlsruhe
Postfach 69 80
Vincenz-Priessnitz-Straße 1
W-7500 Karlsruhe, FRG

Juris Hartmanis
Department of Computer Science
Cornell University
5149 Upson Hall
Ithaca, NY 14853. USA

Volume Editor

Ivan Tomek
Jodrey School of Computer Science, Acada University
Wolfville, Nova Scotia BOP 1X0, Canada

ISBN 3-540-55578-1 Springer-Verlag Berlin Heidelberg New York
ISBN 0-387-55578-1 Springer-Verlag New York Berlin Heidelberg

© Springer-Verlag Berlin Heidelberg 1992
Printed in Germany

ADDITIONAL INFORMATIONAL: The pagination is vi, followed by one unnumbered page, followed by viii–x, followed by one unnumbered page, followed by 2–615. There are black-and-white illustrations. The height is 24.2 centimeters. There are bibliographies throughout the book. There is no index. According to the local authority file, the series is traced as Lecture Notes in Computer Science. It is a numbered series.

Fig. 10.7d. Unedited OCLC bibliographic record.

```
OCLC: 25833324        Rec stat:  p
Entered: 19920423     Replaced: 19920801     Used: 19920112
Type:       a  Bib lvl: m  Source:         Lang:     eng
Repr:          Enc lvl:    Conf pub: 0     Ctry:     gw
Indx:       0  Mod rec:    Govt pub:       Cont:     b
Desc:       a  Int lvl:    Festschr: 0     Illus:    a
               F/B:      0  Date tp:  s     Dates:    1992,
1    010          92-16823
2    040          DLC $c DLC $e OCL $d NLC [Modified by
author]
3    020          3540555781 (Springer-Verlag Berlin
Heidelberg New York)
4    020          0387555781 (Springer-Verlag New York
Berlin Heidelberg)
5    050 00       LB1028.5 $b I11635 1992
6    082 00       371.3/34 $2 20
7    049          KHNN
8    245 00       Computer assisted learning : $b 4th
International Conference, ICCAL '92, Wolfville, Nova
Scotia, Canada, June 17-20, 1992 : proceedings / $c I.
Tomek (ed.).
9    260          Berlin ; $a New York : $b Springer-Verlag,
$c c1992.
10   300          x, 615 p. : $b ill. ; $c 25 cm.
11   440  0       Lecture notes in computer science ; $v 602
12   504          Includes bibliographical references.
13   650  0       Computer-assisted instruction $x
Congresses.
14   650  0       Intelligent tutoring systems $x
Congresses.
15   650  0       Education $x Data porocessing $x
Congresses.
16   700  1       Tomek, Ivan
17   711 20       ICCAL '92 $d (1992 : $c Wolfville, N.S.)
```

Rewrite the fields that need editing.

Fig. 10.8a. Part of top of container.

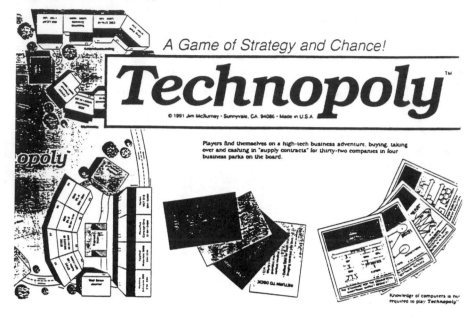

Fig. 10.8b. Part of side of container.

2 to 4 players, ages 10 to adult
See box bottom for additional information ⇩

ADDITIONAL INFORMATION: The game is in color. It is in a container that has the dimensions of 3 x 50 x 26 centimeters. The following pieces are included: one board, play money, 25 Wall Street Journal cards, 26 Federal Register cards, four playing pieces, one die, 32 computer supply contracts, one directions leaflet, one glossary leaflet, one score sheet packet, and one sample score sheet.

Fig. 10.8c. Unedited OCLC bibliographic record.

```
OCLC: 25813085        Rec stat:   c
Entered: 19920514    Replaced: 19920514    Used: 19930114
Type:       r  Bib lvl: m  Source:     d  Lang:     eng
Type mat: g  Enc lvl: I  Govt pub:      Ctry:     cau
Int lvl:  e  Mod rec:    Tech:       n  Leng:     nnn
Desc:       a  Accomp:     Dat tp:     s  Dates:    1991,
1     040        KHN $c KHN [Modified by author]
2     020        0962947105
3     090        LT2360.M23 $b T4
4     049        KHNN
5     245 00     Technopoly
6     260        Sunnyvale, Calif. : $b Jim McBurney, $c
c1991.
7     300        1 game (1 board, play money, 25 Wall
street journal cards, 26 Federal register cards, 4
playing pieces,1 die, 32 computer supply contracts, 1
directions leaflet, 1 glossary leaflet, 1 score sheet
packet, 1 sample score sheet) : $c col. : $e in box 3 x
50 x 26 cm.
8     500        For ages 10 to adult.
9     520        A board game designed to simulate the
high-tech business world.
10    650. 0     Management games.
11    650 1      Management games.
```

Rewrite the fields that need editing.

Fig. 10.9a. Cover of June 1994 issue.

Mecklermedia

ADDITIONAL INFORMATION: *Computers in Libraries* is published by Mecklermedia Corporation. It has illustrations and is 28 centimeters in height. Prior to 1993 it was published monthly with a combined issue in July/August. Starting in 1993 it has been published monthly except for combined issues in July/August and November/December. It has been selectively indexed in *Computer & Control Abstracts*, *Electrical and Electronic Abstracts*, and *Physics Abstracts* since February 1989. The ISSNs for these abstract services are 0036-8113, 0036-8105, and 0036-8091 respectively. *Computers in Libraries* is also available in microfiche from University Microfilms.

Fig. 10.9b. Contents page of June 1994 issue.

On the Cover

Our specially commisioned cover is the work of Dennis Hayes. he is the Assistant Art Director at the Connecticut Law Tribune in Fairfield, Connecticut.

32

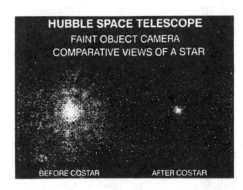

40

Columns

42

Internet Librarian

Departments

Computers in Libraries (ISSN 1041-7915) is published ten times per year (July/August, November/December combined issues) by Mecklermedia Corporation, 11 Ferry Lane West, Westport, CT 06880, (203) 226-6967; Internet: meckler@jvnc.net; CompuServe: 70373.616; AppleLink: meckler. Copyright © 1994 Mecklermedia Corporation. All rights reserved. Subscription: $87.00 (£67.50) per year. Please add $18 for subscriptions to Canada and Central and South America.

Fig. 10.9c. Unedited OCLC bibliographic record.

```
OCLC: 18848244        Rec stat:  c
Entered: 19881206     Replaced: 19910823     Used: 19920309
Type:       a  Bib lvl: s  Source:    d   Lang:     eng
Repr:          Enc lvl:    Govt pub:       Ctry:     ctu
Phys med:      Mod rec:    Conf pub: 0     Cont:     ^^^^
S/L ent:    0  Ser tp:  p  Frequn:    m    Alphabt: a
Desc:       a              Regulr:    n    ISDS:    1
                           Pub st:    c    Dates:   1989-9999
1    010          89-641907    $z sn88-3549
2    040          NSD $c NSD $d NYG $d HUL $d COO $d HUL $d
DLC $dNST $d DLC $d OCL $d DLC $d NST $d EYM $d IUL $d
OCL $d NST$d HUL $d NSD $d IUL $d AGL $d NST $d MYG $d
NST $d CAS $d NST $d KHN [Modified by author]
3    022 0        1041-7915
4    050 00       Z678.9.A1 $b S6
5    049          KHNJ
6    210 0        Comput. libr.
7    222  0       Computers in libraries.
8    245 00       Computers in libraries.
9    260          Westport, CT : $b Meckler, $c c1988-
10   310          Monthly (except for a combined issue in
July/Aug.)
11   500          Title from cover.
12   650  0       Libraries $x Automation $x Periodicals.
13   650  0       Library science $x Computer programs $x
Periodicals.
14   650  0       Minicomputers $x Library applications $x
Periodicals.
15   650  0       Information technology $x Periodicals.
16   780 00       $t Small computers in libraries $x 0275-
6722 $w (DLC)  84649849 $w (OCoLC)7208194
17   780 05       $t Systems librarian & automation review
$g June 1989 $x 0890-8354 $w (DLC)sn 86002554 $w
(OCoLC)14473187
18   780 05       $t Small computers in libraries. Buyer's
guide & consultant directory $g 1989 $x 0896-9485 $w
(DLC) 87658700 $w (OCoLC)16349013
19   936          Vol. 9, no. 3 (Mar. 1989) LIC
```

Rewrite the fields that need editing.

11

Answers to Exercises

This chapter contains the edited OCLC bibliographic records for the exercises in chapter 10. Figure 11.1 is the edited OCLC bibliographic record for Figures 10.1a-10.1c, etc. The fields that have been edited are listed below the edited OCLC bibliographic record with an explanation of the editing.

Fig. 11.1. Edited OCLC bibliographic record.

```
OCLC: 22887888      Rec stat:  p
Entered: 19901120   Replaced: 19920307    Used: 19930310
Type: a  Bib lvl:  m  Source:           Lang:    eng
Repr:    Enc lvl:     Conf pub:  0  Ctry:    cau
Indx: 1  Mod rec:     Govt pub:       Cont:    b
Desc: a  Int lvl:     Festschr:  0  Illus:   a
         F/B         0  Dat tp:    s   Dates:   1991,
1    010         90-25432
2    040         DLC $c DLC [Modified by author]
3    020         0871566494 : $c $25.00
4    050 00      QH95.8 $b .S73 1991
8    092         574.52637 $b St13, 1991
6    049         KHNN
7    100 2       Stafford-Deitsch, Jeremy.
8    245 10      Reef : $b a safari through the coral world
/ $c photographs and text by Jeremy Stafford-Deitsch.
9    260         San Francisco : $b Sierra Club Books, $c
c1991.
10   300         200 p. : $b col. ill. ; $c 29 cm.
11   504         Includes bibliographical references (p.
194-195) and index.
12   650   0     Coral reef biology.
13   650   0     Coral reefs and islands $x Pictorial
works.
14   650   0     Coral reef fauna $x Pictorial works.
15   650   0     Coral reef biology $x Pictorial works.
```

Changes:

```
8    092         574.52637 $b St13, 1991 (Slash removed; Cutter
number from C.A. Cutter's Three-Figure Author Table and date added)
7    100 2       Stafford-Deitsch, Jeremy. (First indicator)
8    245 10      Reef : $b a safari through the coral world
/ $c photographs and text by Jeremy Stafford-Deitsch.
(Prescribed punctuation for other title information; Rule 1.1A1 or 2.1A1)
9    260         San Francisco : $b Sierra Club Books, $c
c1991. (Prescribed punctuation for publisher and date; Rule 1.4A1 or
2.4A1)
10   300         200 p. : $b col. ill. ; $c 29 cm.
(Prescribed punctuation for illustrative matter and dimensions and rounding
to the next whole centimeter; Rules 1.5A1 or 2.5A1 and 2.5D1)
11   504         Includes bibliographical references (p.
194-195) and index. (If the bibliographical references are all
together, the pages are given. Cataloging Service Bulletin no. 47, p. 33)
14   650   0     Coral reef fauna $x Pictorial works.
(Second indicator)
15   650   0     Coral reef biology $x Pictorial works.
(Second indicator)
```

Fig. 11.2. Edited OCLC bibliographic record.

```
OCLC: 23771145       Rec stat:  p
Entered: 19900530    Replaced: 19920131    Used: 19930330
Type: a  Bib lvl:  m  Source:        Lang:    eng
Repr:    Enc lvl:     Conf pub:  0   Ctry:    enk
Indx: 1  Mod rec:     Govt pub:      Cont:    b
Desc: a  Int lvl:     Festschr:  0   Illus:
         F/B:       0 Dat tp:    s   Dates:   1990,
1    010        90-38362
2    040        DLC $c DLC $d UKM [Modified by author]
3    015        GB90-638
4    019        20415246
5    020        0415048338
6    043        e-uk-en $a e-uk---
7    050 00     DA380 $b .H49 1990
8    092        942.06 $b H55, 1990
9    049        KHNN
10   100 1      Hill, Christopher, $d 1912-
11   245 12     A nation of change and novelty : $b
radical politics, religion, and literature in
seventeenth century England / $c Christopher Hill.
12   260        London ; $a New York : $b Routledge, $c
1990.
13   300        xii, 272 p. ; $c 23 cm.
14   504        Includes bibliographical references and
index.
15   651  0     England $x Civilization $y 17th century.
16   651  0     England $x Church history $y 17th century.
17   651  0     Great Britain  $x Politics and government
$x History and criticism.
18   650  0     English literature $y Early modern, 1500-
1700 $x History and criticism.
19   651  4     Great Britain $x History $y Stuarts, 1603-
1714.
20   653        England, 1603-1714.
```

Changes:

```
OCLC: 23771145        Rec stat:  p
Entered: 19900530    Replaced: 19920131    Used: 19930330
Type: a  Bib lvl:  m  Source:          Lang:    eng
Repr:       Enc lvl:     Conf pub:  0   Ctry:    enk
Indx: 1  Mod rec:      Govt pub:      Cont:    b
Desc: a  Int lvl:      Festschr:  0   Illus:
         F/B:      0  Dat tp:    s    Dates:   1990,
```
(These are bibliographical references)
8   092   942.06 $b H55, 1990 (Cutter number from *C.A.*
Cutter's Three-Figure Author Table and date added)
10   100 1   Hill, Christopher, $d 1912- (Subfield code for
date)
11   245 12   A nation of change and novelty : $b
radical politics, religion, and literature in
seventeenth century England / $c Christopher Hill.
(Second indicator)
12   260   London ; $a New York : $b Routledge, $c
1990. (If the first place is not in the United States, then a subsequent
U.S. place should be listed; Rule 1.4C5)
13   300   xii, 272 p. ; $c 23 cm. (Prescribed punctuation
for dimensions)
14   504   Includes bibliographical references and
index. (Tag)
15   651 0   England $x Civilization $y 17th century.
(Tag and second subfield code)
16   651 0   England $x Church history $y 17th century.
(Tag and second subfield code)
17   651 0   Great Britain $x Politics and government
$x History and criticism. (Tag and second subfield code)
```
```

Fig. 11.3. Edited OCLC bibliographic record.

```
OCLC: 24953861      Rec stat:   c
Entered: 19911113   Replaced: 19921117    Used: 19930305
Type: a  Bib lvl:  m  Source:         Lang:    eng
Repr:    Enc lvl:     Conf pub:  0    Ctry:    enk
Indx: 1  Mod rec:     Govt pub:       Cont:    b
Desc: a  Int lvl:     Festschr:  0    Illus:
         F/B:      0  Dat tp:    s    Dates:   1992,
1    010         91-43589
2    040         DLC $c DLC $d UKM $d FPU [Modified by
author]
3    015         GB92-13922
4    019         26363363
5    020         0198522355 (cloth) : $c  30.00 (est.)
($47.50 U.S.)
6    050 00      QA273.6 $b .B377 1992
7    082 00      519.2/4 $2 20
8    049         KHNN
9    100 1       Barbour, A. D.
10   245 10      Poisson approximation / $c A.D. Barbour,
Lars Holst, Svante Janson.
11   260         Oxford [England] : $b Clarendon Press ; $a
New  York : $b Oxford University Press, $c 1992.
12   300         x, 277 p. ; $c 24 cm.
13   440  0      Oxford studies in probability ; $v 2
14   490 0       Oxford science publications
15   504         Includes bibliographical references (p.
[264]-272) and index.
16   650  7      Poisson, distribution de. $2 ram
17   650  7      Approximation, theorie de l'. $2 ram
18   650  0      Poisson distribution.
19   650  0      Approximation theory.
20   653  0      Approximation
21   700 1       Holst, Lars.
22   700 1       Janson, Svante.
```

Changes:

```
10   245 10      Poisson approximation / $c A.D. Barbour,
Lars Holst, Svante Janson.
```
("And" is not on title page; Rule 1.1F1)
```
11   260         Oxford [England] : $b Clarendon Press ; $a
New  York : $b Oxford University Press, $c 1992.
```
(If the title page does not list a U.S. publisher, but there is one listed elsewhere in the publication, LC lists the U.S. publisher. *Cataloging Service Bulletin* no. 47, p. 11-12)
```
12   300         x, 277 p. ; $c 24 cm.
```
(Prescribed punctuation for dimensions; Rule 1.5A1 or 2.5A1)
```
13   440  0      Oxford studies in probability ; $v 2
```
(Prescribed punctuation for number; Rule 1.6A1 or 2.6A1)
```
14   490 0       Oxford science publications
```
(Tag and indicator for series not traced)
```
15   504         Includes bibliographical references (p.
[264]-272) and index.
```
(First page of bibliography does not have a page number)

Fig. 11.4. Edited OCLC bibliographic record.

```
OCLC: 19269647      Rec stat:  c
Entered: 19890130   Replaced: 19921024    Used: 19930405
Type: a  Bib lvl:  m  Source:         Lang:     eng
Repr:       Enc lvl:     Conf pub:  0   Ctry:     txu
Indx: 0  Mod rec:     Govt pub:       Cont:     b
Desc: a  Int lvl:     Festschr:  0    Illus:
         F/B:       0 Dat tp:    s    Dates:   1989,
1    010          89-4223//r92
2    040          DLC $c DLC [Modified by author]
3    020          0882142178
4    041 1        eng $h lat
5    050 00       PA6522.M2 $b B6 1989
6    082 00       873/.01 $2 19
7    049          KHNN
8    100 0        Ovid, $d 43 B.C.-17 or 18 A.D.
9    240 10       Metamorphoses. $l English.
10   245 10       Ovid's Metamorphoses / $c translated by
Charles Boer.
11   260          Dallas, Tex. : $b Spring Publications, $c
c1989.
12   300          xxi, 359 p. ; $c 23 cm.
13   440  0       Dunquin series ; $v 17
14   500          Translation of: Metamorphoses.
15   504          Includes bibliographical references (p.
xxi).
15   650  0       Metamorphosis $x Mythology $x Poetry.
16   650  0       Mythology, Classical $x Poetry.
17   700 1        Boer, Charles, $d 1939-
```

Changes:

```
OCLC: 19269647      Rec stat:  c
Entered: 19890130   Replaced: 19921024    Used: 19930405
Type: a  Bib lvl:  m  Source:         Lang:     eng
Repr:       Enc lvl:     Conf pub:  0   Ctry:     txu
Indx: 0  Mod rec:     Govt pub:       Cont:     b
Desc: a  Int lvl:     Festschr:  0    Illus:
         F/B:       0 Dat tp:    s    Dates:   1989,
```
(There is no index, but there is a bibliography)
5   050 00   PA6522.M2 $b B6 1989 (First Cutter number should
be in subfield a)
8   100 0   Ovid, $d 43 B.C.-17 or 18 A.D. (First
indicator)
9   240 10   Metamorphoses. $l English. (First indicator)
13   440 0   Dunquin series ; $v 17 (Tag and prescribed
punctuation; Rule 1.6A1 or 2.6A1)
15   504   Includes bibliographical references (p.
xxi). (Bibliography note not given)

Fig. 11.5. Edited OCLC bibliographic record.

```
OCLC: 22400239        Rec stat:   c
Entered: 19900918     Replaced: 19910130     Used: 19910521
Type: a  Bib lvl:  m  Source:    d    Lang:    eng
Repr:    Enc lvl:  I  Conf pub:  0    Ctry:    dcu
Indx: 1  Mod rec:     Govt pub:       Cont:    br
Desc: a  Int lvl:     Festschr:  0    Illus:   a
         F/B:      0  Dat tp:    s    Dates:   1990,
1    040        APT $c APT $d AEV [Modified by author]
2    020        0871875535 $z 0871875533
3    090        JK610 $b .F29 1990
4    049        KHNR
5    245 00     Federal regulatory directory.
6    246 14     Congressional Quarterly's federal
regulatory directory.
7    250        6th ed. / with a revised introduction by
Cornelius M. Kerwin.
8    260        Washington, D.C. : $b Congressional
Quarterly, $c [c1990].
9    300        xvi, 986 p. : $b ill. ; $c 24 cm.
10   504        Includes bibliographical references and
indexes.
11   651  0     United States $x Executive departments $x
Directories.
12   650  0     Administrative procedure $z United States.
13   710  2     Congressional Quarterly, inc.
```

[*] Field 90—Some libraries may add "x" to the end of 1990.

The information on the page that looks like a title page verso indicates that LC has cataloged this title as a serial. The copy cataloger needs to watch for cases like this and determine the library's policy on individual records for each edition versus a serial record for all editions.

Changes:

```
OCLC: 22400239      Rec stat:  c
Entered: 19900918   Replaced: 19910130    Used: 19910521
Type: a  Bib lvl:  m  Source:     d   Lang:    eng
Repr:    Enc lvl:  I  Conf pub:   0   Ctry:    dcu
Indx: 1  Mod rec:     Govt pub:       Cont:    br
Desc: a  Int lvl:     Festschr:   0   Illus:   a
         F/B:      0  Dat tp:     s   Dates:   1990,
```
(There are bibliographical references)

2   020   0871875535 $z 0871875533 (The ISBN in the book differs from the one on the OCLC bibliographic record. The one in the book was accepted in subfield a by OCLC. The one in the OCLC record was placed in subfield z)

3   090   JK610 $b .F29 1990 (Decimal added before Cutter number and date added because it is 6th edition. Some libraries may add "x" to the end of 1990)

5   245 00   Federal regulatory directory.

6   246 14   Congressional Qualterly's federal regulatory directory. (Replaces 500 field)

7   250   6th ed. / with a revised introduction by Cornelius M. Kerwin. (Numerals and abbreviations should be used. Statement of responsibility relating to edition; Rule 1.2C1 and Appendixes B.9, C.3B1, and C.8A)

8   260   Washington, D.C. : $b Congressional Quarterly, $c [c1990]. ("Inc." not listed on title page; Rule 1.4D2. Date not from prescribed source. Some libraries may treat the page as the verso of the title page and not put the date in brackets; Rule 2.0B2)

9   300   xvi, 986 p. : $b ill. ; $c 24 cm. (Last numbered Roman numeral page is not given; Rule 2.5B2. This is a common mistake when there is a break in the Roman numerals)

10   504   Includes bibliographical references and indexes. (This field has been omitted)

Fig. 11.6. Edited OCLC bibliographic record.

```
OCLC: 25048160       Rec stat:  c
Entered: 19911211    Replaced: 19931113    Used: 19950314
Type: a  Bib lvl:  m  Source:        Lang:   eng
Repr:    Enc lvl:     Conf Pub:  0   Ctry:   nyu
Indx: 0  Mod rec:     Govt pub:      Cont:
Desc: a  Int lvl:     Festschr:  0   Illus:
         F/B:      1  Dat tp:    s   Dates:  1992,
1    010          91-46564//r932
2    040          DLC $c DLC [Modified by author]
3    020          0670839809 : $c $22.00 ($27.90 Can.)
4    043          n-us-az
5    050 00       PS3563.C3868 $b W35 1992
6    082 00       813/ .53 $2 20
7    049          KHNN
8    100 1        McMillan, Terry.
9    245 10       Waiting to exhale / $c Terry McMillan.
10   260          New York, N.Y., U.S.A. : $b Viking, $c
1992.
11   300          xiv, 409 p. ; $c 24 cm.
12   650  0       Afro-American women $x Fiction.
13   650  0       Afro-American men $x Fiction.
14   650  0       Friendship $x Fiction.
15   651  0       Phoenix (Ariz.) $x Fiction.
16   655  7       Love stories. $2 gsafd
```

Changes:

```
OCLC: 25048160       Rec stat:  c
Entered: 19911211    Replaced: 19931113    Used: 19950314
Type: a  Bib lvl:  m  Source:        Lang:   eng
Repr:    Enc lvl:     Conf Pub:  0   Ctry:   nyu
Indx: 0  Mod rec:     Govt pub:      Cont:
Desc: a  Int lvl:     Festschr:  0   Illus:
         F/B:      1  Dat tp:    s   Dates:  1992,
(This book is fiction)
8    100 1        McMillan, Terry. (First indicator)
12   650  0       Afro-American women $x Fiction. (Tag)
13   650  0       Afro-American men $x Fiction. (Tag)
15   651  0       Phoenix (Ariz.) $x Fiction. (Tag)
(User note: this has a 655 field for the genre of the item)
```

Fig. 11.7. Edited OCLC bibliographic record.

```
OCLC: 25833324        Rec stat:  p
Entered: 19920423    Replaced: 19931025      Used:
199502152
Type: a  Bib lvl:  m  Source:          Lang:    eng
Repr: a  Enc lvl:     Conf pub:  1     Ctry:    gw
Indx: 0  Mod rec:     Govt pub:        Cont:    b
Desc: a  Int lvl:     Festschr:  0     Illus:   a
         F/B:      0  Dat tp:    s     Dates:   1992,
1    010         92-16823
2    040         DLC $c DLC $d OCL $d NLC [Modified by
author]
3    020         3540555781 (Springer-Verlag Berlin
Heidelberg New York)
4    020         0387555781(Springer-Verlag New York Berlin
Heidelberg)
5    050 00      LB1028.5 $b I11635 1992
6    082 00      371.3/34 $2 20
7    049         KHNN
8    111 2       ICCAL '92 $d (1992 : $c Wolfville, N.S.)
9    245 10      Computer assisted learning : $b 4th
International Conference, ICCAL '92, Wolfville, Nova
Scotia, Canada, June 17-20, 1992 : proceedings / $c I.
Tomek (ed.).
10   260         Berlin ; $a New York : $b Springer-Verlag,
$c c1992.
11   300         x, 615 p. : $b ill. ; $c 25 cm.
12   440  0      Lecture notes in computer science ; $v 602
13   504         Includes bibliographical references.
14   650  0      Computer-assisted instruction $x
Congresses.
15   650  0      Intelligent tutoring systems $x
Congresses.
16   650  0      Education $x Data processing $x
Congresses.
17   700 1       Tomek, Ivan.
```

Changes:

```
OCLC: 25833324       Rec stat:  p
Entered: 19920423    Replaced: 19931025     Used:
199502152
Type: a  Bib lvl:  m  Source:           Lang:     eng
Repr: a  Enc lvl:     Conf pub:  1      Ctry:     gw
Indx: 0  Mod rec:     Govt pub:         Cont:     b
Desc: a  Int lvl:     Festschr:  0      Illus:    a
         F/B:      0  Dat tp:    s      Dates:    1992,
```
(This is a conference publication)
```
8    111 2      ICCAL '92 $d (1992 : $c Wolfville, N.S.)
```
(Conference qualifies for main entry; Rule 21B2)
```
9    245 10     Computer assisted learning : $b 4th
International Conference, ICCAL '92, Wolfville, Nova
Scotia, Canada, June 17-20, 1992 : proceedings / $c I.
Tomek (ed.).
```
(First indicator)

Fig. 11.8. Edited OCLC bibliographic record.

```
OCLC: 25813085       Rec stat:  c
Entered: 19920514    Replaced: 19920514    Used: 19930114
Type:       r  Bib lvl: m  Source:    d  Lang:    eng
Type mat: g  Enc lvl: I  Govt pub:     Ctry:    cau
Int lvl:  e  Mod rec:    Tech:      n  Leng:    nnn
Desc:       a  Accomp:     Dat tp:   s  Dates:   1991,
1    040        KHN $c KHN [Modified by author]
2    020        0962947105
3    090        LT2360.M23 $b T4
4    049        KHNN
5    245 00     Technopoly $h [game]
6    260        Sunnyvale, CA : $b Jim McBurney, $c c1991.
7    300        1 game (1 board, play money, 25 Wall
street journal cards, 26 Federal register cards, 4
playing pieces, 1 die, 32 computer supply contracts, 1
directions leaflet, 1 glossary leaflet, 1 score sheet
packet, 1 sample score sheet) : $b col. ; $c in box 3 x
50 x 26 cm.
8    521        For ages 10 to adult.
9    520        A board game designed to simulate the
high-tech business world.
10   650  0     Management games.
11   650  1     Management games.
```

Changes:

```
5    245 00     Technopoly $h [game]  (GMD; Rule 10.1C. LC uses
this GMD)
6    260        Sunnyvale, CA : $b Jim McBurney, $c c1991.
(Abbreviations for California, Cataloging Service Bulletin no. 51, p. 50)
7    300        1 game (1 board, play money, 25 Wall
street journal cards, 26 Federal register cards, 4
playing pieces, 1 die, 32 computer supply contracts, 1
directions leaflet, 1 glossary leaflet, 1 score sheet
packet, 1 sample score sheet) : $b col. ; $c in box 3 x
50 x 26 cm. (Subfield code for dimensions and prescribed punctuation
before dimensions; Rule 1.5A1 or 10.5A1)
8    521        For ages 10 to adult. (Tag)
```

Fig. 11.9. Edited OCLC bibliographic record.

```
OCLC: 18848244      Rec stat:  c
Entered: 19881206   Replaced: 19910823   Used: 19920309
Type:     a  Bib lvl: s  Source:   d  Lang:    eng
Repr:        Enc lvl:    Govt pub:     Ctry:    ctu
Phys med:    Mod rec:    Conf pub: 0  Cont:    ^^^^
S/L ent:  0  Ser tp: p  Frequn:   m  Alphabt: a
Desc:     a              Regulr:   n  ISDS:·   1
                         Pub st:   c  Dates:   1989-9999
1    010         89-641907    $z sn88-3549
2    040         NSD $c NSD $d NYG $d HUL $d COO $d HUL $d
DLC $dNST $d DLC $d OCL $d DLC $d NST $d EYM $d IUL $d
OCL $d NST$d HUL $d NSD $d IUL $d AGL $d NST $d MYG $d
NST $d CAS $d NST $d KHN [Modified by author]
3    022 0       1041-7915
4    050 00      Z678.9.A1 $b S6
5    049         KHNJ
6    210 0       Comput. libr.
7    222  0      Computers in libraries.
8    245 00      Computers in libraries.
9    260         Westport, CT : $b Meckler, $c c1988-
10   300         v. : $b ill. ; $c 28 cm.
11   310         Monthly (except for combined issues in
July/Aug.and Nov./Dec.) $b 1993-
12   321         Monthly (except for a combined issue in
July/Aug. $b 1989-1992.
13   362 0       Vol. 9, no. 1 (Jan. 1989)-
14   500         Title from cover.
15   510 2       Computer & control abstracts $x 0036-8113
$b Feb. 1989-
16   510 2       Electrical and electronic abstracts $x
0036-8105 $b Feb. 1989-
17   510 2       Physics abstracts $x 0036-8091 $b Feb.
1989-
18   530         Available on microfiche from University
Microfilms.
19   650  0      Libraries $x Automation $x Periodicals.
20   650  0      Library science $x Computer programs $x
Periodicals.
21   650  0      Minicomputers $x Library applications $x
Periodicals.
22   650  0      Information technology $x Periodicals.
23   780 00      $t Small computers in libraries $x 0275-
6722 $w (DLC)  84649849 $w (OCoLC)7208194
24   780 05      $t Systems librarian & automation review
$g June 1989 $x 0890-8354 $w (DLC)sn 86002554 $w
(OCoLC)14473187
25   780 05      $t Small computers in libraries. Buyer's
guide & consultant directory $g 1989 $x 0896-9485 $w
(DLC) 87658700 $w (OCoLC)16349013
26   936         Vol. 9, no. 3 (Mar. 1989) LIC
```

268 / Answers to Exercises

Changes:

> 10   300   v. : $b ill. ; $c 28 cm. (Field 300 missing;
> Rule 12.5)
> 11   310   Monthly (except for combined issues in
> July/Aug.and Nov./Dec.) $b 1993- (Frequency changed; Rule
> 12.7B1 and Field 310)
> 12   321   Monthly (except for a combined issue in
> July/Aug. $b 1989-1992. (Former frequency; Rule 12.7B1 and Field
> 321)
> 13   362 0   Vol. 9, no. 1 (Jan. 1989)- (Field 362 missing;
> Rule 12.3)
> 15   510 2   Computer & control abstracts $x 0036-8113
> $b Feb. 1989- (Field 510 missing; Rule 12.7B17. Some libraries will
> not add)
> 16   510 2   Electrical and electronic abstracts $x
> 0036-8105 $b Feb. 1989- (Field 510 missing; Rule 12.7B17. Some
> libraries will not add)
> 17   510 2   Physics abstracts $x 0036-8091 $b Feb.
> 1989- (Field 510 missing; Rule 12.7B17. Some libraries will not add)
> 18   530   Available on microfiche from University
> Microfilms. (Field missing; Rule 12.7B16 and Field 530)

Useful Tools
for the Copy Cataloger

Anglo-American Cataloguing Rules. 2d edition, 1988 revision. Prepared by the Joint Steering Committee for Revision of AACR. Edited by Michael Gorman and Paul W. Winkler. Chicago: American Library Association, 1988.

Anglo-American Cataloguing Rules, Second Edition, 1988 Revision. Amendments 1993. Prepared under the direction of the Joint Steering Committee for Revision of AACR. Chicago: American Library Association, 1993.

Bibliographic Formats and Standards. Dublin, Ohio: OCLC Online Computer Library Center, 1993.

Cataloging Service Bulletin, No. 1- . Washington, D.C.: Library of Congress, 1978- .quarterly.

Cataloging User Guide. 2d ed. Dublin, Ohio: OCLC Online Computer Library Center, 1993.

Library of Congress Rule Interpretations. 2d ed. Washington, D.C.: Library of Congress, 1989- . Looseleaf, with updates.

PRISM Basics CBT Course. Dublin, Ohio: OCLC Online Computer Library Center, 1994.

Selective Glossary of Cataloging Terms

Note: Words italicized in an entry have their own entries.

Access Point: A name, term, etc. that can be used to search for an *item*.

Accompanying Material: Dependent materials intended to be used with the main *item*.

Added Entry: Any *access point* except the *main entry*.

Alternative Title: A second title by which a *work* may be known. The two titles are always joined on the *chief source of information* by the word "or." The alternative title is part of the *title proper*.

Area: A major section of the bibliographic description of a *bibliographic record*. There are eight areas.

Author Number: See *Cutter Number*.

Authority Control: The process of maintaining consistency in the form used for an *access point* when there are variant forms of the name or term.

Authority File: A group of *authority records*.

Authority Record: A record containing the established form of name or term and the variant forms that have been referred to that form.

Bibliographic Record: The complete description of one item, including all *access points* and *call number*.

Bibliographic Utility: An organization that produces a bibliographic database from members' *bibliographic records.*

Binder's Title: The title placed on a book by the bindery when it is rebound.

Book Number: See *Cutter Number.*

Call Number: A number composed of *classification number* and *Cutter number.* It may also contain *workmark,* date, volume number, and copy number. It is used to place a book with books on the same subject, and it serves as an address when retrieving the item.

Caption Title: The title appearing on the first *page* of the text.

Catalog: A group of *bibliographic records* representing the *items* in a collection.

Cataloging: The process of describing an *item* in a collection. Cataloging enables a user to determine if the library has an item and the item's suitability, and it provides a location device via the *call number.*

Cataloging in Publication: See *CIP.*

Chief Source of Information: The preferred source for the required information for a *bibliographic record.*

CIP (Cataloging in Publication): A partial *bibliographic record* contained in the *item.* It is prepared by the Library of Congress from galley proofs.

Classification Number: The first part of a *call number* that places the *item* with other items covering the same subject.

Close Copy: A *bibliographic record* for a different *edition* of the *item.*

Collation: See *Physical Description.*

Collective Title: An inclusive title assigned to an *item* containing several *works.*

Colophon: A statement at the end of a book containing information about the author, title, and publication details.

Content: In the context of a *MARC* record, it is the data (text) of the record.

Content Designation: In the context of a *MARC* record, it is the definition of the codes in the record structure.

Cooperative Cataloging: The sharing of *bibliographic records* to be used for *cataloging*.

Copy Cataloging: Preparation of a *bibliographic record* by using or adapting one already prepared by someone else.

Cover Title: The title on the cover of an *item*.

Cutter Number: The second part of a *call number* that arranges *items* within the same *classification number* in alphabetical order by *main entry*.

DDC: Dewey Decimal Classification.

DLC: The OCLC symbol for the Library of Congress.

Delimiter: One of the characters standardized by the American Standard Code for Information Interchange (ASCII) that enables computers to communicate with each other.

Descriptive Cataloging: The component of *cataloging* that consists of physically describing the *item* and assigning author and title *access points*.

Download: See *Export*.

Edition: All copies of a *work* made from the same type setup or the same plates and issued by the same entity.

Element: A subunit of an *area* of description.

End Papers: See *Lining Papers*.

Entry: See *Access Point*.

Exact Copy: A *bibliographic record* for the *edition* being cataloged.

Export: To move data from one computer to another.

Extent of the Item: The first *element* of the *physical description area*, which gives the number and the specific material designation of the units of the *item*. For books it is the number of *pages*, *volumes*, *leaves*, or columns.

Facsimile: A reproduction of a *work* with the exact content and a simulation of the original appearance.

Field: A subunit of data in a *bibliographic record*.

Fixed Field: The 008 field plus part of the *leader*; it is often displayed in paragraph form with mnemonic *tags*.

Format: The physical presentation of an *item*.

Galley Proof: A copy of a work, before it is made into pages, that is used for examination and correction.

Half Title: A brief title on a *page* preceding the *title page*.

Heading: A name, term, etc. at the head of a record used as an *access point* to the *item*. Used more in relation to a card catalog than an online catalog.

Impression: An exact copy of a *work* made at a different time. Also called *printing*.

Imprint: See *Publication Distribution Area*.

Indicator: A two-character code that further defines a data *field*.

International Standard Book Number (ISBN): An internationally agreed-upon number that uniquely identifies a *monographic item*.

International Standard Serial Number (ISSN): An internationally agreed-upon number that uniquely identifies a *serial item*.

ISBN: See *International Standard Book Number*.

ISSN: See *International Standard Serial Number*.

Issue: A copy of a *work* with minor but well-defined variations.

Item: A physical entity, as opposed to an intellectual entity. See also *work*.

Item Record: A record containing information (i.e. bar code number, *volume* number, copy number, and circulation status) about a specific *item*.

Jacket: A paper wrapper that goes around the cover of a book.

Kindred Copy: See *Close Copy*.

LC: Library of Congress.

LCC: Library of Congress Classification.

Leader: The first 24 positions in a *MARC* record that contain coded information that allows the computer to process the record.

Leaf: One of the folded sections of the sheet of paper that forms part of a book. Each side of a leaf forms a *page*; thus, a leaf consists of two pages.

Lining Papers: The paper glued to the inside front and back covers. Also called *end papers*.

Main Entry: The main *access point* for an *item*; it is used in citing the item.

MARC (MAchine-Readable Cataloging): A series of rules for coding bibliographic data into a form that can be understood and manipulated by a computer.

Material (or Type of Publication) Specific Details Area: An *area* for cartographic materials, music, computer files, *serial* publications, and microforms to record details that are specific to those *formats*.

Member Copy: Cataloging copy (*bibliographic record*) prepared by another member of the utility.

Member Record: See *Member Copy*.

Monograph: A publication that is complete in one or a finite number of parts.

Near Copy: See *Close Copy*.

Note Area: The part of a *bibliographic record* that contains general information that is not already in the record.

OCLC (Online Computer Library Center): One of the *bibliographic utilities* in North America.

Original Cataloging: Preparation of a *bibliographic record* without reference to other bibliographic records for the same *item* or records for different *editions* of the item.

Other Title Information: Information on the *title page* that qualifies or further expands the *title proper*. Formerly known as *subtitle*.

Page: One side of one of the folded sections of a sheet of paper that forms part of a book. For the paper to be a page, there must be printed information on both sides of the folded section.

Pagination: The paging of a book.

Parallel Title: The *title proper* of an *item* in another language.

Physical Description Area: The part of the *bibliographic record* that contains the extent of the *item*, illustrative matter, and dimensions. Formerly known as *collation*.

Plates: *Leaves* or *pages* bearing illustrations with or without text that are not part of the main *pagination* of the text.

Printing: See *Impression*.

PRISM: Computer architecture of the OCLC system.

Publication Distribution Area: The part of the *bibliographic record* that contains the place, name, and date of all publication, distribution, and issuing activities. Formerly known as *imprint*.

Record Directory: A list of *fields* in a *MARC* record that gives their lengths and starting positions.

Record Structure: The codes used to identify the *elements* of information (i.e. *tags*, *indicators*, and *subfield codes*) in a *MARC* record.

Recto: The *page* on the right side of an open book, usually bearing an odd page number.

Romanize: To convert a name or term in a nonroman alphabet (e.g., Japanese) into roman characters.

Running Title: The title listed on each *page* or *leaf*.

Serial: A publication issued in parts and intended to continue indefinitely.

Series: A group of *items* on the same subject matter, usually published by the same publisher. Each item bears a series title in addition to its own title.

Series Area: The part of the *bibliographic record* that contains the series to which the *item* belongs.

Series Title Page: A page bearing the *series* title and other information related to the series.

Set: A group of books closely related in content. Also called a multipart item.

Shared Cataloging: See *Cooperative Cataloging*.

Shelflist: *Bibliographic records* of all *items* in a collection filed in the order that the books are arranged on the shelves.

Signature: The *pages* or *leaves* made from one huge sheet of paper that comprise part of a book.

Spine Title: The title listed on the spine of a book.

Standard Number: A number that is internationally agreed upon, mainly *ISBN* or *ISSN*.

Statement of Responsibility: A list of the individuals or groups responsible for the intellectual or artistic content of the *item*.

Subfield: A subunit of data in a *field*.

Subfield Code: A two-character code that further subdivides a *field* of data.

Subject Cataloging: The component of *cataloging* that consists of assigning subject headings and a *classification number*.

Subseries: A *series* within a series. Its title may be dependent on the title of the main series.

Subtitle: See *Other Title Information*.

Tag: A three-digit number used to identify a specific data *field*.

Title Proper: The main title of an *item*.

Tracings: All the *added entries* for an *item*. Used more in relation to a card catalog than an online catalog.

Transliteration Table: A table of characters (letters and numbers) used in converting one alphabet into another.

Uniform Title: The form of title used to bring all variant forms of a title together under the *main entry*.

Variable Field: The subunits of data in a computer record.

Variable Control Field: A *field* in a *MARC* record that contains a single data element or a series of fixed-length data elements.

Variable Data Field: A *field* in a *MARC* record that contains data.

Variant Copy: See *Close Copy*.

Verso: The *page* on the left side of an open book, usually bearing an even page number.

Verso of Title Page: The *page* following the *title page*; the backside of the title page.

Volume: A part of a *work*.

Work: An intellectual entity, as opposed to a physical entity. See also *Item*.

Workmark: One or two lowercase letters at the end of a *Cutter number*. In *DDC call numbers*, it represents the title. In *LCC* call numbers, it represents a *facsimile* or variant *edition*.

Index